ONLY IN
BUDAPEST

D1313132

Duncan J. D. Smith

ONLY IN
BUDAPEST

A Guide to Unique Locations,
Hidden Corners and Unusual Objects

Photographs by
Duncan J. D. Smith

**The
Urban
Explorer**

For Roswitha,
without whom the following pages could not have been written,
also Győző and Szabolcs Szivák of Kőbánya,
and the Roma children of Józsefváros

Contents

ÓBUDA (District III)

PEST (Central and Inner Suburbs: Districts V–IX)

Introduction

"All foreigners, who have visited Budapest, talk about
it with praise, even those who are in the position
to make a comparison between the Hungarian capital
and the most beautiful and famous cities of foreign lands."

Lajos Kossuth (1883)

Budapest is surely one of the most dramatic, and at the same time least known, capital cities in Europe. Straddling the mighty Danube (*Duna*), Buda on the west bank and Pest on the east, it is also one of the most fascinating. The relatively few available guidebooks offer the undemanding visitor an amazing (and effortlessly accessible) array of museums, churches, historic buildings and eateries, reflecting the history of the city from Roman and Magyar times, via the Ottoman and Habsburg Empires, up to the present day. However, for those with a little more time on their hands, and for those who want to *discover* something of the place for themselves, this new guide has been expressly written. It only takes a few minutes of planning, and a glance at a decent street map*, to escape the crowds and the orchestrated tours and discover a different Budapest.

Based on personal experience, and footslogging all twenty-three of the city's districts (*kerületek*), the author will point the explorer in a new and unusual direction. This is the Budapest of Roman ruins, medieval ramparts and Turkish tombs; hidden courtyards and colourful old market halls; unfrequented museums brimming with fascinating objects; secret caves and thrilling hillside railways; Transylvanian houses and Art Nouveau bath buildings; not to mention a former power station and an old Ukrainian river barge both recently refurbished as arts' centres! It is also a city with a dark and turbulent past, its myriad monuments to the revolutions of 1848 and 1956, forgotten Jewish cemeteries, bombed-out structures and Stalin-era statues still bearing grim witness to terrible times.

As would be expected, many of these curious locations, all of which are both visible and visitable, are to be found within the narrow streets of the ancient Castle Hill of Buda (Vár and Víziváros in District I) and the old medieval walled town of Pest (Belváros in District V). However, a similar number lie *outside* these long-established areas of occupation, for instance in Óbuda (District III), the former Roman town of Aquincum north of Buda, as well as the environs of the rolling Buda Hills to the west (Districts II, XI, XII and XXII). Equally interesting are the Inner Suburbs surrounding old Pest (Districts VI, VII, VIII and IX), spread out beyond the nineteenth century Habsburg Boulevard known as the Kiskörút. These are bounded by a further, outer Boulevard, the Nagykörút, beyond which are the city's sprawling Outer Suburbs (Districts IV, XIII–XVI in the north and Districts X, XVII–XXI and XXIII in the south). Using Budapest's extensive transport network of underground trains (*metró/földalatti*), suburban trains (*HÉV/vonat*), trams (*villamos*), trolleybuses (*trolibusz*) and buses (*autóbusz*), the explorer can quite quickly reach all the places described within the following pages – and that's without detracting whatsoever from the sense of personal discovery that each of these places has to offer. Indeed, directions have been kept to a minimum so as to leave the visitor free to find their own particular path. Whether exploring the maze of tunnels below Castle Hill, searching Buda for Islam's most northerly sacred site, rattling along under the suburbs of Pest on Continental Europe's oldest underground railway, or visiting religious ruins on Margaret Island, it is hoped that the visitor will experience a sense of having made the discovery for his or her self.

In embarking on these mini-odysseys in search of Budapest's tangible historical legacy the author would only ask that telephones are switched off in places of worship (which should not be visited during services), and due respect is shown in the quiet city courtyards and backstreets that are home and workplace to many Hungarians. Other than that, treat Budapest as a giant oyster containing many precious pearls – I just hope you enjoy finding them as much as I did.

Duncan J. D. Smith
Budapest – Vienna

* Most street maps of Budapest, for example the Falk Cityplan Extra, cover Castle Hill, central Pest and the inner suburbs; the invaluable Network Map of Budapest Transport Ltd. (BKV), available from the Budapest Tourism Office, details tram, bus, metro and rail routes across all twenty-three districts of the city.

After each entry there is a selection of others within walking distance, wherever applicable.

The dates given after the names of Hungary's various monarchs are the actual years they reigned for, whereas those given after important non-royal personalities relate to their birth and death.

An alphabetical list of opening times of museums and other places of interest mentioned in the text can be found at the back of the book.

The legendary Turul Bird on Castle Hill

1 The Legend of the Turul Bird

District I (Vár), the Turul bird monument at Szent György tér
on Castle Hill (Várhegy)
Bus 16 from M1/M2/M3 Deák Ferenc tér; Funicular railway
from Clark Ádám tér

In 430 AD, during the period historians refer to as the Age of Barbarians, Attila and his Huns swept into what is now Hungary making it a base for further incursions into Europe; Roman Aquincum, on the site of modern Óbuda, had already fallen to them in 409AD (see no. 34). Meaning 'person' in Mongolian, the Huns were a confederacy of Turkic-speaking nomads from Central Asia, who conquered the Romans and their vassals but never actually took Rome itself. They were soon replaced by waves of nomadic Avars and Bulgars from Asia, whilst more sedentary Slavs populated the lands west of the Danube.

It was against this backdrop of mass migrations that the earliest Hungarians (Magyars) came into being. It is thought that the first Hungarian homeland was in the for-
ests between the River Volga and the Urals in Western Russia from where in 500BC proto-Magyars moved south into the Central Volga region, encountering Turkic-speaking peoples moving west during the first centuries AD. However, not until 700–850AD did proto-Magyar tribes appear in the historical record whilst serving as vassals for the Khazar Empire of Southern Russia. Under High Prince Álmos (858–895) they seceded from the Khazar yoke and occupied present-day Ukraine from where they undertook raids deep into Frankish Europe. In c.887 seven proto-Magyar tribes (still celebrated in the seven tent-shaped towers of Buda's Fishermen's Bastion and in the statues at the base of the

Prince Árpád on Heroes' Square

column on Heroes' Square) elected a new High Prince named Árpád. However, in 895, whilst the tribes were away raiding Europe, Bulgars and Pechenegs devastated the proto-Magyar villages. This prompted Árpád to lead his people across the Verecke Pass in the northern Carpathians and on to the Great Hungarian Plain (Nagyalföld). In doing so Árpád (c.895–c.907) became the first true Magyar ruler.

Arriving in c.900 they soon conquered the entire Carpathian Basin, with Árpád building a summer residence on Csepel Island in the Danube and his co-ruler, the chieftain Kurszán, constructing a fortress in what is now modern Óbuda (see no. 84). The tribes successfully pushed the Bulgars south of the Danube and continued to plunder Western Europe until their eventual defeat by the German King Otto I at the Battle of Augsburg in 955.

To consolidate the Magyar homeland and legitimize it in the eyes of the neighbouring Holy Roman Empire, Árpád's grandson Géza (c.971–997) decided to convert his people to Christianity; accordingly he was baptised together with his son, Vajk, who would take the name István (Stephen) (997–1038) on his accession to the Hungarian throne on January 1st 1001 (see nos. 25 & 40). A crown was even sent to the new monarch from Pope Sylvester II in Rome.

Hungarians have long been fascinated by the folklore surrounding their origins. One such story is today represented by a huge, sword-wielding bronze sculpture of the mysterious Turul bird, which has perched in Szent György tér outside the Royal Palace on Buda's Castle Hill since being created by Gyula Donath in 1905. Hungary's Austrian conquerors, keen to legitimize their rule and well aware of the Hungarian interest in myth and legend, were responsible for commissioning the statue, as well as others surmounting golden balls on the top of Freedom Bridge (Szabadság híd).

The word Turul is an ancient one (from the Turkish *togrul* or *turgul*, meaning 'falcon') and is mentioned twice in legends describing the shaping of Hungary. In the first, Árpád's grandmother Emese is informed in a dream by the Turul that her child will be the father of a great nation: that child was Álmos, Árpád's father. In the second, the leader of the Magyar tribes dreams that eagles are attacking their horses whereupon the Turul appears to protect them, carrying the sword of Attila the Hun and leading them on to the land of Hungary.

As to the ultimate origins of Árpád's ancestors experts are still unclear. Linguistically, it is known that the Hungarian (or Magyar) language is not of Indo-European origin but rather a branch of the Finno-Ugric language group, which forms a sub-group of the Altaic-Uralic language family of Finns, Lapps, Turks, Mongolians, Estonians and Siberians. Not surprisingly the Soviets played up the Siberian links; similarly, the Eurocentric Habsburgs stressed the Finnish connection. However, recent archaeological evidence from north-west China suggests a likely far eastern origin.

Turul birds on Freedom Bridge

The origin of the name 'Hungary' is thought to derive from an old Slavic word for the early Magyars, derived from the Bulgaro-Turkic On-Ogur ('people of the ten arrows'), to which the letter 'h' was added erroneously because of confusion with the Huns. Regarding the name 'Magyar', the Hungarian word for 'Hungarian', according to legend it is derived from the name Magor, the son of Nimrod in the Hebrew Bible, from whom the Hungarians were thought to have descended.

Other places of interest nearby: 2, 3, 4, 5

2   Buda by Funicular

District I (Vár), the Buda Castle Funicular Railway (Budavári sikló)
between Clark Ádám tér and Szent György
tér on Castle Hill (Várhegy)
The lower station on Clark Ádám tér is reached by Tram 19 along
the Buda embankment; Bus 16 from M1/M2/M3 Deák Ferenc tér

The Buda Castle Funicular Railway
arriving at Clark Ádám tér

Visitors to Buda's Castle Hill can make their ascent by a variety of means, including bus as well as an elevator rising up from Dózsa György tér (next to the stop for Buses 5, 16 and 178 and Tram 18) to the south-west. For the healthy explorer the best method is by foot thereby offering an opportunity to explore the winding streets of the Víziváros district on the north-eastern slopes of Castle Hill. Translated as 'Water Town', due to its proximity to the river where fishermen's cottages and docks once existed, Víziváros is one of the city's oldest districts with medieval houses and Baroque churches still standing on its winding streets.

However, the most unusual means of ascent to the Castle District is by funicular or cliff railway (sikló). It takes just two minutes to rise from Clark Ádám tér to the upper station in Szent György tér at the Buda Royal Palace (from where horse-drawn carriages await visitors who wish to travel in luxury) and affords wonderful views of the

Danube and Pest in the process. The funicular was built in 1870 in order to transport clerks and other employees up to the Royal Palace and Castle District, an administrative area at that time. The UNESCO-protected conservation area is now dominated by museums, although the President of the Hungarian Republic (Magyar Köztársaság) also resides here.

Invented in the 15th century a funicular railway (from the Latin word *funiculus* meaning 'thin rope' or 'cord') is an ingenious combination of hoist and railway track used in especially steep locations where traditional railways, relying on the friction between wheels and track, would not be effective. A powered winch is used to haul one car upwards by cable along an inclined track, whilst also using it to act as a counterweight for the car travelling downwards at the same time. In this way the winch merely has to provide enough force to overcome the difference in weight between the two cars (namely the weight of the passengers they contain) together with any friction within the system.

Buda's funicular was constructed on the orders of Ödön Széchenyi, whose father Count István Széchenyi masterminded the building of the nearby Chain Bridge (see no. 42). Like so much of Castle Hill the funicular railway suffered considerable damage during the Second World War and was extensively rebuilt in 1986 during which time it was electrified. Its two stepped carriages are accurate copies of those used on the original railway, their names – Margit and Gellért – referring to two of the city's famous saints (see nos. 13, 40 & 72).

Near the funicular's lower station on Clark Ádám tér is the so-called Zero Kilometre Stone from where all the city's distances are calculated. A little further downstream can be found Miklós Ybl's arcaded stairway (Bazár) leading up into the Palace Gardens (Várkert), as well as his neo-Renaissance Palace pumping station (Kioszk) built in the 1870s.

Other places of interest nearby: 1, 3, 4, 5

3 Scars of the Second World War

District I (Vár), the former Ministry of Defence at Színház utca
on the south side of Dísz tér on Castle Hill (Várhegy)
Bus 16 from M1/M2/M3 Deák Ferenc tér;
Funicular railway from Clark Ádám tér

Towards the end of the Second World War, the fabric of both Budapest and Vienna suffered terrible damage from both allied bombing and months of bloody combat as Soviet troops wrested the two cities from the hands of the German *Wehrmacht*. Today, visitors to Vienna would be hard pressed to find any physical evidence of the conflict, except for a couple of monuments erected long after the event. With help from the American brokered Marshall Plan its battered buildings were rapidly pulled down and replaced or else perfectly restored. For Budapest, however, reconstruction has been a slower process, indeed many of the walls of Pest are still pockmarked with bullet holes from this time (though many date from the 1956 Uprising). The most notable example is the former Ministry of Defence on the south side of Dísz tér on Castle Hill. A neo-Baroque building that had housed

the ministry since the late 19th century it was gutted by fire during the war and remains entirely and deliberately unrestored as a monument to the violence of war.

The bullet-ridden former Ministry of Defence on Dísz tér, Castle Hill

Following the First World War and the Treaty of Trianon, under which Hungary lost two-thirds of its territories to neighbouring states, some economic stability had returned with the government of Count István Bethlen. However, with the crash of 1929 and the labour discontent that followed, Hungary's regent Admiral Miklós Horthy appointed the right-wing Gyula Gömbös as Prime Minister. Gömbös dreamt of a Hungarian-

Italian-German Fascist axis and sought closer ties with the Nazis in the hope of reversing Trianon.

As in Vienna, anti-Semitism became rife as the increasingly discontent *petit bourgeoisie* sought a scapegoat (see no. 62). By 1938 Hungary was allied with Nazi Germany and the first so-called Vienna Awards returned part of former Northern Hungary (present-day Slovakia) to them (Northern Transylvania followed in 1940). Despite a brief respite under a new Prime Minister, Count Pál Teleki, who distrusted the Nazis, Hungary was soon assisting Germany in the invasion of Yugoslavia.

However, by early 1943 the Hungarian 2nd Army had been all but wiped out on the Russian front and German troops, fearing a Soviet invasion, entered Budapest in March 1944. They were accompanied by Adolf Eichmann, who together with the SS (*Schutzstaffel*) had established a Jewish ghetto in Budapest by October 1944, from where some of those incarcerated were deported to the concentration camp at Auschwitz-Birkenau in Southern Poland (see the poignant wall plaque at the Józsefvárosi railway station) (see no. 49).

In October 1944, following a plea for an armistice, Hungary's regent Admiral Horthy was kidnapped by the SS, and the Fascist Arrow Cross party under Nazi puppet Ferenc Szálasi took control of Hungary. It wasn't long, however, before the Soviets closed in on Budapest, embarking on a months-long artillery battle with the Germans for control of Pest. Meanwhile, German troops made a last stand in the maze of streets on Castle Hill, the remaining citizens cowering in the labyrinth of tunnels that run through the limestone rock below (see no. 4). It soon became the worst siege since that of Stalingrad. Following fierce fighting the Germans eventually surrendered on February 13th 1945 by which time Soviet artillery had reduced the area to ruins. Of the tens of thousands of Axis troops who broke out only 785 are thought to have made it back to the safety of German lines.

The task of restoring the shattered city fell to the Soviet military government who were quick to install Communists in all positions of power; a situation that would exist until the fall of Communism in 1989. As for the lucrative draw of the Marshall Plan, Stalin convinced the leaders of his Central and Eastern European satellite nations to resist it because of the Americans' proviso that all recipients undertake economic liberalisation. As a result the painstaking reconstruction of Budapest was a far slower and more piecemeal affair than that of Vienna, although it would be a no less careful one (witness for example the magnificent reconstruction of the neo-Baroque Royal

Palace, not to mention the Museum of Military History (Hadtörténeti Intézet és Múzeum) occupying an old barracks at nearby Tóth Árpád sétány 40, which was seriously damaged during the conflict).

Most of Buda's buildings were restored back to their previous Baroque appearance although at Táncsics Mihály utca 20 there is an interesting attempt at an entirely new structure merely painted to match the old. Another important casualty of the fighting was the 13th century Franciscan Church of Mary Magdalene at Kapisztrán tér 6, built for Hungarian-speaking worshippers – German speakers heard mass in the Church of Our Lady (now called the Matthias Church). During the Ottoman period the Mary Magdalene Church was the only church to initially receive special dispensation to remain a Christian place of worship and not be converted into a mosque. Later in the 18th century it became the official church for the Buda Castle garrison. Having survived so much, its nave and chancel were eventually destroyed by modern weapons, leaving only its patched-up 15th century tower (Mária Magdolna-torony) and a single reconstructed window to tell the sorry tale.

The ruined Church of Mary Magdalene on Kapisztrán tér, Castle Hill

As well as the Museum of Military History on Castle Hill, the Hungarian National Museum (see no. 55) also contains very informative displays relating to both the First and Second World Wars.

Other places of interest nearby: 1, 2, 4, 5

4 History under the Hill

District I (Vár), the Hospital in the Rock Museum
(Sziklakórház Múzeum) at Lovas út 4/C on Castle Hill (Várhegy)
Bus 16 from M1/M2/M3 Deák Ferenc tér;
Funicular railway from Clark Ádám tér

Castle Hill is best known for its sprawl of winding streets and Gothic houses, reconstructed in the Baroque style by the Austrian Habsburgs after they had taken the area from the Ottoman Turks (see no. 9). Not so well known is the fact that for almost every street on the surface there is a tunnel of at least the same length running through the rocks below.

Entrance to the Buda Castle Labyrinth on Úri utca, Castle Hill

Geologically speaking Castle Hill is a narrow rocky ridge just over 1.5 kilometres long and 60 metres high that is made up of limestone and marl. These calcareous stones can be excavated easily both by the action of water over millennia, as well as through the efforts of man over a far shorter period. Indeed, it is these qualities combined with the existence of thermal springs that first drew prehistoric man to find refuge in the Buda Hills (Budai-hegység) as long as 4,000 years ago (see nos. 13 & 14).

Today, a part of this hidden subterranean labyrinth can be explored by entering the inconspicuous doorway of the so-called Buda Castle Labyrinth (Budavári Labirintus) at Úri utca 9. The name 'labyrinth' is well deserved since it gives access to a network of passageways and galleries stretching for almost ten kilometres beneath the hill. Originally, the labyrinth was a series of naturally hollowed-out caves and manmade chambers used as cellars, wells and other storage facilities, and were unconnected. However, the Ottoman Turks joined many of them together for military and economic purposes and it is a 1200 metre-long section of such tunnels, reaching a depth of 16 metres and covering an area of 4,000 square metres, which can be visited today.

The resulting casemate system was perfect for the hasty relocation of troops from one part of the hill to another and was also useful in giving an attacker the impression that there were more troops posted than actually existed. In the 1930s the tunnels were reinforced with concrete and made into a shelter capable of holding up to 10,000 citizens in the event of an attack. Many of Budapest's inhabitants would cower here during the last bloody months of the Second World War. The German army also used the passageways when they made their last desperate stand against the Russian army, who were advancing inexorably towards them through the streets of Pest.

For a real taste of life beneath Castle Hill during wartime visit the Hospital in the Rock Museum (Sziklakórház Múzeum) at Lovas út 4/C. Used originally in part as a wine cellar, this underground network of tunnels and chambers was fortified during the early

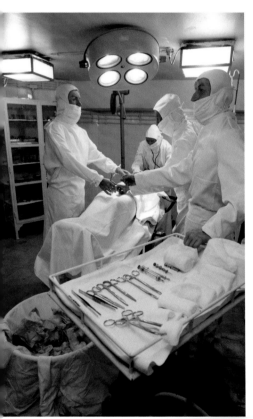

The operating theatre in the Hospital in the Rock Museum

years of the Second World War, for use as a military hospital and shelter. During a highly informative guided tour of the complex the still-intact hospital will be visited, installed here because Castle Hill was once part of the Government Quarter. It contains a fully-equpped operating theatre, x-ray facilities, and generators independent of the city's power network. The only features that are not original are the lifelike waxwork doctors and nurses, whose pained expressions only add to the grim atmosphere of the place.

The hospital was originally designed to hold around 300 wounded civilians and soldiers, together with 40 medical staff working in shifts. By February 1945, however, and the last days of the Soviet Siege of Budapest, more than 700 patients were crammed into the windowless wards.

Wartime operations centre in the Hospital in the Rock Museum

The suffering, not to mention the smell, must have been appalling. A decade later the complex was reactivated to treat victims of the 1956 Uprising.

Then, between 1958 and 1962, the shelter was further strengthened to withstand potential nuclear and chemical attacks during the Cold War era. A visit to the shelter is another memorable part of the tour and includes features such as a decontamination chamber, secure water reserves, and air filtration system. Civil defence drills were still being staged here as late as the 1980s during which time governmental caretakers ensured all the equipment was in full working order – just in case. Only then was the facility eventually mothballed and returned to being used as a storage cellar. Looking back on those paranoid times it is understandable why considerable secrecy surrounded the hospital and shelter, and why its declassification only occurred in 2002.

Other places of interest nearby: 1, 3, 5, 6

5 Of Mummies and Alchemists

District I (Vár), the Golden Eagle Pharmacy Museum (Arany Sas
Patikamúzeum) at Tárnok utca 18 on Castle Hill (Várhegy)
Bus 16 from M1/M2/M3 Deák Ferenc tér;
Funicular railway from Clark Ádám tér

An alchemist's laboratory in the Golden Eagle
Pharmacy Museum on Tárnok utca

Even visitors without any interest in the history of medicine will find the tiny Golden Eagle Pharmacy Museum on Tárnok utca a fascinating place. It is located in a 15th century house with a Baroque facade, making it one of the oldest extant buildings in the Castle District. The collection itself is truly eclectic, detailing the history of pharmacy from the Middle Ages up to the 17th century. This is told by means of several cabinets of curiosities as well as two reconstructed rooms, one a medieval alchemist's workshop and the other a Baroque pharmacy, the building itself having been the first pharmacy in the district (for an example of an old fashioned pharmacy still in use visit the Opera Patika at Andrássy út 26, in business since 1889).

Scholars are still entranced by the work of the alchemists, those proto-scientists who believed that all matter was composed of the four elements (earth, water, fire and air) and whose work took them in-to the realms of mysticism and magic. Their two intertwined goals were the 'philosopher's stone', a mythical substance that would enable the transmutation of common metals into gold, and the 'universal panacea', a remedy that would cure all disease and prolong life indefinitely. With its elements of physics, medicine, metallurgy and religion, alchemy is now seen as a precursor to the modern science of chemistry.

A highlight of the museum is this ancient Egyptian mummy's head

Somewhat surprising in a pharmacy museum, to modern eyes at least, is the head of an ancient Egyptian mummy to be found in one of the museum's cabinets. The word 'mummy' comes from the Arabian *mumiya*, meaning 'bitumen' or 'pitch', a black tar-like substance that oozes out of certain mountains in the Middle East. The ancient Persians used it for medicinal purposes. When the Arabs invaded Egypt and first discovered the preserved bodies of ancient Egyptians they noticed they had a dark coating (actually a dessicated mixture of bodily fluids and unctions used in the mummification process) that reminded them of *mumiya* – and so the word mummy was born. For centuries Europeans apothecaries had sold black powder made from *mumiya* as a "cure all" medicine for epilepsy, coughs, headaches, stomach ailments and all manner of other complaints. Only when supplies ran out did they turn to the mummies of ancient Egypt, grinding thousands of them to dust in the mistaken belief that they had been deliberately coated in real *mumiya*. As late as 1908 "mummy powder" could still be found listed in the trade catalogues of certain pharmaceutical suppliers!

Other places of interest nearby: 3, 4, 6, 7

6 The Oldest Coffee House in Town

**District I (Vár), the Ruszwurm Coffee House
at Szentháromság utca 7 on Castle Hill (Várhegy)
Bus 16 from M1/M2/M3 Deák Ferenc tér;
Funicular railway from Clark Ádám tér**

It was the Hungarian poet and novelist Dezső Kosztolányi (1885–1936) who remarked, "After its Turkish baths, the Hungarian café is the most oriental feature (of Budapest). It is where we spend our lives". Whilst myriad bars and other fashionable venues are today burgeoning in Budapest, the traditional coffee house (*kávéház or kávézó*) and bathhouse remain integral parts of the Budapest scene.

The world's first coffee house opened in Istanbul in 1554 and no doubt coffee was being sold exclusively to (and brewed exclusively by) Turks in the Ottoman town of Buda during the same period (see no. 46). Europe's first coffee house did not open in Venice until 1647, followed by London (1652), Paris (1660) and Hamburg (1677). Meanwhile, in Vienna in 1683 attempts by Turkish troops under Grand Vizier Kara Mustafa to capture the city were thwarted, heralding the retreat of the Ottomans from their European adventure. It was for many years recounted how bags of curious green beans, found amongst the Ottomans' abandoned possessions and thought originally to be camel fodder, were claimed by Polish adventurer Georg Franz Kolschitzky and made into coffee. However, in reality it was not until 1685 that Emperor Leopold I (1658–1705) granted a licence to sell coffee and tea in Vienna to an Armenian trader called Johannes Deodatus. A year later, a Christian European alliance (including the Habsburgs) ejected the Ottomans from Buda, destroying much of Castle Hill in the process; the country's first coffee house eventually opened in Pest in 1714 and one in Buda opened soon after.

Despite this relatively late start, the coffee houses of Vienna and Budapest stand quite apart from those of other countries, in both the architecturally fascinating venues they occupy – from the small and cosy to the grand and elegant – and in the way they have willingly fulfilled a unique social rôle in the lives of both cities. Thus, by the early 19th century they had become popular meeting places not only for the fashionable but also the down-at-heel; students, intellectuals, artists and 'Bohemians' used the coffee house, rather than their unheated attics, as an open forum for discussion.

The oldest extant coffee house in Budapest is the Ruszwurm on Castle Hill, founded in 1827 and still purveying not only excellent coffee and cakes but also Biedermeier charm in its nostalgic furnishings. Its pastry chef was imprisoned for his support of the 1848 Revolution against the Habsburgs, a revolt that was itself orchestrated from another coffee house, namely the Pilvax across the river in Pest (see no. 48). Whilst in prison he met a Hungarian commander, Rudolf Linzer, after which it is said he named his now famous shortcake and apricot jam biscuit.

At the end of the century the coffee house (of which there were now over 300!) provided the backdrop for the so-called *Belle Époque*, a brief Golden Age of cultured living snuffed out by the Great War. Each with a unique atmosphere and story, Budapest's *Belle Époque* coffee

Budapest's oldest coffee house is the Ruszwurm on Szentháromság utca, Castle Hill

houses are now legendary: the Gerbeaud, patronised by Elisabeth, Empress of Austria, the Astoria with its marble columns and gilt-edged mirrors favoured by Nazi officials (see no. 49), and the Centrál Kávéház at Károlyi utca 9, once popular with the literary set, all located in fashionable District V. Not surprisingly the grand boulevard of Andrássy út boasts several grand coffee houses too, namely the Lukács (see no. 69), with its ghosts of the Communist secret police, the faded grandeur of the Művész at number 29, and the elegant Café Callas at number 20. In District VIII, at Múzeum körút 12, there is the Múzeum Kávéház with original murals by Károly Lotz. The recently renovated New York Café at Erzsébet körút 9–11 can also be added to this list, its marble balconies once boasting 400 periodicals. The architect of this sumptuously appointed coffee palace, Alajos Hauszmann, was also responsible for the reconstruction of the Royal Palace on Castle Hill. It is difficult to imagine that during the 1940s such coffee hous-

es had been closed down under the Communists, who viewed them as breeding grounds for anti-Soviet gossip and converted them into sports shops, post offices and self-service restaurants!

Coffee and cake at the Művész coffee house on Andrássy út

The Ruszwurm is actually a cukrászda, that is a small coffee house that doubles up as a cake shop. It is renowned not only for its sweet pastries but also its savoury pogácsa scones, made with pork fat and cumin. Other classic cukrászdák include Auguszt at Kossuth Lajos utca 14–16 and Szalai at Balassi Bálint utca 7, both long-established family concerns in District V. Traditional menu favourites include curd cheese-filled pastry pockets (túrós táska) and dumplings (túrógombóc), shortcrust poppyseed crescents (pozsonyi kifli), vanilla and caramel-topped puff pastry squares (francia krémes), rum-soaked sponge squares with chocolate sauce, walnuts, raisins and crème anglaise (somlói galuska), baked dough balls dipped in butter and walnuts (aranygaluska) and strudels (rétes). The Hungarians are adamant they, not the Viennese, invented the strudel, although they concede that its distinctive flaky pastry probably derives from the baklava pastry of the Turks. It is true that the best wheat flour, with a high gluten content for elasticity, came originally from Hungary and had to be imported by the Austrians. The Hungarians use a far greater variety of fillings too, including not only apples (almás) but also cherries (meggyes), poppyseeds (mákos), curd cheese and even savoury fillings, such as cabbage sautéed in lard with ground pepper and caramelized sugar.

Other places of interest nearby: 4, 5, 7, 8

7 Treasures of the Painted Church

District I (Vár), the Matthias Church/Buda Church of Our Lady
(Mátyás-templom/Budavári Nagyboldogasszony templom)
at Szentháromság tér 2 on Castle Hill (Várhegy)
Bus 16 from M1/M2/M3 Deák Ferenc tér;
Funicular railway from Clark Ádám tér

Castle Hill (*Várhegy*) was first settled and fortified in the 13th century by King Béla IV (1235–70) of the Árpádian Dynasty, in the wake of the devastating Mongol (Tartar) invasion of 1241. This formed a part of the king's decree that fortified towns be built across Hungary. Béla also ordered that Hungarians previously living at the foot of the hill move up to the Castle Hill itself, where they settled around the Mary Magdalene Church (see no. 3); similarly, Germans living in Pest congregated around the Church of Our Lady, founded by the king in 1255 (the Germans named the area 'Ofen' (meaning 'oven') after the many lime kilns they encountered on the hill.

With the accession of the House of Anjou, Louis I the Great (Nagy Lajos) (1342–82) started to build a walled castle for his royal court on the hill, which he moved there from Visegrád in 1346, a move finalised in 1408. It was a structure embellished later by Sigismund (Zsigmond) of Luxembourg (1387–1437), by which

The spire and polychrome roof of the Matthias Church on Castle Hill

Intricate floral frescoes inside the Matthias Church

time Buda had become the country's new capital. The stage was thus set for the arrival of one of Hungary's greatest royal personages, namely the non-dynastic Renaissance King Mátyás (Matthias) 'Corvinus' Hunyadi (1458-90), crowned King of Hungary in 1458 at the age of just fifteen (see no. 46).

The new king's father was the powerful noble János Hunyadi, whose efforts had checked the early expansion of the Ottoman Empire. With his lands secure for the time being, King Matthias set about transforming Castle Hill into a seat of learning and luxury that would become the envy of Europe (see no. 9). The king married twice, firstly the twelve-year-old Catherine Podjebrad of Bohemia, who died quickly in childbirth, and secondly in 1476 Beatrice, daughter of the King of Naples, whose part in transforming the court from a medieval to a Renaissance one should not be underestimated.

Both marriages were celebrated in the Church of Our Lady, giving rise to the building's popular name of the Matthias Church (Mátyás-templom). However, the church seen by visitors today would probably be unrecognisable to King Matthias, having been through many changes in its 750-year history – including its conversion into a Turkish mosque. Between 1874 and 1896 the architect Frigyes Schulek removed all later additions and restored the church as he thought it would have appeared when first erected in the 13th century, albeit in a somewhat romanticised way in order to reflect the prevailing nationalist spirit of the age. Consequently, as with his nearby Fisherman's Bastion (Halászbástya) (1903), the church is decorated with a mass of Hungarian folk motifs and pseudo-medieval ornamentation, every surface carved, every inch of wall painted in a heady, eclectic, almost eastern style. The result is something extraordinary, from the ornately sculpted gothic spire, soaring 80 metres into the sky, to the roof of dazzling polychrome tiles made at the Zsolnay ceramics factory.

The interior of the church has many unique features too, including the main entrance (Mary Portal) with its 14th century relief depicting the death of the Virgin, inside which is a column capital depicting two men opening a book that is the oldest *in situ* sculpture in Budapest. There is also the Loreto Chapel containing a Gothic triptych, the Béla Chapel, where the tombs of the 12th century King Béla III (1172–96) and his wife Anne of Châtillon can be found, and everywhere the intricate floral frescoes of Bertalan Székely. In a side room is the Museum of Ecclesiastical Art containing religious relics (including a dessicated Saintly foot!), a copy of the crown of St. Stephen, a sculptured Black Madonna and some masterly gold monstrances.

When King Matthias died heirless in 1490 the powerful Black Army of mercenaries that had helped him conquer Vienna in 1485 was disbanded. This, together with a peasant revolt against the nobles in 1514, did much to destabilise the cultured and ordered kingdom Matthias had created. On August 26th 1526 the Turks led by Suleyman the Magnificent, Sultan of the Ottoman Empire, routed the Hungarians at the Battle of Mohács in southern Hungary and plundered Buda of its royal treasure, ransacking Pest into the bargain (fortunately the church treasures were removed safely to present-day Bratislava). Buda's first Golden Age thus came to an abrupt end and Hungary would not regain full control of her affairs for several centuries.

Matthias adopted the epithet 'Corvinus' from the Hunyadi family coat of arms that included a raven, the Latin for which is corvus. The coat of arms is carved part way up the outside of the south tower of the church and also hangs beside the main altar. Legends abound as to why the raven was chosen, including one in which the bird was successfully hunted down after having stolen the king's signet ring. Others invoke the family's property called Raven's Rock whilst another relates how, whilst the young Matthias was imprisoned in Prague, his mother would send letters to him carried by a raven. Today, ravens with rings in their beaks even adorn the old Corvin Cinema in Pest (see nos. 37 & 61).

Other places of interest nearby: 5, 6, 8, 9

8 The Historical Hilton

District I (Vár), the Hilton Budapest hotel (Hilton Szálló)
at Hess András tér 1-3 on Castle Hill (Várhegy)
Bus 16 from M1/M2/M3 Deák Ferenc tér;
Funicular railway from Clark Ádám tér

A modern hotel that opened on January 1st, 1977 would hardly seem the sort of place that visitors looking for unusual sights would head for and yet the Hilton Budapest is a rare exception, occupying an historic site on Castle Hill next to the famous Matthias Church (Mátyástemplom) (see no. 7). What makes it so different is not only the manner in which architect Béla Pintér has made its modern structure blend in with the surrounding Baroque and neo-Gothic structures, but also that within its fabric the remains of two actual historic structures have been sensitively incorporated. Little wonder the president of the Hilton chain dubbed it "the pearl in the whole string"!

The hotel's main entrance is set within the facade of a late 18th century Jesuit College built in the so-called Zopf Style, a German/Central European variant of late Baroque (Rococo) characterised by the use of strapwork mouldings on the façade. The rest of the facade comprises the early Gothic remains of a Dominican monastery built in 1254, its old church tower now housing the hotel's casino. Incorporated into the stonework of the tower is a relief depict-

Looking westwards towards the Matthias Church (left) and the Hilton Hotel (right) on Castle Hill

ing the Renaissance King Matthias (Mátyás) 'Corvinus' Hunyadi (1458–90).

Inside the hotel, on the lefthand side, there is a plate glass window in the bar through which more of the monastery ruins can be viewed forming a wonderfully theatrical courtyard that is sometimes used for *al fresco* summer opera performances and affording a spectacular view out across the city. Several stone columns from the nave of the old church of St. Nicholas have been reused here for added effect. For a closer look the courtyard may be entered from the outside to the rear of the building; look out for an ancient milestone that once marked the boundary of the Roman Empire two thousand years ago. The adjacent restaurant, aptly named The Dominican, offers panoramic views too – as well as gourmet cuisine and fine Hungarian Tokaj wine.

Relief of King Matthias incorporated into the modern Hilton Hotel

Visitors to the nearby mock-medieval Fishermen's Bastion may notice on its east side the statues of the monks Julianus and Gellért, the latter not to be confused with Saint Gellért whose statue stands on Gellért Hill. The monks remind us that the Hilton Hotel is built on the historic site of a Dominican monastery friary.

Castle Hill has another restaurant concealed within historic surroundings, namely the Rivalda at Színház utca 5-9, its pretty courtyard once part of a Carmelite nunnery whose former church is now the auditorium of the National Dance Theatre (see no. 20); Beethoven performed here in 1800.

Other places of interest nearby: 6, 7, 9

9 Gothic Glimpses on Castle Hill

District I (Vár), Országház utca 18, 20 and 22 on Castle Hill
(Várhegy)
Bus 16 from M1/M2/M3 Deák Ferenc tér;
Funicular railway from Clark Ádám tér

Although the two ancient settlements of Buda and Pest were merged in 1873 their characters remain very distinct. Whereas Pest is a flat swathe of commercial concerns and housing developments, broken up by grand 19th century boulevards and shopping arcades, Buda's Castle Hill is a 60-metre high craggy fastness crowned with a palace, medieval ramparts and narrow cobblestoned alleyways.

Castle Hill was first settled and fortified in the 13th century by King Béla IV (1235–70), and then permanently inhabited as a royal residence by Sigismund (Zsigmond) of Luxembourg (1387–1437), who became Holy Roman Emperor in 1433; later it was turned into a seat of learning and luxury by the Renaissance King Matthias (Mátyás) 'Corvinus' Hunyadi (1458–90) (see no. 46). Having been repeatedly laid waste by everyone from the Mongols (Tartars) (1241) and the Ottomans (1541) to the Habsburgs (1686) and the Soviets (1945), much of Castle Hill is of necessity a reconstruction, albeit a reasonably convincing one (see no. 3). However, if one knows where to look, jutting out from the oft-rebuilt walls can still be found some authentic elements surviving from the original 14th and 15th century medieval town, built after the withdrawal of the Mongols but before the Ottoman occupation.

The best place to commence this Gothic odyssey is the basement of the Budapest History Museum (Budapesti Történeti Múzeum) in Wing E of Buda's former Royal Palace, where there is a fascinating plaster model showing the various medieval remains so far discovered on Castle Hill (the palace building above has itself been re-built numerous times, notably in late 18th century Rococo style by Empress Maria Theresa (1740–80), in 19th century neo-Baroque style for Emperor Franz Joseph I (1848–1916) after damage sustained during the 1848 Revolution, and finally in its present style following the ravages of the Second World War). A further, much steeper flight of stairs leads further down to a labyrinthine Gothic vaulted undercroft (*gótikus terem*), where parts of the medieval royal palace of King Matthias can be visited, including remains of a 14th century Gothic Chapel only discovered in the 1960s and reconsecrated. In addition to its famed library (the Bibliotheca Corviniana, a few volumes from which are displayed in the neighbouring National Széchenyi Library (Országos Széchenyi Könyvtár) in Wing F) the palace is reputed to have had hot running water, poet-musicians, wine-spouting fountains and a hall large enough to host horseback tournaments!

Next-door in Wing C of the former Royal Palace there is the Hungarian National Gallery (Magyar Nemzeti Galéria), on the ground floor of which is the Medieval and Renaissance Stone Collection (*Lapidarium*) containing many beautifully sculptured fragments from the old palace. In its cellar is the Palatine Crypt (*Nádor kripta*), built by the Habsburgs in 1715 as part of a Baroque reconstruction of the Palace and occupying the former site of the medieval Chapel of St. Sigismund.

Leaving the palace and entering the Castle District proper to the north (*Várnegyed*) takes one along Tárnok utca where, amongst the later Austrian Baroque rebuilding, there are some corbelled, 14th century merchants' houses at numbers 14 and 16. Inside the entranceway at number 13 can be seen some curious arched wall niches known as *sedilias*. The function of these distinctively Gothic features is controversial with some commentators believing them to be defensive posts, suggested by the fact that they are usually found just inside arched entranceways that gave horsedrawn vehicles access to a building's courtyard. By the same token they could have had a trading purpose, some being enhanced with the addition of a counter, or else they may have been purely decorative. On the other hand, the fact that *sedilias* are more usually found in rows of three inside Gothic churches, as seats for the clergy, suggests that they were used as such by servants. A left turn at the top of the street, opposite the Matthias Church (Mátyástemplom), runs into Szentháromság utca, where further *sedilias* can be seen at number 5.

Gothic corbels form part of a Baroque façade on Országház utca, Castle Hilla

Gothic sedilias concealed in a passageway on Úri utca

Turning right along Úri utca ('Gentlemanly Street'), which runs along the western ramparts of Castle Hill, produces yet more Gothic features, notably at numbers 32 and 48, incorporated into the neatly plastered ochre-coloured facades of later Baroque buildings. At this point a narrow lane, Dárda utca, leads eastwards past an old archway onto Országház utca, where a row of houses at numbers 18, 20 and 22 gives an impression of how the Castle District might have looked in the Middle Ages (there are further *sedilias* at numbers 2 and 9). Italian craftsmen working on the Royal Palace once lived here.

Continuing eastwards Fortuna köz leads onto Hess András tér, where again *sedilias* can be found inside the Fortuna Restaurant. Finally, leading away from Hess András tér along the eastern ramparts of Castle Hill is Táncsics Mihály utca, where at number 26 is a medieval Jewish Prayer House, or *Bethel*, excavated in 1964. Sephardic Jews arriving in Buda in the wake of the Ottoman conquest established and used it during the 16th and 17th centuries, although it contains Jewish gravestones collected from the surrounding area that date as far back as 1268. Directly opposite at number 23 is an older and larger synagogue from the late 15th century, still buried underground and awaiting excavation.

Other places of interest nearby: 6, 7, 8

10 The Saviour of Mothers

District I (Tabán), the Semmelweis Museum of Medical History (Semmelweis Orvostörténeti Múzeum) at Apród utca 1-3
Tram 18 from M1 Déli Pályaudvar, 19 along the Buda embankment; Bus 7 from Ferenciek tere

Tucked away between Castle Hill and Gellért Hill is a valley known as the Tabán (see nos. 27 & 30). Before a devastating fire in 1810 and clearance in 1933 for sanitary reasons its winding streets and single-storey houses would have resembled Vienna's bustling wine village of Grinzing. Little now remains except for its Baroque parish church (Tabáni plébániatemplom) on Szarvas tér, known also as the Church of St. Catherine of Alexandria, which stands on the site of a 12th century chapel (a copy of an important fragment of which, known as *The Tabán Christ*, is in a niche below the organ). There is also a horseshoe-shaped corner building at Szarvas tér 1, built in the early 1700s as The Golden Stag Inn (Arany Szarvas vendéglő) and named after a relief depicting a stag chased by hounds above its portico (another historic inn sign is that of the Red Hedgehog Inn (Vörös Sün Ház) at Hess Andras tér 3, Buda's only inn until 1784).

However, most fascinating of all is the manor house at Apród utca 1–3 where the famous Hungarian physician Ignác Semmelweis was born in 1818. Semmelweis graduated in Vienna in 1844 and began working as an assistant in a hospital there, where he noticed a dramatic difference in the mortality rates of mothers suffering from Puerperal (or Childbed) Fever in two different wards. On investigation, Semmelweis discovered that the ward with the lower death rate

The birthplace of Ignác Semmelweis on Apród utca, now the Semmelweis Museum

was run by midwives, who tended to keep their environment clean, whilst the higher mortality rate belonged to a ward managed by medical students, who often attended births directly after conducting autopsies. When a friend died from septicaemia after cutting himself with a scalpel during a dissection Semmelweis's suspicions were confirmed: insanitary conditions facilitated the transfer of "cadaveric material" and "putrid particles" directly into the open wounds of previously healthy patients. In 1847 his theory was put to the test and students were encouraged to wash their hands in bowls containing a disinfecting solution of lime chloride. Within two years the mortality rate in the hospital had plumetted and Semmelweis was dubbed the "Saviour of Mothers". Regrettably, his professional colleagues were unimpressed, continuing with their insanitary habits and returning him to Budapest on the pretext of Hungary's rebellion against the Habsburgs in 1848. Although in time Semmelweis built up a successful gynaecological and obstetrics practice, he gradually became embittered and depressed. He died on August 13th 1865 twelve days after being admitted to a mental asylum back in Vienna, some say from streptococcal blood poisoning from an infected finger, although such irony has been recently cast into doubt.

The tomb of Ignác Semmelweis in the Kerepesi Cemetery

Aged just 47 Ignác Semmelweis was buried in Budapest's Kerepesi Cemetery (see no. 58). It was not long, however, before Semmelweis came to be seen as a martyr to the cause of medicine, his opinions on surgical cleanliness becoming standard practice. Today, Budapest's University of Medicine (Semmelweis Orvostudományi Egyetem), where he taught in the 1800s, as well as a street in the city are both named after him.

Meanwhile, his birthplace in the Tabán has been transformed into the Semmelweis Museum of Medical History and is one of the largest of its type in the world. The collection traces the history of medicine from ancient times and includes exhibits such as the diagnostic bones of a South

African witch doctor, Roman surgical instruments excavated at nearby Aquincum, etched glasses used for drinking spa water, a Far Eastern opium pipe and a copy of a medieval chastity belt. There is also the gilded wood interior of the Holy Ghost Pharmacy (1813), brought here from Király utca in Pest, and now used to display apothecary jars from across Hungary. Most unusual are the anatomical models that were once used as study aids in the University of Medicine's world-renowned Department of Anatomy. The Holy Roman Emperor Joseph II (1780–90) commissioned the models from the Florentine physiologist Felice Fontana and the Tuscan anatomist Paolo Mascagni during a visit to Florence in 1780. They are rendered in beeswax for added realism. Unfortunately, much of the collection was lost through neglect when study practices changed, as well as through irreparable damage inflicted during the siege of

Quite rightly, Ignac Semmelweis has a Budapest street named after him

Budapest in the winter of 1944–45. Thankfully, the most highly prized model depicting the lymphatic system of the female body has survived to this day. Finally, amongst the medical books displayed in the Semmelweis Memorial Room can be seen a seven-volume set of Osler's *Modern Medicine* given by former American President George Bush Senior to József Antall, a onetime director of the museum, who latterly became Hungary's first democratic Prime Minister (1990–93) of the post Soviet era.

Other places of interest nearby: 2, 11, 12

11   A Much Loved Empress

District I (Tabán), the statue of Empress and Queen Elisabeth
(Erzsébet királyné szobor) on Döbrentei tér
Tram 18 from M1 Déli pályaudvar, 19 along the Buda
embankment; Bus 7 from Ferenciek tere

Standing in a small square on the Buda side of the Elisabeth Bridge
(Erzsébet híd) is a seated statue of Empress and Queen Elisabeth,
wife of the Habsburg Franz Joseph I (1848–1916), Emperor of Austria
and King of Hungary. Created by György Zala in 1937 it commemorates the assassination of the Empress by Italian anarchist Luigi
Luccheni on September 10th, 1898 whilst she was boarding a steamer

A pensive statue
of Elisabeth,
Queen of Hungary
on Döbrentei tér

on Lake Geneva. The statue once stood on the other side of the river in Pest but was removed in 1947 and brought to this location four decades later after anti-Fascist resistance fighters blew up an earlier statue of a right-wing politician who had encouraged Hungary's alliance with Nazi Germany.

The statue of Elisabeth is unusual on two counts: firstly, it is one of the city's rare figurative tributes to a member of the often-oppressive Habsburg monarchy (see no. 13) and secondly locals decorate it occasionally with floral tributes. To understand why Hungarians continue to hold the Austrian Empress, or 'Sisi' as her admirers know her, in such high esteem is not difficult to understand. Elisabeth was born on December 24th 1837 into the eccentric German Wittelsbach dynasty (one of her cousins was the so-called "Mad" King Ludwig

One of several locations in Budapest named after Elisabeth

II of Bavaria). In the summer of 1853 she accompanied her mother and older sister, Helene, on a trip to the resort of Bad Ischl in Upper Austria where they hoped Helene would catch the eye of their cousin, the young Emperor Franz Joseph. In reality it was the fifteen-year-old Elisabeth he noticed and after a very public whirlwind romance the two were married in Vienna the following spring.

Almost immediately Elisabeth encountered difficulties with the rigid protocol of the Viennese court but despite this dutifully bore the Emperor three children, including the eagerly awaited male heir to the throne, Rudolf. With rumours circulating of her husband's infidelities and denied any part in her childrens' upbringing, which was undertaken by the Emperor's mother, the domineering Archduchess Sophie, Elisabeth's behaviour grew erratic as her marriage unravelled. In 1860 in order to avoid Vienna and its stifling routines Elisabeth embarked on a life of travel, seeking solace in Madeira, horseriding in England, building a palace in Corfu and, most controversially of all, fraternising with her Hungarian subjects (accompanied by her Hungarian ladies-in-waiting she satisfied her famously sweet tooth at Budapest's Gerbeaud coffee house).

Although loved by the Viennese today, Elisabeth's pro-Hungarian sentiments during her lifetime appalled many of them. Sympathising with the cause of Hungarian nationalism she spoke Hungarian fluently, wrote letters to her family in Hungarian and played a part in the eventual acceptance of the Dual Monarchy by the Hungarian populace following the Austro-Hungarian Compromise Agreement of 1867, whereby Franz Joseph I remained Emperor of Austria and was crowned King of Hungary. The Compromise allowed Hungary to manage its own domestic affairs, build its own Parliament and opened up Buda, Óbuda and Pest to foreign capital. The three towns were unified in 1873.

Looking eastwards across Elisabeth Bridge towards Pest

Elisabeth and the Emperor were reconciled briefly at their coronation in the Matthias Church (Mátyás-templom) in Budapest, where a bust of the empress can be found in the Museum of Ecclesiastical Art (see no. 7). It was during this time that the Gödöllő Palace north-east of Budapest was presented to the couple as a gift.

Although Elisabeth's contribution to the politics of the day should not be overstated, after all her fabled obsession with her looks and weight probably consumed much of her time, it cannot be denied that she had a common touch that the Emperor couldn't begin to match. Consequently, at a grass roots level, mid-19th century Hungarians could relate to the troubled young Empress – and she to them.

Early in the morning of January 30th 1889 Elisabeth's only son Crown Prince Rudolf committed suicide, together with his seventeen-year-old mistress, in his hunting lodge at Mayerling; Rudolf's humiliated wife, Princess Stephanie, would later be rejuvenated by Budapest cosmetics pioneer Dr. Erno Laszlo in the 1920s. The Empress wore black for the rest of her days and grew increasingly frail and reclusive.

It was whilst she was on her way to take tea with Baroness Rothschild in Montreux that the Empress was stabbed, dying of her wounds within an hour or two. Her assassin had been fixed on killing the Duke of Orléans but when he didn't appear decided upon the Empress instead (for no reason other than she was famous), whose presence had been unwisely announced in a local paper. Both Austrians and Hungarians alike mourned deeply for the death of their Empress – and the enduring legend of Sisi was born. A visit to her last resting place today, in Vienna's Kaisergruft where the Habsburgs have been buried for centuries will reveal her sarcophagus draped not only in Austrian red and white but also the distinctive red, white and green of the Hungarian flag.

Other locations named after the Empress include Erzsébet körút running through District VII, Erzsébet tér and the Hotel Erzsébet at Károlyi utca 11 in District V, and the Elisabeth Tower in the Buda Hills (see no. 22); the elegant Elisabeth Bridge, connecting Belváros in District V with Gellérthegy in District XI, was begun in 1897 and remained the world's longest suspension bridge until 1926, only to be blown up by retreating German troops in 1945 and rebuilt in 1964; finally there is District VII, called Erzsébetváros, reflecting Habsburg influence on the development of Pest in the late 19th century (similarly, Terézváros was named after Empress Maria Theresa (1740–80), Krisztinaváros after her daughter, Józsefváros after Emperor Joseph II (1780–90), Lipótváros after Emperor Leopold II (1790–92), and József nádor tér after the Palatine (or Nádor) Archduke Joseph of Habsburg, son of Leopold and Imperial representative in Hungary).

Other places of interest nearby: 10, 12, 13

12 The Ottomans' Bathing Legacy

District I (Tabán), the Rudas Thermal Baths (Rudas Gyógyfürdő)
at Döbrentei tér 9
Tram 18 from Déli pályaudvar, 19 along the Buda embankment;
Bus 7 from Ferenciek tere

No other city in the world has more active thermal springs bubbling below its surface than Budapest – approximately 120 around Castle Hill and its surroundings, percolating up through the limestone with a combined daily output estimated at 70 million litres. The presence of abundant spring water first drew prehistoric man to Castle Hill 4,000 years ago (see nos. 13 & 14) and the Romans built an aqueduct to channel water from the springs to their military baths (see no. 34). The Order of the Knights Hospitallers had bathhouses here in the 13th century, the Renaissance King Matthias (Mátyás) 'Corvinus' Hunyadi (1458–90) had his own bathing facility below his palace at the foot of Castle Hill and Buda's early Jewish community used the waters for their ritual bathing. However, it was not until the Ottoman occupation of Buda in the mid-16th century that the warm, mineral-laden and mildy radioactive waters were first extensively exploited, using the technology of the Turkish bath, or *Hamam*.

Islam forbids that the body be immersed fully in still water and insists on running water ablutions only. Consequently, traditional *Hamam* baths consist of three inter-connected rooms, namely a hot room for soaking up steam and scrubbing, a warm room for washing with soap and water and a cool room for relaxing. The *Hamam* is a place for social gathering, ritual cleansing and an important part of any town's architectural landscape, the latter provided by the iconic dome of the hot room, its ceiling pierced by small apertures allowing shafts of light to penetrate the steamy darkness within. In Ottoman Buda, being far away from the restrictions of Constantinople, the *Hamam*s were augmented with hot and cold plunge pools ranged around the central hot room. Still adhered to today, the classic progression through an Ottoman-period bath in Buda is as follows: dry sauna, shower and cool pool, relax in the hot room, then the humid steam room and finally the cold plunge.

Most atmospheric of the remaining Ottoman baths are the Rudas Thermal Baths (Rudas Gyógyfürdő), constructed by Sokoli Mustapha, Pasha of Buda from 1566–78, whose name appears on a plaque marking the site of the springs on the cliff behind. His name also appears in the bath's main columned octagonal chamber, the dome above it inlaid with coloured glass. The Rudas contains six pools of differing temperature (from 16–42 °C), three saunas, and two steam rooms and offers both massage and rheumatic/respiratory cures.

Within a stone's throw of the Rudas, to the north, are the Rác Thermal Baths (Rác Gyógyfürdő) at Hadnagy utca 8–10 (the word 'rác' means 'Serb' in Hungarian, the area having once been inhabited by Serbians). Although now part of a luxury hotel with a 19th century façade and lobby by Miklós Ybl the domed octagonal main pool is still resolutely Ottoman.

The Ottoman Király Thermal Baths on Fő utca

To the north of Castle Hill, is Buda's third Ottoman bath building, the Király Thermal Baths (Király Gyógyfürdő) at Fő utca 82–84 (District II). Like the Rudas and the Rác it too is built on the riverbank but differs in that its original facade is still visible. The baths were begun by Arslan, Turkish governor of Buda from 1565–66, and completed by his successor Pasha Sokoli Mustapha in 1570. It was Arslan who built a wall around the Víziváros district – inside which the baths are situated – allowing them to be used safely by the Ottoman garrison. In 1796, long after the Turkish withdrawal, and having had several different owners, the baths were bought by the König family (the word 'Király' being Hungarian for König, or King) and it was they who added the neo-Classical wings seen today. The Király now has four pools (26–40 °C), saunas, camomile-scented steam rooms and offers massage and rheumatic/arthritic cures.

Other places of interest nearby: 10, 11, 13

13 The Budapest Bastille

District XI (Gellérthegy), the Citadel (Citadella) at Citadella
sétány on Gellért Hill (Gellérthegy)
Tram 18 from M1 Déli pályaudvar, 19 along the Buda embankment, 47, 49 from Kálvin tér; Bus 7 from Ferenciek tere to
Móricz Zsigmond körtér then Bus 27

The western bank of the Danube in Budapest is characterised by the
outline of two hills, namely Castle Hill (Várhegy), with its narrow
streets and medieval foundations, and the less-frequented Gellért Hill
(Gellérthegy) to the south, separated by the saddle of land known as
the Tabán (below part of which is a hidden reservoir).

Archaeological remains have shown that early man was first
drawn to Gellért Hill by the presence of thermal springs that formed
caves around its lower slopes; most significantly there is settlement evidence for the Celtic Eravi tribe in the Late Iron Age (4th
century BC) whose citadel (or *oppidum*) occupied the summit of
the hill. Unfortunately, the hill's
reputation during historic times
has been a less than peaceful
one. Not only was it reputed to
be a haunt of witches but during or shortly after the reign of
Hungary's first Christian king, St.
Stephen (István) (1001–1038), it
was here that the Venetian Bishop
Gellért, who had been assisting
the king to convert his people to
Christianity, was beaten to death
by reluctant pagan chieftains and
then placed in a barrel and rolled
into the Danube (see no. 40).
Today, a bronze statue of Gellért,
Hungary's first Christian martyr,
looking out over the Elisabeth
Bridge (Erzsébet híd), at the bottom of the hill that carries his
name.

The statue of Bishop Gellért on Gellért Hill

Crowning the summit of

Gellért Hill are the white walls of the so-called Citadel, a circular fortress erected by the Austrian army following their brutal suppression of the anti-Habsburg Revolution of 1848–49 (see nos. 39, 48 & 56). Visible for miles around and with cannon poking out from its battlements towards Castle Hill and Pest, the Citadel's function like that of the Paris Bastille was to remind the city's inhabitants who their masters were.

Habsburg fortifications on the Gellért Hill Citadel

Following the Austro-Hungarian Compromise Agreement of 1867 and the creation of the Dual Monarchy, the fortress was abandoned, parts of it symbolically demolished in 1894 and in 1897, the rest becoming the property of the Hungarian Government. Having served variously as a prison, an anti-aircraft battery and a hostel for the homeless the Citadel today provides visitors with one of the most spectacular views over Budapest (see no. 22).

Perched on the Citadel's ramparts is the Freedom Monument (Szabadság-szobor), erected by the Soviets to commemorate the freeing of the city from German forces at the end of the Second World War (see no. 39). The sense of liberation would be shortlived as an equally repressive Communist regime quickly replaced its Fascist predecessor (see no. 14). With the eventual declaration of the Third Hungarian Republic in 1989, however, the monument was shorn of its Communist symbols and the erection of two pieces of the recently demolished Berlin Wall on the hill confirmed the city's newfound sense of independence.

To the west of Gellért Hill there is an important nature reserve on Sas Hill (Sas-hegy), home to the rare Hungarian Meadow Saxifrage, St. Stephen's Pink, Buda Hare's Tail grass, the Pannonian Lizard and the unique Bull Spider.

Other places of interest nearby: 12, 14, 15

14 The Chapel in the Rock

District XI (Gellérthegy), the Cave Church (Sziklatemplom/
Sziklakápolna) just off Verejték utca on Gellért Hill
(Gellérthegy)
Tram 18 from M1 Déli pályaudvar, 19 along the Buda embank-
ment, 47, 49 from Kálvin tér; Bus 7 from Ferenciek tere

Just opposite the entrance to the Gellért Thermal Baths, at the
southern foot of Gellért Hill, there is an outcrop of rock containing
a natural cavern. Archaeological evidence has shown that primitive
man inhabited such caves 4,000 years ago (see no. 13). In the early
middle ages local tradition relates how a charitable hermit named
Iván made a subterranean home for himself here, dispensing cures to
the sick with the help of the therapeutic waters that bubbled up near

The entrance to the Cave Church
of St. Paul on Gellért Hill

the cave's entrance. By rights
this historic cave should have
been named after Iván the
hermit – but this was not to
be. Indeed, somewhat confus-
ingly, the place was known for
centuries as either St. Gellért's
or St. Stephen's Cave because
of tales relating to these historical characters that were
played out on Gellért Hill (see
nos. 13 & 40).

In the 1920s the Paulite
monks converted the cave
into a pilgrims' chapel. The
Paulites are the only monastic
order of purely Hungarian origin and were founded in 1308
by Özséb, canon of Esztergom,
following the Mongol (Tartar)
invasion of 1241. They named
themselves after a 3rd-century
Egyptian hermit called Paul,
who entered the desert in order
to be closer to God. His only

companion during this period of self-imposed seclusion was a raven, trained to bring him a mere half a slice of bread a day (a charming painted architectural fragment in the Budapest History Museum depicts the saint with his raven). Originally, the Paulites had built a monastery in c. 1300 in the Buda Hills that was destroyed during the Ottoman invasion and replaced by a Baroque successor still extant in Pest (see no. 23).

In 1931 Count Gyula Zichy, archbishop of Kalocsa, by whose efforts the Paulite Order had been re-established after 150 years of inactivity, expanded the Gellért cave chapel into a series of interconnected chapels, where Polish refugees would take shelter during the 1940s (note the wall plaque in the Polish Chapel). In 1934 the

The Paulite Monastery at the foot of Gellért Hill

order was also responsible for constructing the monastery against the hillside on the riverbank below, a combination of Modern and Hungarian neo-Romanesque styles to a design by Károly Weichinger.

Tragically, by the 1950s both chapel and monastery had been seized by the Communists, the order dissolved, the Father Superior executed and the chapel walled up. It was not until August 1989 that the Cave Church and the monastery were eventually returned to the Paulites for reconsecration (an ugly lump of the cave chapel's concrete blocking wall is preserved to the right of the entrance). In the main chapel today can be seen a small apex stone with a relief of St. Paul, his faithful raven still perched on his shoulder.

Other places of interest nearby: 13, 15

15 Baths of the *Belle Époque*

District XI (Gellérthegy), the Gellért Thermal Baths, (Gellért Gyógyfürdő) at the Danubius Gellért Hotel, Kelenhegyi út 4
Tram 18 from M2 Déli pályaudvar, 19 along the Buda embankment, 47, 49 from Kálvin tér; Bus 7 from Ferenciek tere

During the early years of the 20th century thermal bathing became a craze across Europe and those cities blessed with natural springs were transformed as visitors flocked to take the curative waters. Boasting more thermal springs than any other city in the world, *fin de siècle* Budapest was in the vanguard of European spa cities, becoming a renowned centre for both leisure and therapeutic bathing and boasting cures for up to forty different ailments. The city's old Ottoman-period baths took on a new lease of life (see no. 12) and at least one Budapest entrepreneur made a fortune for himself bottling and selling spa water (see no. 66).

The most tangible reminder of these times is the trio of elegant new thermal bath complexes (*gyógyfürdő*), built to satisfy and capitalise on the huge demand for bathing facilities in what became known as the *Belle Époque*, a brief Golden Age of elegant living prior to the First World War. Foremost amongst these are the Gellért Thermal Baths designed by three architects (Artúr Sebestyén, Ármin

Art Nouveau splendour at the Gellért Thermal Baths

Hegedűs and Izidor Stark) between 1912 and 1918 as part of the glamorous, late Art Nouveau Gellért Hotel. They occupy the former site of an Ottoman mudbath facility demolished when the Szabadság Bridge was erected (the Aquincum Hotel Baths at Árpád fejedelem útja 94 in Óbuda (District III) still offer natural mud remedies). Using water from a medicinal spring already exploited in the 13th century, the baths are renowned for a foyer embellished with sea-green Art Nouveau pyrogranite tiles from the famous Zsolnay ceramic factory (see

Swimming back in time at the Gellért Thermal Baths

no. 54), as well as its oft-photographed colonnaded and glass-roofed indoor pool. The waters of the Gellért's four thermal pools (26–38 °C) are suffused with carbonic gases recommended for patients with blood pressure and heart troubles.

Secondly is the Széchenyi Thermal Baths (Széchenyi Gyógyfürdő) at Állatkerti körút 11 (District XIV) in City Park. This was the first public bathhouse to be built in Pest, using a thermal spring discovered in 1879 by Zsigmondy Vilmos, whose statue stands proudly outside; at 74–75 °C they are the hottest thermal springs in the city. With its luxuriously appointed, domed neo-Baroque bathhouse erected in 1913 it was the biggest spa complex in Europe and is still visited by a million people annually! A popular pastime in the vast outside pool (opened in 1927) is to play chess, something that looks somewhat bizarre in winter when the ghostly figures are shrouded in steam. The south wing contains a dozen pools at varying temperatures for the treatment of arthritic, rheumatic and respiratory disorders; drink-

ing the water is said to be effective against gall bladder disease.

Budapest's third great *Belle Époque* baths are the Lukács Thermal Baths (Lukács Gyógyfürdő) to the north of Castle Hill at Frankel Leó utca 25–29 (District II). Constructed during the 1920s the complex incorporates a four-pool thermal centre built on the site of the Ottoman bath of Bey Veli that was remodelled in the 1880s (see the old lily-strewn pond and Turkish bath building across the road). Its hard sulphurous spring waters (17–50 °C) have been used to treat those with locomotive, muscular and nervous disorders, as witnessed by the many votive plaques in the leafy forecourt. The opportunity to taste the pungent waters from an old

Neo-Baroque architecture at the Széchenyi Thermal Baths in City Park

marble drinking hall near the entrance should not be missed. The two outdoor swimming pools are where the city's intellectuals often met during the 1970s and 80s and still do. It should be remembered, however, that Budapest historic baths, whether Ottoman or *Belle Époque*, account for just half a dozen of the city's fifty or so bathing facilities currently in operation.

It is actually possible to experience the splendour of a Belle Époque bath building without getting wet! The glorious Hungária fürdő at Dohány utca 42-44 (District VII), which until just a few years ago was a ruin threatened with demolition, has been superbly restored, and is now the luxury Zara hotel. The hotel foyer located beneath a vast barrel-vaulted ceiling is where the main pool was originally located.

Other places of interest nearby: 13, 14

16 Floating History on the Danube

District XI (Lágymányos), the A38 barge moored on the Buda
side of the Danube 150 metres south of the Petőfi Bridge
Tram 4, 6 around the Nagykörút

One of Budapest's most unusually located cultural venues must
surely be the A38 barge moored on the banks of the Danube near the
Petőfi Bridge. Formerly a Ukrainian stone-carrying ship it celebrated
its first year as one of Budapest's most fashionable venues on May 1st
2004 – the day Hungary joined the European Union.

The A38 is 85.25 metres long and 15.5 metres wide and was built in
1968, its name being the abbreviation for *Artemovszk*, a discontin-
ued prototype of the Soviet *okskiy* barge type. Having been bought
and towed to Budapest by an ambitious private enterprise called
Zászlóshajó Ltd. the barge underwent an 18-month conversion (the
total cost being 3 million Euros). Its cavernous insides offered 2000
square metres of useable space enabling a group of architects, maritime engineers and acoustic experts to create a unique floating venue.

The resulting blend of Communist-era engineering, industrial
heritage and state-of-the-art equipment has proved extremely popular with both artists and audiences alike. At its heart is a 300 square
metre multipurpose venue in the former hold that can accommodate 600 standing and 250-seated people. It plays host to a varied
programme of events from classical musical through jazz and rock
to the latest DJ performances. On the deck above is a glass-walled

The A38 barge, now a floating cultural venue, moored near Petőfi Bridge

restaurant and bar whilst above that is a third floor offering an open terrace bar for dancing, studio and conference room. The bar has been voted one of the world's best by readers of renowned travel publisher, Lonely Planet.

Another historic ship moored permanently on the Danube can be found farther upstream, at the Vigadó tér landing stage (District V). It is the Kossuth Museum Ship and is an adjunct of the city's Transport Museum (see no. 77). This splendid old Danube paddle steamer was built for the Hungarian Royal Inland & Maritime Navigation Company in the Ganz-Danubius shipyard in Újpest in 1913. It was originally named *Archduke Ferdinand* but with the collapse of the Habsburg Empire in 1919 it was re-named *Rigó* and later *Leányfalu* in 1930. After being taken to Austria at the end of the Second World War it was returned to Budapest in 1947 and became the property of the Hungarian-Russian Navigation Company. In 1953 it was converted to oil and given the superstructure it still has today. Eventually in 1976, after becoming the property of the Hungarian Navigation Company, the ship was decommissioned and languished back in the docks at Újpest serving as a houseboat. Thankfully during the 1980s the potential of this floating piece of Budapest history was recognised and in 1986 it was modernised and opened to the public. Subsequent restoration has seen the renamed *Kossuth* become home to the elegant Old Timer Ship Restaurant (Vénhajó Étterem). In complete contrast the nearby Spoon Café & Lounge occupies a modern triple-deck boat, offering a convertible winter garden on the roof and an oriental bar below the water line.

Other nautical-themed restaurants include the Admiral Restaurant at Belgrád rakpart 30, its wood-panelled walls resembling an old-fashioned schooner, and the novel Verne Étterem-Restaurant at Váci utca 60, designed to look like Captain Nemo's Nautilus submarine. For those who really want to feel the flow of the river beneath their feet there is also the Fortuna Hotel Boat (Fortunahajó) moored at Szent István park's lower quay near the Margaret Bridge (District XIII).

17 The Park of the Toppled Statues

District XXII (Budatétény), Memento Park (Szoborpark)
on the corner of Balatoni út and Szabadkai utca
Direct bus service (including tour) leaves from M1/M2/M3 Deák
Ferenc tér daily at 11am; alternatively Tram 47 from Deák Ferenc
tér to Újbuda Központ, then Bus 150 to Memento Park

From the German army's surrender of Buda's Castle Hill on February 13th 1945 (see no. 3) until the first free elections held in March 1990, Budapest was effectively in Communist hands. The task of rebuilding the war-damaged city, complete with Communist iconography, fell to the Soviet military government who quickly placed loyal Hungarian Communists in many positions of power. Despite only taking 17% of the vote during the November 1945 election, the Soviet authorities demanded the Hungarian Communist Party remain in control. As a result, a Communist dictatorship was gradually introduced by nationalising private property, suffocating opposition parties, limiting personal freedoms and establishing a secret police force (ÁVO, later the ÁVH).

Statue of a Russian soldier moved from Gellért Hill to Memento Park

By 1949 thousands of dissenters had been rounded up and dispatched on one-way tickets to the Soviet Union and incoming General Secretary Mátyás Rákosi (1945–56) had traditional Hungarian Communist leaders executed as foreign spies (see no. 69). With compulsory industrialisation, the nationalisation of schools and the homogenisation of the city's social identity in favour of a classless society, the Communist stranglehold on Hungary was complete.

Stalin's death in 1953 brought only the briefest respite and in 1956 Khrushchev's Kremlin installed another tough General Secretary in the shape of Ernő Gerő (July–October 1956). Despite Hungarians eventually revolting against the oppressive Russian yoke in October of the same year (see no. 37), the Soviet grip soon tightened again as the Russians installed yet another General Secretary, namely János Kádár (1956–88). However, there was a growing need to appease the disgruntled population and Kádár, who had implemented a bloody revenge against the revolutionaries, offered amnesties in 1963 to some of those jailed after the 1956 Uprising.

By 1968 Kádár's radical new economic reforms were breaking with traditional Communist thinking and permitted controlled private enterprise (a watered-down version of Soviet despotism termed 'Goulash Communism'!). By the time of Kádár's death in 1989 Hungary's links with its old Warsaw pact neighbours had reached breaking point. Having now also grown reliant on foreign trade and facing rising inflation and a series of mass protests, the so-called Reform Communists gave way to free elections. With them the traditional Communist party in Hungary was defeated, a new Hungarian Republic was proclaimed on October 23rd 1989 and the end of Communism in Europe was heralded (the withdrawal of Soviet troops in 1991 is still celebrated in Hungary each June 24th with the Budapesti Búcsú (Budapest Departure) street festival).

A very tangible change to the cityscape of Budapest that occurred as a result of these changes was the rapid removal of nearly all Communist street propaganda. The names of Marx Square, Lenin Boulevard and the Avenue of the People's Republic were obvious victims, as were other "symbols of tyranny" such as the red star (still considered as inflammatory as the Nazi swastika), which were forbidden by law (see no. 39). Similarly the many statues of Soviet 'greats', Hungarian Communist leaders, Workers' Movement heroes, soldiers and proud factory workers found themselves quickly and unceremoniously uprooted from the city's parks and squares and dumped in a farmer's field out in District XXII. Today these fascinating examples of monuments in the so-called Socialist Realism style form what is surely one of Europe's more unusual collections of sculpture, namely Memento Park (see no. 75).

Entered via a gateway inscribed with Gyula Illyés's poem *One Sentence on Tyranny* ("Where there is tyranny, Everyone is a link in the chain") the park was the brainchild of two enterprising young Hungarians who felt these forlorn sculptures still had a valuable story to tell. Typical are the Cubist granite statues of Marx and Engels at the entrance, which once graced the former Communist Party Headquarters at Széchenyi rakpart 19 (District V), the huge Russian soldier that once adorned the Freedom Monument (Szabadság-szobor) on Gellért Hill (see no. 39) and the so-called *Stand to!* by István Kiss from Dózsa György út (District XIV).

Noteworthy too is the monument to Béla Kun that once stood on Vérmező út (District I). Kun was the founder of the Hungarian Communist Party and leader of a shortlived Hungarian Soviet Republic in 1919 (known variously as the Republic of Councils, or Commune), the second Communist government to be founded in Europe after Russia itself. Following the First World War and the collapse of the Habsburg Monarchy, Hungary had declared total independence from Austria. However, faced with losing two-thirds of its territories

Stand to! by István Kiss in Memento Park

under the Treaty of Trianon, the government of the newly independent First Hungarian Republic under Mihály Károlyi had resigned and handed power to the Social Democrats. They in turn made a coalition with Kun's new Hungarian Communist Party in an attempt to woo Soviet support against the dictates of the Western Allies. However, with support from Moscow not forthcoming due to the Russian Civil War, the anti-Communist Romanian army crushed Kun's ambitions and the former Habsburg Admiral Miklós Horthy (1920–44) took power as regent with a Christian-right coalition parliament. Hungary had begun its inexorable slip from short-lived Communism via right wing Conservatism towards a pro-Fascist regime.

The sculptor of the Béla Kun monument was Imre Varga, a favoured artist under the Kádár regime, who despite such an apparent handicap is now something of a household name in Hungary (see no. 62; Varga's Sculpture Museum is at Laktanya utca 7 in Óbuda (District III)).Before leaving Memento Park glance at the gift shop selling CDs of rousing Proletariat anthems that are played through a 1950s radio.

18 The Budafok Calvary and the Champagne Castle

District XXII (Budafok), the Calvary (Kálvária Domb)
on Kálváriahegy utca
Tram 47, 49 around the Kiskörút to Móricz Zsigmond körtér,
then Bus 33 to Tóth József utca

Alighting from the number 3 bus in Budafok brings one face to face with the statue of a wine taster, a reminder that here is an historic wine-producing area. Further evidence of this activity can be discovered by walking up Tóth József utca and turning left along Pannónia utca, where the entrances to several old subterranean wine cellars are visible. It is said that the limestone hills of Budafok are riddled with 100 kilometres of such tunnels. A little further along, at Veréb utca, there is even an entire house constructed underground, now preserved as the Cave Dwelling Museum (Barlanglakás Múzeum).

Returning to the main street, a right hand turn leads onto Kereszt utca, off which Temető utca (Cemetery Street) leads to Budafok's small and peaceful, tree-lined burial ground. Continuing along Kereszt utca one reaches Kálváriahegy utca and shortly to a hidden architectural treasure – the Budafok Calvary. Following the Turkish

The little-known Baroque Calvary of Budafok

occupation, Budafok became an important centre of Catholic religious life and so it is not surprising to find a wayside Calvary here, an expression of religious devotion rendered in stone as ordered by the Council of Trent during the Counter Reformation. Such structures subsequently became a common feature of Baroque settlements. The Budafok Calvary is an elaborate example and was built in 1832 on the crest of a hill, mimicking Mount Golgotha near Jerusalem. Its focal point is a group of three crosses bearing Jesus and the two thieves, with Mary Magdalene and St. John looking on; directly below is the Holy Grave, its entrance secured with bars of wrought iron. Beyond the calvary is Stáció utca leading to a steep flight of stairs used by pilgrms. The stairs

The József Törley mausoleum above Budafok

are a deliberate imitation of Christ's own way to the Cross and are broken periodically by columns bearing painted Stations.

At the bottom of the hill is Savoyai Jenő tér with its onion-domed Baroque church from where Plébánia utca leads upwards between two vintners' castles. On the left is the so-called Cognac Castle and on the right, at Anna utca 1–3, the rambling *chateau*-style mansion of the Törley Champagne family. Founded here in 1882 because of the extensive limestone caves, which guarantee the necessary stable temperature (12–13 °C) for producing sparkling wines (as in the Champagne region of France), the Törleys eventually became Imperial and Royal Court Supplier to the Habsburgs. Twelve to fourteen million bottles of Champagne are still produced here annually. Towards the top of the hill is Panoráma utca, leading up to the mausoleum of the family's founding father, József Törley, erected in 1909 and from where there is an extensive vista.

19 Runic Gravestones and the Ribcage Mortuary

District XII (Németvölgy), the Farkasréti Public Cemetery
(Farkasréti temető) at Németvölgyi út 99
Tram 59 from M2 Széll Kálmán tér; Bus 8 from Erzsébet híd

Traditional wooden grave markers
in the Farkasréti Cemetery

The end of the line for the number 59 tram from Széll Kálmán tér is the Farkasréti temető – the Wolf's Meadow Cemetery. Whereas Budapest's two other great cemeteries occupy flat land, their burial plots and footpaths laid out geometrically (see nos. 58 & 81), Farkasréti occupies a saddle of land between rolling hills (Mártonhegy and Sas-hegy) and valleys (Németvölgy and Farkasvölgy), its tombs separated by groves of horse chestnut and ash trees. Little wonder that its opening in 1894 was criticised by those who wanted the area reserved for recreation. At the end of the Second World War its headstones provided a macabre backdrop for close-combat fighting between German and Soviet troops, some of them still pockmarked with gunshot.

Visitors come to Farkasréti today to see the graves of composers Béla Bartók and Zoltán Kodály (Plots 42 and 20, respectively), as well as the conductor Sir George Solti who died in Antibes in 1997, buried alongside Bartók (see no. 70). Also interred here, somewhat surprisingly, is post-war General Secretary of the Hungarian Communist Party Mátyás Rákosi (1945–56), whose hardline Stalinist policies saw the imprisonment of 100,000 people and the execution of another 2,000 (see no. 69); there is a plaque bearing his name near the main entrance.

Less well known is the grave of Katalin Karády, the Hungarian Marlene Dietrich, who sheltered persecuted Jews during 1944 (see no. 63). Indeed, the Farkasréti cemetery has a distinct Jewish burial ground accessible from Érdi út (see no. 59).

The Farkasréti Cemetery is also home to some traditional wooden grave markers and unusual grave inscriptions, the latter written in the runic Székely alphabet. The Székelys are a distinct ethnic group historically centred in Transylvania and speaking in Hungarian dialect. Still fiercely patriotic and adhering strongly to their traditions, the origins of the Székelys remain uncertain. Some historians suggest they were a part of the original westward migration of the Magyars from the Volga region, settling in Transylvania prior to Prince Árpád's main advance onto the Great Hungarian Plain (Nagyalföld) in c.900AD (see no. 1). Others believe they were of Turkic origin, possibly related to the Scythians, who merely joined the trek west. Others still see them as Hungarians dispatched to Transylvania to protect the borders.

A further curiosity in store at Farkasréti is a surprising mortuary, just inside the main entrance on the right hand side, designed by Imre Makovecz. Like Ödön Lechner, Béla Lajta and Károly Kós before him, Makovecz has conjured up a distinctly Hungarian style – a Hungarian version of Organic Architecture – by drawing on ancient folk forms (see nos. 67, 78 & 82). A creative dissident during the Communist era, Makovecz's graceful, predominantly wooden structures were the exact opposite of the prevailing Soviet concrete blocks. Banned from working in cities and from teaching he honed his unique style in rural villages and forest settlements. With the end of Communism he became widely recognised and represented his country at the Seville Expo in 1992, his work reflecting Hungary's struggle for independence as well as challenging materialistic values. His Farkasréti temple designed in 1977 is entered through winged doors leading into what can only be described as a giant human ribcage rendered in timber; the dead are placed in caskets where the heart would be.

Other Organic structures by the Makovecz school include his Yurt-style homes on Törökvész utca (District II), based on the traditional houses of felt and poles used by the nomads of Central Asia, and a curious rooftop structure on a building at Szentkirályi utca 18 (District VIII).

Other places of interest nearby: 20

20 Gizi Bajor's Museum of the Theatre

District XII (Németvölgy), the Gizi Bajor Theatre Museum
(Bajor Gizi Színészmúzeum) at Stromfeld Aurél út 16
Bus 102 from M1 Déli Pályaudvar; Tram 59 from M2 Déli
Pályaudvar

From the 1850s onwards, the gentle rolling hills west of Castle Hill –
Sváb-, Isten- and Orbánhegy, for example – were used for the construction of private villas and summer chalets. One such villa, contructed at
the turn-of-the-century, was the glamorous home of Hungarian actress
Gizi Bajor (1893–1951).

Renowned for her charm, looks and great versatility Bajor
excelled in a wide range of roles from Shaw to Shakespeare. After her
death, and at the instigation of fellow actress Hilda Gobbi, the villa
and its garden were turned into the Gizi Bajor Theatre Museum. The
collection not only illustrates the process of mounting a theatrical
production but is also a tribute to the many stars of Hungarian theatre
and early cinema, such as the tragic stage heroine Mari Jászai and the
"fairhaired wonder" Emilia Márkus. Although little-known outside
their native land, their faded sepia photographs and other memora-
bilia, set alongside the actresses' own personal possessions, regularly
bring a nostalgic tear to the eye of returning expatriates. For everyone
else it is an opportunity to realise the national importance of theatre
and cinema in early 20th century Hungary (see no. 61).

Until the late 18th century Hungarian theatre had essentially been German theatre. This changed in 1784 when the enlightened Habsburg Emperor Joseph II (1780–90) encouraged Magyar-language theatre by converting a Carmelite

Actress Gizi Bajor's former villa in the Buda Hills

nunnery on Castle Hill's Színház utca into the city's first permanent theatre (Várszínház), still functioning today as the National Dance Theatre (Nemzeti Táncszínház). Things never really looked back and theatre played an important part in the revival of national spirits during the late 19th century.

As the population of Budapest rose from 400,000 in 1880 to a million in 1905 (the fastest rise of any city other than Chicago) so theatres were opened to satisfy demand (see no. 67). Typical was the Comedy Theatre (Vígszínház) opened in 1896 at Szent István körút 14 (District XIII) and its sister the Pesti Színház at Váci utca 9 (District V). It was Ferenc Molnár, a playwright for the Vígszínház, who in the 1920s wrote *Liliom*, made later into the famous musical *Carousel* by Rogers and Hammerstein.

The Comedy Theatre on Szent István körút

Despite Budapest's theatres being nationalised in 1949 by the Communists they have managed to remain refreshingly vibrant, varied and numerous (55 listed at the last count!). An important venue for most established theatre professionals is the National Theatre (Nemzeti Színház) at the suitably named Bajor Gizi Park 1 in District IX, adjacent to the Közvágóhíd HÉV station. Count István Széchenyi, builder of the Chain Bridge, erected the first National Theatre in the 1830s, which was followed by several other venues and is currently housed in a modern building built in 2002. The façade of the old theatre now stands bizarrely half-submerged in a small lake.

Other places of interest nearby: 19

21 The Children's Railway

District XII (Széchenyi-hegy), the Children's Railway
(Gyermekvasút) starting at Széchenyi Hill (Széchenyi-hegy)
and finishing at Hűvösvölgy
Cogwheel railway to first station at Széchenyi-hegy; Tram 61
from M2 Széll Kálmán tér to end station at Hűvösvölgy

The Cogwheel Railway departing for the Buda Hills

An unusual way of exchanging the urban sprawl of Buda for the wooded solitude of the Buda Hills (*Budai-hegység*) is by means of the Cogwheel Railway (Fogaskerekű vasút). Opened in 1874 it is the third oldest such railway in Europe. Its lower station is at Szilágyi Erzsébet fasor 47 in the Városmajor area, opposite the Budapest Hotel (District II), two stops on Tram 61 from Széll Kálmán tér. The station is actually on one side of the Stadt Mayeroff Park, which was laid out in the 1780s by József Tulherr using 3,000 different species of which some of his elms are still standing. From here the railway makes its 25-minute ascent of Széchenyi-hegy (427 metres), a part of the Svábhegy range where Budapesters built summer villas from the 1850s onwards.

At the terminus another park will be found at the far side of which is a second unusual mode of transport, namely the so-called Children's Railway. This 12-kilometre long narrow-guage line, which winds its way through the leafy Buda Hills to Hűvösvölgy, was the brainchild of the onetime Communist Minister for Transport Ernő Gerő and was declared a gift from the Soviet people (see no. 17). In order to help prepare children for adult life he planned a railway that would be staffed entirely (except for the driver) by members of a Communist youth organisation called the Pioneers. Originally called the Pioneer Railway, the first section of track was laid in 1948 with the rest constructed as part of Hungary's first 5-Year Plan. Children aged 10–14 years who produced good academic results – as well as a letter of approval from their parents – were selected to man the stations and the cheery red rolling stock. Although today renamed the Children's Railway, and hauled by diesel rather than steam engines (although a vintage 1950 steam engine is occasionally pressed into service), the line is still supervised by youngsters, whose predecessors are depicted in a 1950s-era mosaic above the ticket office.

The railway has eight stations in total offering passengers the opportunity to alight and explore at their leisure. The second station at Normafa, for instance, where the forest proper begins, has a popular café serving beer in summer and mulled wine in winter; it was named after a visit by soprano Rozália Klein in the mid-19th century who was so moved by the vista that she sang the grand aria from Bellini's *Norma* under a nearby beech tree (subsequently lost in a gale in 1927). The Budakeszi-erdő Park Trail also begins hereabouts with trails leading back down into Buda as well as north-westwards towards the Budakeszi game reserve (Budakeszi Vadaspark), where wild boar roam free. From the fourth startion, Virágvölgy, can be reached the charming Zugliget hills and the Disznófő Forrás ('Pig's Head Spring') that flows through the former hunting grounds of King Matthias (Mátyás) 'Corvinus'

A steam engine working on the Children's Railway

A proud young ticket collector
on the Children's Railway

Hunyadi (1458–90). From the fifth station, János-hegy, a path leads to the city's highest point where there is both an elaborate lookout tower as well as the upper station for a chairlift (see no. 22). At the sixth station of Szépjuhászné there is a restaurant and the remains of a once-renowned medieval monastery (see no. 23,) whilst from the seventh station of Hárs-hegy a further two lookout towers can be reached. Finally, at the end station of Hűvösvölgy (meaning 'refreshing valley'), there is the Nagy-rét picnic area and the justifiably popular Náncsi Néni restaurant at Ördögárok út 80, a veritable oasis of Hungarian cooking. The valley itself lies at the southern end of a series of hills called Hármashatár-hegy ('Three Frontiers Hill'), popular with walkers for the last two centuries and where the well-to-do built villas during the 19th century.

22 A Belvedere Tower in the Buda Hills

District XII (János-hegy), the Elisabeth Tower (Erzsébet-kilátó)
on John's Hill (János-hegy)
Bus 291 from M3 Nyugati pályaudvar, then chairlift to
János-hegy;
Children's Railway to János-hegy

Without a doubt the best panoramic views of Budapest are available from the slopes and summits of the Buda Hills (*Budai-hegység*) on the west bank of the Danube. Several of these excellent vantage points, for example the lookouts on Kis-Hárs-hegy (362 metres) and Nagy-Hárs-hegy (454 metres), are accessible via the Children's Railway, which winds its way northwards through the wooded foothills (see no. 21).

Best of all is the Elisabeth Tower, atop John's Hill (János-hegy), which at 527 metres is the highest point within the city limits. On a clear day the view from its balcony extends some 80 kilometres towards the Mátra Hills in the north-east, the Bakony range to the south-west and the start of the Great Hungarian Plain (Nagyalföld) on the far eastern horizon. The tower was built in 1911 and named after Empress Elisabeth, the ill-fated wife of Emperor Franz Joseph I (1848–1916), who on occasion walked to the top of the hill herself (see no. 11). The architect was Frigyes Schulek, renowned for designing the neo-medieval Fishermen's

The Elisabeth Tower on John's Hill,
Budapest's highest point

Bastion (Halászbástya) (1903) on the site of a former fish market on Castle Hill, which itself affords a wonderful vista over the historic medieval district of Víziváros eastwards across the Danube to Pest.

For a good view westwards of the Buda Hills themselves visit the Museum of Military History at Tóth Árpád sétány 40 on Castle Hill (the cannonballs in the museum's walls date from 1849 when Hungarian rebels captured Buda from the Habsburgs). Another fine vista is from the Citadel on Gellért Hill, south of Castle Hill, built by the Habsburgs in the wake of the 1848 Revolution in order to prevent any further uprisings against their authority. Rising 235 metres high and selected for its obvious strategic vantage points over Buda, Pest and the Danube, it is today equipped with telescopes for use by tourists rather than guns for soldiers (see no. 13).

Moving down onto the Danube itself, two bridges offering extensive views both upstream and down are Petőfi híd and Margit híd. The latter was Budapest's second permanent bridge, constructed in the 1870s by a French firm, although only the 'elbow' where it connects with Margaret Island is original (added in 1900) the rest having been destroyed during the Second World War. On Margaret Island itself there is a splendid reinforced concrete water tower built in 1911 with a lookout gallery at the top (see no. 72).

Within Pest the most notable location to offer views of the city is the circular balcony around the cupola of St. Stephen's Basilica, giving a 360° vista from a height of 65 metres (see no. 40). For those wishing to see beyond the earthly limitations offered by the vantage points described above there is the Uránia Astronomical Observatory (Uránia Csillagvizsgáló) at Sánc utca 3/B (District I), as well as the Planetarium (Planetárium) in Népliget (District X).

John's Hill is also accessible by means of a 15-minute long scenic chairlift ride (Libegő) constructed in the 1970s that departs from the corner of Zugligeti út and Csiga út, itself reached via Bus 155 from Széll Kálmán tér.

Other places of interest nearby: 23

23 A Hidden Medieval Monastery

District II (Kurucles), the Budaszentlőrinc monastery ruins
(Budaszentlőrinc Pálos Kolostor) near the junction of
Budakeszi út and Jánoshegy út
Bus 22 from M2 Széll Kálmán tér; Children's Railway to
Szépjuhászné

Well concealed amongst the wooded Buda Hills (*Budai-hegység*) close
to the famous Children's Railway (see no. 21) are the scant remains of
the Budaszentlőrinc monastery. How this once famous and wealthy
building came to be represented by so few stones is representative
of the story of Budapest itself. Surprisingly little of the city's fabric
is actually very old, its buildings having fallen victim to wave upon
wave of invaders and conquerors that have swept across through the
Carpathian Basin in which Budapest lies.

The Budaszentlőrinc monastery was built in c.1300 by the
Paulites, the only monastic order of pure Hungarian origin, who
took their name from a 3rd century Egyptian hermit named Paul (see
no.14). By 1304 a regional assembly was meeting here, instead of
the mother monastery 22 kilometres away at Pilisszentkereszt, and
the monastery remained the focus of Paulite religious life throughout
the Middle Ages. Within a very few years it had attracted various
church privileges as well as land donations and we can only assume

The ruins of the Budaszentlőrinc Monastery in the Buda Hills

it became a very significant establishment. This seems all the more likely when in 1381 the remains of Paul himself were brought to Buda at the request of King Lajos I (1342–82), on the occasion of a peace treaty with the Republic of Venice. Initially placed in the Chapel of Buda Castle the relics were soon brought to the monastery itself, which consequently became an important centre for pilgrims.

Historical records from the early 15th century show that new buildings and altars were being added to the monastery at this time and it is said that even King Matthias (Mátyás) 'Corvinus' Hunyadi (1458–90), whose hunting lodge was in woods nearby (now an overgrown site on Szerb Antal utca), would come here to quench his thirst in the monastery's fine wine cellar after hunting expeditions. Chronicles also detail a new vestry and congregation hall "of marvel-

lous beauty" installed in 1512 by General Gergely Gyöngyösi, as well as an organ.

However, during the 1541 Ottoman occupation of Buda the monastery was burnt down, its contents looted and its 25 remaining monks ousted (already reduced from an original 500 as a result of the Reformation). Although the Ottomans were expelled in 1686 the monastery is not mentioned again until 1746 when the Archbishop of Esztergom sent out an expedition to locate its remains. In 1847 the first archaeological excavations were undertaken to ascertain the ground plan

King Matthias out hunting
in a sculpture by Alajos Stróbl
on Castle Hill

of the monastery, followed by further digging in 1934 and an eventual preservation of the site in the 1990s by the newly created Department for the Protection of Settlement Heritage.

Of the relatively few walls remaining many have been re-buried, but of those still visible an impression of the old monastery can be gained. They include the southern and western walls of the church, part of the vestry and later sanctuary, and all of the southern side chapel complete with three altar pedestals. Also visible are parts of a patterned brick floor and some architectural carvings (three finely carved fragments from the actual red marble sarcophagus of the hermit Paul are today preserved in the Budapest History Museum).

This, however, is not the end of Budapest's Paulite story. In 1699 they moved into a ruined Turkish mosque in Pest and by 1756 had transformed it into a new seat for the Hungarian Paulite Order where the cult of St. Paul would thrive for a further thirty years. The monastery's church, now the University Church on Egyetem tér in District V, was completed in 1742 and has statues of the hermits St. Paul and St. Anthony on its west façade. It also contains some exhuberantly carved timber made possible by the order's acquisition of forests in the north; notable are the main door and choir stall doors carved by one Brother Felix. There is also a copy of the *Black Madonna* of Częstochowa. The monastery itself at Papnövelde utca 7 contains a little-known architectural gem, namely the intact Baroque library of the Central Seminary of Pest (Pálos Könyvtár) completed in c.1775 and open by appointment only (the street name Papnövelde utca means Seminary Street). The Paulite Order was eventually abolished by decree of the Habsburg Emperor Joseph II (1780-90) on August 20th, 1786 and the church given to the University. The Paulites would not be heard of again this time until the 1920s (see no. 14).

Other places of interest nearby: 22

Modernist architecture on Napraforgó utca in Buda

24 From Bauhaus to Buda

District II (Kurucles), the Napraforgó utca housing estate
Tram 61 from M2 Széll Kálmán tér

In 1920 the influential Hungarian architect Béla Lajta passed away
(see no. 67). Around the same time his contemporary Károly Kós
gave up Hungary for his native Transylvania (see no. 82). Together
with Ödön Lechner, who had died in 1914, the three had trawled
Hungary's legendary and historic past for suitably potent design
motifs with which to decorate their buildings and so re-assert national identity (see no. 78). In doing so they had been the creators of
Hungary's first truly national architectural style.

With the dawn of the 1920s, however, the use of ornament for
ornament's sake was rejected and old-fashioned craftsmanship was
sidelined in favour of new technological innovations and the intro-
duction of reinforced concrete. This was the age of Walter Gropius
and the German Bauhaus movement, of the austere functionalism
of Vienna's Adolf Loos, of Le Corbusier and Mies van der Rohe
and of the beginnings of what would eventually be known as the
International Style.

Hungary too had its proponents of this new movement – known
as Modernism – for example Farkas Molnár and László Vágó, adherents as opposed to creators of the style, but no less important for
that. In common with their counterparts elsewhere in Europe they
worked not only on villas for their *avant-garde* patrons but also
tackled the problems of providing public housing. Anyone interested
in the development of modern architecture in general, and the work
of these early Hungarian Modernists in particular, should jump on
a bus or a tram and head out to Napraforgó utca (Sunflower Street)
in Buda. Here, in 1931 on the steep banks of the Ördögárok River,
several up-and-coming architects were given the task of creating
comfortable yet affordable housing for Budapest's lower middle
class. The resulting estate was modelled on the famous German
Werkbund's *Weissenhofsiedlung*, a housing exhibition that had been
held in Stuttgart in 1927. Twenty-two detached and semi-detached
houses were built, each with their own patch of garden as well as a
roof terrace, the latter being one of the architectural elements of Le
Corbusier's Five-Point Programme. Molnár's effort can still be seen
at number 15 whilst Vágó was responsible for numbers 1 and 11;

number 2 is by the noted architect Gyula Wälder. The distinctive streamlined cube and cylinder forms, flat roofs, cantilevered balconies, smooth-rendered walls and curved windows have given these buildings a timeless, almost futuristic quality, validating the old adage that "Function creates form". Although the houses proved ultimately to be beyond the means of average families they are today much sought after.

Another notable architect involved in the Napraforgó utca project was the former Olympic gold medallist swimmer Alfréd Hajós, responsible for the house at number 17 (see no. 59). Turning to architecture long after his swimming success back in 1896 he was the architect behind the eponymous Alfréd Hajós National Sports Pool (Hajós Alfréd Nemzeti Sportuszoda) built on Margaret Island in 1935 (see nos. 72 & 79), as well as the Hotel Andrássy at Andrássy út 111 erected in the same decade (District VI).

Probably Budapest's first ever Modernist public building was the Átrium Cinema and apartment block at Margit körút 53 designed by the architect Lajos Kozma in 1935-36; the building's constructional elements were originally colour coded with white for walls, black for fixed metal frames and red for moving ones; a line of green over the doorway was the building's only real decoration.

25 An Unusual Park for the Millennium

District II (Rózsadomb), Millennium Park (Millenáris Park)
at Fény utca 20–22
M2 to Széll Kálmán tér; Tram 4, 6 around the Nagykörút

In 1896 Budapest celebrated in considerable style the thousand years since the conquest of the Carpathian Basin by Prince Árpád, with monuments and grand buildings springing up across the city (see nos. 1, 44 & 76). The thousand years since the crowning of the nation's first king, St. Stephen (István) and the founding of the Hungarian state in 1001 AD, were celebrated with considerably less fuss (see no. 40). However, it too has left a tangible mark on Budapest's urban landscape in the shape of the Millennium Park north of Castle Hill.

Finished in 2001 the Millennium Park was commissioned by the FIDESZ-MDF government, on the site of the former headquarters of the Ganz Electrical Works (Ganz Villamossági Művek). Once a powerful foundry and electrical factory, the works began life in 1844 as the Ganz Iron Works, a small cast-iron factory a few roads away to the east (see no. 27). Rapid growth saw the opening of the Electrical

Buda's Millennium Park was once the Ganz Electrical Works

Works in 1897 and it was here that the world's first electric railway engine was manufactured. The company soon became respected throughout Europe and eventually employed 2,000 workers, although much of its fabric would be severely damaged in the Second World War.

During the ensuing Communist era the works were again expanded and they continued in business well into the 1990s. However, being now entirely surrounded by housing meant that the issue of urban pollution was pressing and with a decline in output due to changing markets the relocation of the factory to the countryside became inevitable (now operating under the name Ganz Transelektro Rt.).

Subsequently, the cavernous structures of the old Electrical Works have been ingeniously adapted for re-use as an events and exhibition centre. This involved the demolition of a pair of tall buildings and a chimney in the late summer of 2000 and the removal of 120,000 cubic metres of rubble from the site. The remaining buildings were retained for historic and aesthetic reasons, for example a former machine-assembly hall known as Building E that has now become a 600-seat theatre. Similarly, Building B erected in 1911–12 as a giant assembly plant has become an auditorium and Building D, among the first to be erected on the site, is now a small exhibition hall. (The presence of the Millennium Park is also bringing other attractions into the area, for example currently there is a fascinating exhibition in which visitors can experience the world as sensed by the visually impaired).

The surrounding area has been landscaped loosely into a park that represents a stylised microcosm of Hungary itself, a small pool representing Lake Balaton and a miniature cornfield and undulating vineyard symbolising the country's agricultural regions. One can only imagine what King Stephen would have made of it all!

Other places of interest nearby: 26, 27

26 A Baroque Odyssey

District I (Víziváros), the Church of St. Anne
(Szent Anna-templom) at Batthyány tér 7
M2 to Batthyány tér

It is said that when the Turks took control of Castle Hill in 1541 it was done so without a single shot being fired; the area was then peaceably transformed into a provincial Ottoman town. By contrast, the removal of the Ottomans by Habsburg forces in 1686 resulted in massive destruction as a result of which the area was rebuilt in typically triumphant Baroque style, a style that originated in Italy. This in turn was largely laid to waste during the Second World War when Soviet artillery pounded Castle Hill in order to oust German troops who

The twin spires of the
Baroque Church of
St. Anne on Batthyány tér

had dug themselves in there. Consequently, much of what is seen on Castle Hill today is of necessity a reconstructed palimpsest: 20th century walls mimicking original Baroque walls atop ancient medieval foundations. Thankfully, in addition to a few secular Baroque buildings (e.g. houses on Bécsi kapu tér and the Erdődy Palace at Tancsics Mihály utca 7) Budapest's many Baroque churches have fared better and make for an interesting thematic journey in their own right.

Beginning in Buda, on the banks of the Danube, the twin-spired Church of St. Anne on the southern side of Batthyány tér is one of the city's best. It was begun in 1740 to the designs of Kristóf

A detail on the former Church of the Wounds of St. Francis on Fő utca

Hamon and eventually completed in 1805 by Matthias Nepauer, husband of Hamon's widow and one of Hungarian Baroque's most renowned practitioners. Above the tympanum outside can be seen the God's-eye-in-the-triangle motif representing the Holy Trinity, a Baroque symbol widely used in the 18th century, whilst inside are statues framed by black marble columns that symbolise the Temple of Jerusalem. Most unusual is the old presbytery next door that now contains the Angelika Kávéház, imbued with a special atmosphere by light streaming in through the stained glass windows. Nearby, at Batthyány tér 4, there is the former White Cross Inn (Fehér Kereszt Fogadó) where Casanova reputedly stayed and next-door is an example of a building in the so-called *Zopf* Style, a German/ Central European variant of late Baroque (Rococo) characterised by the use of strapwork mouldings and carved lintels on the façade (*Zopf* means 'plait', which the mouldings resemble).

Bounding the north side of the square, at Fő utca 41, is a former

Franciscan friary converted into a poor hospital in the mid-18th century by the nuns of St. Elizabeth. Today it is an old people's home while its Baroque church serves the city's German-speaking Catholics. Over the doorway are carved a pair of hands bearing the stigmata relating to its original name as the Church of the Wounds of St. Francis.

To the south of Castle Hill may be found the Tabán Parish Church (St. Catherine of Alexandria) (see no. 10), as well as Krisztinaváros Parish Church (Our Lady of the Snows) in Krisztina tér. The latter was built in 1797 and replaced a wooden chapel famous for an icon of the Holy Virgin, brought back from Re in Northern Italy by a chimney sweep who had survived the plague of 1649. The icon, which still resides in the church, was even visited by Empress Maria Theresa (1740–80), who authorised the Buda council to name the area after her daughter Kristina. It was here too that the great 19th century reformer Count István Széchenyi and his wife Crescentia Seilern were married in 1836 (see no. 42). Another interesting Baroque structure is the Parish Church in Óbuda (District III) far to the north (see no. 32).

Meanwhile, across the river in Pest, this Baroque odyssey continues in District V with the Servite Church (from where Szervita tér derives its name), the Inner City Church, the oldest in Pest (see no. 46), and the University Church, converted from a ruined mosque and featuring some glorious woodwork (see no. 23).

Our tour finishes in District VIII with the Parish Church of Józsefváros on Horváth Mihály utca, fronted by a statue of Péter Pázmány, the Archbishop of Esztergom, who led Hungary's Counter Reformation.

Other places of interest nearby: 27

27 Staircases, Stoves and the Art of Forging

District II (Rózsadomb), the Foundry Museum (Öntödei Múzeum) at Bem József utca 20
M2 to Batthyány tér; Tram 4, 6 around the Nagykörút

One of Budapest's more obscure museums, and one that is often unfairly omitted from many guidebooks, is its Foundry Museum. This is surprising when one considers that it is located just off the busy Margit körút close to both the Ottoman Király Thermal Baths (see no.12) and the attractive Uniate Church, the latter built in 1760 with money donated by one of Buda's master bakers (see no. 51). Perhaps it is the somewhat uninspiring name that is off-putting? Whatever the reason, this museum should not be missed for it provides a fascinating glimpse into the era of the Industrial Revolution in Hungary.

The museum is suitably located in the old Ganz Ironworks and as such is Central Europe's only museum of smelting and casting to be established inside a former foundry. A Swiss immigrant Ábrahám Ganz founded the company in 1844 as a small cast-iron works. Within a generation the company would change from being a producer of stoves and other domestic items into a significant heavy machinery manufacturing plant, including Ganz's own patented 'chill cast' railway wheels and railway crossing points, as well as corn milling rollers patented later under the direction of his colleague and successor, András Mechwart.

By 1878 the factory's electrical department had been established, resulting in 1884 in the development of the world's first transformer that made it possible to conduct electricity over long distances. It was here too that the electricity meter was first invented. In 1897 Mechwart established the huge new Ganz Electrical Works, a few roads away to the west, in order to build on the company's global prowess in electrical technology; that site is occupied today by the Millennium Park where some of the old buildings have been re-used as a cultural centre (see no. 25).

Thankfully, the building housing the original foundry, erected in 1858–62, has been preserved. It is Hungary's only example of a structure with a Howe-type timber and iron-trussed roof, so named after its inventor William Howe of Massachusetts. Within the building can be seen the original chilled casting shop together with its iron-melting ovens and casting moulds illustrating the little-known history of metal, iron and steel moulding in Hungary over the last thousand years. There is also an extensive collection of actual finished products including rows of ornately decorated cast iron stoves, as well as a splendid example of a so-called 'snail', or spiral, staircase. Outside the museum can be found examples of the foundry's castings, including lamp standards, anchors, railway axles, ships propellers, and public statues.

Although Ganz died in Pest in 1867, his foundry continued in production until closure in 1964. All credit must go to the Foundry Museum's curators for taking a mundane industrial process and transforming it into a collection that will offer something of interest to most visitors.

A ship's propellor outside Buda's fascinating Foundry Museum

Other places of interest nearby: 25, 26, 28

28 The Tomb of the Father of the Roses

District II (Rózsadomb), the Tomb of Gül Baba (Gül Baba türbéje) at Turbán utca 11/Mecset utca 14
Tram 4, 6 around the Nagykörút

Despite the fact that from 1541 Buda's Castle Hill was essentially an Ottoman town for a century and a half, there are very few tangible remains left standing from that period (see no. 46). This is hardly surprising, however, when one considers the wholesale destruction wrought during the Habsburgs' seizure of the fastness in 1686 and the thoroughness of their subsequent rebuilding of the area as a triumphant Baroque town.

The tomb of the dervish Gül Baba on Turbán utca in Rózsadomb

Whilst the new Austrian rulers were happy to leave standing the therapeutic baths they found constructed over the city's numerous thermal springs (see no. 12), not one Islamic mosque or minaret would be left intact. However, at three separate locations in Buda several graves belonging to the area's former Ottoman rulers still remain.

Most celebrated of all is the tomb of Gül Baba at Mecset utca 14 (meaning Mosque Street) in a fashionable residential area of District II. Gül Baba was a *dervish*, an ascetic holy man and initiate of *Sufism*, the esoteric and spiritual branch of Islam. *Sufi* practitioners were regarded as sources of wisdom, enlightenment, poetry and medicine. More specifically, he was a member of the Bektashi *dervishes*, an order prominent in 16th century Turkey where they dominated the *Janissaries*, the Sultan's household troops. It is therefore not surprising that Gül Baba arrived in Buda in 1541 as personal companion to Suleyman the Magnificent, Sultan of the Ottoman Empire, with the intention of creating a religious centre in Buda. Sadly, Gül Baba died soon afterwards during the Ottomans' first victory ceremony held in the Matthias Church-turned-Great Mosque on Castle Hill. Suleyman himself was a coffin bearer at the funeral and Muslims now revere Gül Baba as a saint. His octagonal stone tomb was erected during the governorship of Buda's third pasha, sometime between 1543 and 1548.

A statue of Gül Baba

Four years after the Habsburgs' conquest of Buda in 1686 the Jesuits converted the shrine into a Christian chapel of St. Joseph. However, after their dissolution, a local landowner restored the tomb to its original form for the benefit of both Christians and Bektashi Muslims, it being the latter's most northerly site of pilgrimage. The Turkish government themselves renovated the tomb in 1885, when they uncovered Gül Baba's skeleton (he was 164 centimetres high), and again in 1997, when it was topped off with a golden crescent and enhanced by a statue. The tomb's interior is hung with ceramic plaques bearing Koranic verses, similar to those inscribed here originally by the Turkish traveller Evliya Tselebi in 1663.

Legend relates how it was Gül Baba who introduced cultivated roses to Hungary (some say he wore a rose in his turban), his name meaning 'Father of the Roses' in Turkish. The garden around the tomb is today planted with roses and the area of Rózsadomb, where the tomb is located, translates as Rose Hill in Hungarian. However, it seems more likely that the word 'Rose' (*Gül*) should be taken metaphorically to mean that this man was the rose of his order, a man who had obtained mystical knowledge from Allah himself. Indeed, in some accounts he is called *Gül Dede*, meaning Dervish Rose.

On the northern side of Castle Hill, on the old ramparts close

A fountain in the precinct of the Gül Baba tomb

to the Vienna Gate (Bécsi kapu) commemorating the Habsburgs' successful siege of the fortress in 1686, can be found the grave of the last Turkish Pasha of Buda, Vizir Abdurrahman Abdi Arnaut Pasha. He was killed during the siege and his respectful epitaph reads: "He was a noble enemy, let him rest in peace".

Finally, just outside the Round Bastion at the southern end of the walls surrounding the Royal Palace, there is the area known as the Tabán (after the Turkish word *tabanane*, meaning 'armoury'). It was here, as part of the Ottoman's repopulation of Buda with loyal subjects, that Bosnian Muslims and Serbs were permitted to manufacture gunpowder. This gentle slope overlooking the Gellért Hill was once a Turkish cemetery (*török temető*) from which a handful of turban-topped graves can still be seen.

Artefacts relating to the Ottoman period in Hungary can be found in the Hungarian National Museum (see no. 55), where there is a magnificent portrait of Suleyman, as well as in the Budapest History Museum (Budapesti Történeti Múzeum) in Wing E of Buda's former Royal Palace. Meanwhile, in the Hungarian National Gallery (Magyar Nemzeti Galéria), in Wing C of the Palace, can be found artist Gyula Benczúr's Recapture of Buda (1896) depicting the slain Abdurrahman Pasha overseen by Prince Eugène of Savoy and Charles of Lorraine, the commanders of the victorious Christian armies.

Other places of interest nearby: 25, 27

29 Subterranean Buda

District II (Szemlő-hegy), the Szemlő-hegy Cave
(Szemlő-hegyi-barlang) at Pusztaszeri út 35
Bus 29 from Suburban train HÉV Szépvölgyi út

For those visitors to Budapest interested in speleology, that is the study and exploration of caves, the Buda Hills (*Budai-hegység*) will hold much of interest. The limestone and marl rock underlying these hills contains approximately 160 caves, their galleries extending for many kilometres. Indeed, Budapest is the world's only city to have major cave systems running below its built-up areas. Castle Hill (Várhegy) itself is riddled with a network of natural chambers that have been exploited by man for centuries (see no. 4); considerably more modest is the tiny St. Gellért Cave Chapel on Gellért Hill (see no. 14). All were carved out originally by the same thermal springs that today supply the city's famous baths.

However, in order to experience Buda's caves in their natural state it is necessary to travel northwards to Szemlő-hegy and the eponymous cave system discovered there in 1930 as a result of quarrying operations. The cave was first entered by one Mária Szekula, who was slim enough to squeeze through an opening called "Tű foka", or the Needle's Eye. Now entered through a specially cut adit, the 300 metre-long cave comprises a series of fractures in the rock that have been opened up through the action of thermal

Visiting the Szemlő-hegy Cave
in the Buda Hills

waters over the last 3.5 million years. As the Buda Hills were uplifted so these waters, already saturated in calcium carbonate from calcite veins in the host rock, receded into ponds. This resulted in the precipitation of delicate, pure white formations of Aragonite minerals known popularly as 'Cauliflower' reliefs. Their discovery prompted the first explorers to call the cave "The Underground Flower Garden of Budapest". Similarly, conical accumulations of calcite platelets on the walls and floor of the cave created so-called Pisolite formations, known popularly as 'Peastone', because they resemble peas or bunches of grapes. It is said that the cave's constant temperature (10 °C), dust-free air and almost 100% humidity has a curative effect on those suffering from respiratory problems.

Another cave open to visitors lies north-west from here, namely the Pál-völgy Cave (Pál-völgyi-barlang) at Szépvölgyi út 162. It too boasts air said to have a restorative effect but is primarily visited for its wonderful display of stalactites (hanging from the ceiling) and stalagmites (rising from the ground below). Some of these formations, formed by the endless dripping of mineral-laden waters from the roof as the passages were drying out, have been given specific names, such as The Elephant and The Crocodile. The cave is also a winter roost for bats.

The Pál-völgy cave was discovered in 1904 in an abandoned quarry and part of its 1,200-metre long passage was soon opened up to an inquisitive public. In 1927 electric lighting was installed and in 1944 the cave was designated a protected zone. By 1980 speleogists had discovered 13 kilometres of passages and in 2001 a new tunnel was found connecting it with the Mátyás-hegy cavern on the other side of the valley. The resulting cave system now boasts a total length of almost 30 kilometres making it the longest in Hungary. The Mátyás-hegy cavern itself has a subterranean lake lying 90 metres below its entrance.

Those wishing to further explore the geology of Hungary should head for the Hungarian State Geological Institute (Magyar Földtani Intézet) at Stefánia út 14 (District XIV) (see nos. 54 & 78).

30 Some Most Unusual Museums

District III (Óbuda), the Textile Museum (Textilmúzeum),
Lajos utca 136–138
Suburban train HÉV to Tímár utca; Bus 86 from M2 Batthyány
tér; Tram 17 from Margit híd

Many visitors and even some locals in Budapest are probably quite unaware of one of the city's more incredible cultural statistics: it has approximately 120 museums! Of these many are justifiably well known, containing exhibits of international importance and deservedly appearing in the "must see" listings of most guidebooks. However, Budapest also has more than a few little-known museums that rarely make it into the guides and yet contain fascinating collections that veer between the unusual and the down-right obscure: boring they most certainly are not!

A display of coloured stockings in Óbuda's Textile Museum

Typical amongst this number is Óbuda's Textile Museum at Lajos utca 136–138. It is located in the oldest part of the once vast Goldberger textile factory founded by Jewish entrepreneurs in 1784. Although four generations of the Goldbergers supplied cloth to the Habsburg monarchy their last family member would perish in the Mauthausen concentration camp in Austria during the Second World War (see nos. 59 & 62). The collection includes old looms, stocking machines, fabric printers and some stunning fabric sample books.

Around the corner is the Hungarian Museum of Trade and Tourism (Kereskedelmi és Vendéglátóipari Múzeum) which can be found at Korona tér 1. This unashamedly nostalgic collection focuses on life, leisure, and pleasure during Budapest's *Belle Époque.* Included are relics from the elegant Gerbeaud coffee house and Gundel's Art

Old fashioned shop display in the Museum of Commerce & Catering

Nouveau restaurant, a luxury sleeping car from the days of the Orient Express, and a reconstructed bedroom from the luxury Gellért Spa Hotel. During the 1920s wealthy patrons took flying boats from the hotel to Lake Balaton.

Other unusual museums in Budapest include the Bible Museum (Biblia Múzeum) at Ráday utca 28 (District IX), which contains the first complete Hungarian translation of the Bible (the Vizsolyi Bible) as well as the first printed Greek New Testament issued by Erasmus. A little further out in the same district is the Museum of the Milling Industry (Malomipari Múzeum) at Soroksari út 24. In neighbouring District VIII there is the Flag Museum (Zászlómúzeum) at József körút 68, established in 1995 and the world's first collection of its type, containing flags from across the five continents the majority of which have been donated by presidents and monarchs.

Also in District VIII is the Gas Museum (Gázmúzeum) at Köztársaság tér 20, as well as the Police History Museum (Bűnügyi és Rendőrség-történeti Múzeum) at Mosonyi utca 7, detailing some of Hungary's most famous criminal cases in ghoulish recreations. Related to the emergency services are the Kresz Géza Ambulance Service Museum (District V) and the Firefighting Museum (District X), District X also being home to the Dreher Beer Museum (Dreher Sörmúzeum) at Jászberényi út 7–11 in Kőbánya (see no. 80). Natural historians should enjoy the charming Újpest Butterfly Museum (Újpesti Lepkemúzeum) at Dessewffy utca 26 (District IV).

Meanwhile, for those who like their museums really obscure, there is the Museum of the Hungarian Meat Industry at Gubacsi út 6/b (District IX) and even the Gyula Korom Museum of Hairdressing Equipment at Ady Endre út 131/a (District XIX). Only in Budapest!

Other places of interest nearby: 32, 33

31   Art Amongst the Ruins

District III (Óbuda), the Kiscelli Museum (Kiscelli Múzeum)
at Kiscelli utca 108
Tram 17 from HÉV Margit híd; Bus 160 from HÉV Margit híd

Surely one of Budapest's most picturesquely located and unusually housed museums must be the Kiscelli in Óbuda. Part surrounded by woods at the foot of the Buda Hills (*Budai-hegység*) this secluded museum was originally constructed as a monastery for the Trinitarian Order by the Zichy family, the local landowners (see no. 32). The monastery church was completed in 1760 and its cloister followed in 1784. Much later the building served as a barracks and a military hospital and was eventually purchased by Miksa Schmidt, an antiques dealer and manufacturer of Viennese-style furniture, by whose wishes it was bequeathed to the city in 1935 and transformed into a museum.

On the ground floor of the museum there are some fascinating examples of 19th century trade signs that once adorned the long vanished shops of Óbuda, including a glove, a lobster and a golden key signifying a locksmith. Also here are the entire contents of the old Golden Lion pharmacy dating back to 1794. Upstairs is home to a significant collection of late-19th and 20th century Hungarian art that was a part of the city's original Municipal Art Gallery (Fővárosi Képtár), the majority of which was confiscated and in the 1950s transferred to the Hungarian National Gallery (Magyar Nemzeti Galéria) in Wing C of the former Royal Palace on Castle Hill. The paint-

Doorway of the former Trinitarian Monastery now home to Óbuda's Kiscelli Museum

ings displayed clearly demonstrate the influence that impressionism, cubism and surrealism made on Hungarian art. They include work by the cubist János Kmetty (*City Park*), impressionist József Rippl-Rónai (*My Parents After 40 Years of Marriage; My Brothers Lajos and Ödön*), *plein-air* specialist Károly Ferenczy, leading light of the so-called Transylvanian Nagybánya School, and Margit Anna, a member of the European School of the 1940s. Also represented is Alajos Stróbl, famous for his masterly bronze Matthias Fountain (Mátyás kútja) outside the Royal Palace and the statue of St. Stephen near the Matthias Church (Mátyás-templom), both on Castle Hill.

Of equal interest is the fascinating collection of prints, paintings, engravings and artefacts relating to the development of 18th and 19th century Budapest. They belong to the modern history department of the Budapest History Museum (Budapesti Történeti Múzeum), which is housed here. The old graphic documents are of especial interest to historians when dealing with a city such as Budapest, which has seen so much damage done to its urban fabric. Thankfully, many of the city's architectural icons seen in these images are still standing, for example the Chain Bridge, the Citadel on Gellért Hill and the Central Synagogue on Dohány utca.

Returning downstairs there is a display on the history of Hungarian printing houses in the 18th and 19th centuries including more than twenty antique presses, one of which was used to print the *People's Twelve Demands* during the 1848 Revolution (see no. 56). Aside from the old cloister cells that now contain Baroque sculpture, the most atmospheric part of the museum is the ruined monastery church, its brick walls left stripped of their plaster following bomb damage during the Second World War. The result is a strange work of art in itself – although it is used for contemporary art – that exudes a unique historic and religious resonance all of its own.

The museum stands on Kiscelli Hill (Kiscelli-hegy), named after a little statue of the Virgin of Mariazell in Austria, which once stood here: the German name 'Klein Mariazell' in time became Kiscell.

32 A Vanished District

District III (Óbuda), the Zichy Mansion at Fő tér
Suburban train HÉV to Árpád híd; Bus 86 from
M2 Batthyány tér

A brisk walk up to the viewing terrace of the Kiscelli Museum on Kiscelli Hill (*Kiscelli-hegy*) in Óbuda (District III) offers a broad vista of a seldom-visited part of modern Budapest, now seemingly dominated by a mass of featureless apartment blocks thrown up in the 1960s.

However, hidden amongst the acres of featureless concrete there still exist pockets of bygone Óbuda, for example the foundations of the Cloister of the Poor Clares in the grounds of a school on Perc utca. It was founded in the 14th century by Elizabeth of Poland, wife of Charles I of Anjou (1308–42) and mother of King Louis the Great (1342–82).

The Baroque Zichy Mansion on Fő tér, Óbuda

Óbuda's Jewish synagogue on Lajos utca

Especially interesting are the fascinating remnants of a now predominantly lost Baroque district constructed here in the 17th and 18th centuries following the expulsion of the Turks (see no. 46). A colourful ethnic mix of Serb, German, Jewish and Magyar traders, artisans and fishermen once lived and worked here in an atmosphere of harmony and respect.

Down near Árpád Bridge, in an area now hemmed in by busy roads going to and from Flórián tér, there is a patch of old Óbuda that retains some of the atmosphere of these former times. The focal point is the cobblestoned square of Fő tér around which are arranged a number of restored houses, including the town hall, taverns serving traditional Danube fish dishes and the crumbling Rococo-style Zichy Mansion, at number 1. The mansion was built in 1746–57 for Count Miklós Zichy, a member of a wealthy land owning family responsible for developing Óbuda in the 18th century. It was the commercially savvy Zichy Counts who encouraged Jewish traders to settle in the area in order to help re-build the city's commerce and to contribute to tax revenues. Today, the mansion is home to several museums, including that of modern artist Victor Vasarely and radical poet and artist Lajos Kassák. Of most interest is the Óbuda Local History Museum (Óbudai helytörténeti gyűjtemény), with its items relating to the history and development of the district. Amongst the many artefacts are interesting examples of trade signs that once hung outside the area's long-vanished shops.

On the opposite side of the square at number 4 stands another Baroque house dating back to the 18th century. It was once home to the ethnographer Zsigmond Kun (1893–2000) and until recently housed his collection of 19th and early 20th century Hungarian art. Included were some delightful ceramics from Kun's hometown in Northern Hungary, to where the museum has now been relocated. Kun's time here, like so many aspects of old Óbuda, has now been relegated to the history books.

The district's Jewish community settled in Óbuda during the 18th century and for a while thrived, a monument to their commercial achievement being the Goldberger textile factory (see no. 30). By the 1820s they had erected a neo-Classical synagogue at the end of Lajos utca (on the other side of the flyover), its pediment carrying a carving of the twin tablets of the Ten Commandments (the Decalogue). However, by the end of the Second World War a much-reduced Jewish community was unable to afford the restoration of the synagogue and the forlorn building served as a television studio. In 2010 it was eventually reinaugurated as a synangogue.

Closeby is Óbuda's Baroque Parish Church with two statues in front carrying the Zichy coat of arms. Behind the church is a final remnant of old Óbuda, namely a charming ensemble of single-storied Baroque buildings on Mókus utca and Dugovics Titusz tér, their red roofs standing proud against the oppressive grey backdrop of modern concrete housing units.

Other places of interest nearby: 30, 33, 34

33 Boat Factory Island

District III (Óbuda), the former boatyards on Óbuda Island
(Óbudai Hajógyári-sziget) reached by a footbridge from near
Filatori gát to the middle of the island
Suburban train HÉV to Árpád híd; Tram 1 around the Hungária
körút; Bus 86 from M2 Batthyány tér

Dotted along the Danube (*Duna*) within Budapest's city limits are several islands (*sziget*) noteworthy for their natural as well as their man-made history. For those seeking fresh air and seclusion as an alternative to the city's busy streets a trip to the open parkland of Óbuda Island (Óbudai Hajógyári-sziget) in District III is recommended (access is best made across a bridge from the HÉV suburban train station at Filatori gát, which connects to a network of tracks fanning out across the northern part of the island).

With its vast areas of open parkland it is easy to see why Óbuda Island is popular with children (incidentally, the Emperor Hadrian built a palace here in Roman times), as well as providing the venue for the annual weeklong Sziget Music Festival (originally called Diáksziget Festival, meaning 'Student Island Festival'). The largest popular music event in Central Europe the festival takes place in early August and attracts around half a million people. From here it is almost impossible to imagine that the southern end of the same island was once home to one of Hungary's most important industrial complexes.

Óbuda Island is shaped like an extracted tooth: the park to the north occupying the rounded crown whilst to the south are two elongated peninsulas dangling root-like downstream. In between the peninsulas is a sheltered haven long exploited as a winter port for Danube shipping. From 1836 onwards shipbuilders exploited this convenient geography by using the western peninsula to develop a series of boatyards, thus accounting for its modern name of *Hajógyári-sziget*, or Boat Factory Island. First on the scene was the Austrian Danube Steamship Company (Donau Dampfschiff Gesellschaft, or DDSG), a monopoly which, due to rapidly increasing traffic on the Danube, had by 1867 created a huge shipyard that eventually covered an area of some 30 acres. Concentrating on ships for river navigation it was soon one of the most important industrial concerns in the country.

After the First World War, and with the collapse of the Austro-Hungarian Empire, shipbuilding gradually came to a standstill. Not until 1937 was production revived through the production of components for tankers and U-Boats for the German Navy. After the Second World War the yards came under Russian control and boomed once again by providing ships for Soviet river navigation companies. At one point the Óbuda shipyards were one of the most significant for riverboat production in the world. However, with the collapse of the Soviet Union production could not be maintained and the consequent decline of markets in the East sounded the eventual death knell for the shipyards.

Pleasure boats moored on Óbuda's Boat Factory Island

To reach the site of the old boatyards it is best to leave the HÉV station at Árpád híd and cross to the island by means of a 19th century cast iron bridge. The old quays are now occupied by fishermen, small pleasure cruisers and the occasional rusty hull still being worked on. Like so much of old Óbuda, the winds of political change have blown away much of the former character of the shipyards, with just a few old anchors and pieces of machinery left to tell the story. However, the shipyards are now slowly taking on a new life as the area is redeveloped as offices, film studios, bars and nightclubs, one example being the suitably named Dokk Bistro & Club at Hajógyári-sziget 122.

Other places of interest nearby: 30, 32, 34

34 The Ruins of Roman Aquincum

District III (Óbuda), the Hercules Villa (Hercules Villa)
at Meggyfa utca 19–21
Suburban train HÉV to Filatori gát; Bus 86 from HÉV Margit híd

Although today Buda's Castle Hill would *appear* to be the oldest inhabited part of Budapest, it is actually the modern district of Óbuda (meaning 'old Buda') farther north that can lay legitimate claim to this title. Archaeological evidence unearthed at Békásmegyer in the northern part of Óbuda demonstrates that this part of the riverbank has been inhabited continuously from as early as the 4th millennium BC (Neolithic period), with traces of Iron Age communities dating from c.900BC. These include dovecote-shaped niched sepulchral structures known as *columbaria* containing dozens of cinerary urns.

From the Late Iron Age (4th century BC) there is settlement evidence for the Celtic Eravi tribe, whose citadel (or *oppidum*) was on what is now Gellért Hill (see no. 13). They were drawn to the area by the natural springs they found in caves on the lower slopes of the

Underground heating revealed in a building in Roman Aquincum

Buda Hills (*Budai-hegység*) (see no. 14). They also settled part of the plain on the opposite side of the river.

It was against this backdrop that the Romans arrived, occupying the Celtic settlements in c.10AD and establishing a legionary garrison town by 90AD, centred on what is now Flórián tér in Óbuda. The purpose of such garrisons was to form part of the so-called *limes*, a defensive line of forts along the empire's eastern and northern borders that could effectively repel barbarian attacks as well as protect shipping on the Danube, an important trading route for the Romans.

An inscribed Roman sarcophagus at the Hercules Villa in Óbuda

The town had a population of c.20,000 (6,000 of whom were soldiers) and was laid out on a classic grid pattern. Now dissected by busy roads, the site's many sculptural fragments can be found adorning the walls of the modern underpass, bizarrely juxtaposed between cigarette kiosks and cheap clothing stores. Also visible are the remains of the military baths (*Thermae Maiores*), stumbled upon by workmen in 1778 and now preserved as the Baths Museum (Fürdőmúzeum) beneath a noisy flyover at Flórián tér underpass (Flórián téri aluljáró) 3–5. Such was the excitement at this discovery that Empress Maria Theresa (1740–80) financed further excavations, revealing the familiar layout of tepid, hot, steam and cold baths, together with open-air swimming pool and gymnasium.

The main thoroughfares out of the town were dotted with villas and farms, one of which, the Hercules Villa, was discovered in 1958 by workmen digging foundations for a school. Now surrounded by modern buildings it is named after a mosaic floor depicting Hercules shooting an arrow at the centaur Nessus, who is carrying off his wife Deianeira. Below the villa's floors can be seen evidence of an underfloor heating system (*hypocaust*) and in the garden are displayed numerous sarcophagi from the 3rd–5th centuries. Not far away, on the corner of Nagyszombat utca and Pacsirtamező utca, there is a huge military amphitheatre that could accommodate an estimated audience of 15,000.

Meanwhile, about 3 kilometres to the north (along what is now the modern HÉV suburban railway), the civilian town of Aquincum was established (being the Latinised version of the Celtic name *Ak-ink*, meaning 'ample water'). In 107AD on the order of the Emperor Trajan it became the capital of Pannonia Inferior (now Transdanubia), the eastern part of the Roman border province of Pannonia; the future Emperor Hadrian would be its first governor under whom the town gained city status and an eventual population of c.60,000. The ruins of the city, excavated in the late 19th century and including houses, courtyards, baths and a market place, now make up the Aquincum Museum (Aquincumi Múzeum és Romterület) at Szentendrei út 139. The museum building itself contains some beautiful Roman glass and sculptures, an unusual portable water-powered organ (*hydra*) presented to the firefighters of Aquincum in 228AD, and the original mosaic from the Hercules Villa. The ruins of the town's civilian amphitheatre built c.130–160AD lie just across the road, which itself is the site of the city's old aqueduct; the names of regular spectators can still be seen carved on the seats.

On the opposite bank of the Danube were a series of watchtowers punctuated by two forts guarding vital bridgeheads, namely Trans-Aquincum (on what is now Dagály utca in District XIII) and Contra Aquincum (just east of Március 15. tér in District V); there was also a fort built on Csepel Island (see no. 84). Despite such defences Aquincum fell to the Huns in 409 and their leader Attila may have built a stronghold on the site of the Roman military camp (the so-called "town of Attila"). However, with the disintegration of his empire after his death in 453 it would not be until c.900 that the Magyar tribes under High Prince Árpád would conquer the Carpathian Basin and Óbuda would be settled again (see no. 1).

In 1241 the area was devastated by a Mongol (Tartar) army led by the grandson of Genghis Khan (fortunately they retreated due to the death of Genghis's son Ogedei) prompting King Béla IV (1235–70) to move his people from the unprotected Danube floodplain up to the security of the Castle Hill – until this time probably uninhabited. It is during this period that the old settlement area, called Buda in the historical records until 1261, is renamed Old Buda (hence Óbuda) and the new hilltop settlement and seat of Béla's royal court takes on the name of Buda.

Other places of interest nearby: 32, 33

35 Bunkers, Boar's Skin and Handmade Boots

District V (Lipótváros), cellars of the Pintér Antik antiques gallery at Falk Miksa utca 30
Tram 2 along the Pest embankment, 4, 6 around the Nagykörút

An unexpected surprise whilst walking along the criss-crossing streets of Pest is to stumble upon a few of its more unusual shops, which speak as eloquently about the city's past (and indeed its present) as any museum or historic building. These include opulently appointed department stores from the *Belle Époque*, arcades smothered with Art Nouveau motifs (see no. 45), bookshops piled high with antique tomes (see no. 56) and down-at-heel shop fronts from the Communist era, all of which have become museum pieces in themselves (see no. 55).

To these can be added a further handful of interesting shops, including Pintér Antik on Falk Miksa utca in District V (the 'antiques street'), a fascinating antiques emporium occupying the brick-vaulted bombproof rooms of a former Second World War bunker. It is easy to forget the building's origins whilst wandering amongst the fine furniture and chandeliers. Further to the south, in Belváros, is the Ékes Kesztyű glove store at Régiposta utca 14, a family business making boar's skin leather gloves by hand since 1883. At the other end of the same street is a well-concealed arcade containing a shop selling only buttons.

Meanwhile, out in the

Bombproof cellars on Falk Miksa utca now contain the Pintér Antik gallery

Jewish Quarter at Wesselényi utca 19 (District VII) there is the Siberia shoe shop offering not only hand-crafted shoes and boots with the zaniest designs but also art exhibitions and occasional block parties

Paprika for sale in a Budapest market hall

(the mosaic-adorned building next door was once the city's shoemakers' guild). Farther down the street, at its junction with Síp utca, is the former Árkád Bazár toyshop (1909), with dolls and toy soldiers rendered in tiling on its facade.

Alongside these unusual shops can be added some unusual Hungarian products worth looking out for. These include shimmering Zsolnay ceramic vases (see no. 54), tins of fiery paprika (see no. 52), potent Bull's Blood wine from Eger (see no. 47), CDs of Communist proletariat songs (see no. 17), folk embroidery from Transylvania (see no. 83) and sickly sweet Szamos marzipan made and sold on Párizsi utca in District V. Quite unforgettable is the brown herbal liqueur known as Unicum marketed in a distinctive globular bottle. First created as a cure by royal physician Dr. Zwack, its name, meaning 'a curiosity', was coined after it was tasted by the Habsburg Emperor Joseph II (1780–90), who declared, "Das ist ein Unikum!" Definitely an acquired taste, several million litres of this curious drink are consumed each year.

Stores in Pest that still retain something of their early 20th century flair in terms of fixtures and fittings include Fleisher's bespoke tailor on the corner of Paulay Ede utca and Nagymező utca in District VI that has barely altered since it opened in the 1920s. Also, at nearby Andrassy út 39 is the former department store Párizsi Nagyáruház, its soaring Art Nouveau frontage reminding onlookers that when it opened in 1911 it was a combined luxury shop and casino with a rooftop ice-rink. It now houses the Alexandra Bookstore, with a café in the former ballroom, adorned with a magnificent ceiling painted by Károly Lotz.

Other places of interest nearby: 36, 37, 38, 39, 41

36 Magistrates, *Evita* and the Great Plain Shepherds

District V (Lipótváros), the Ethnographic Museum (Néprajzi Múzeum) at Kossuth Lajos tér 12
M2 to Kossuth Lajos tér; Tram 2 along the Pest embankment

Opposite Budapest's labyrinthine 691-room Parliament building (Országház) can be found another monumental structure, yet one that seems wholly unsuited to its present function, namely as home to the city's Ethnographic Museum. The reason for this is that the building, designed by Alajos Hauszmann (1897), who was also responsible for the opulent New York Café and the rebuilding of the Royal Palace (see no. 6), was originally created as the Palace of Justice, wherein lay the Supreme Court and the Chief Public Prosecutor's Office. This accounts for the overall grandeur of the neo-Renaissance building, its façade bristling with sculptures of magistrates and legislators.

The interior is equally awe-inspiring, especially the formidable entrance hall with its marble staircases and chandeliers, and ceiling fresco by romanticist Károly Lotz depicting *Justitia*, the Roman goddess of Justice typically holding a set of scales. The museum itself,

Statues of lawmakers adorn the Ethnographic Museum on Kossuth Lajos tér

however, which was installed here in 1974, makes little concession to such grandeur and illustrates perfectly the folk art, customs, costumes and way of life of peasants and farmers in the old Hungary before it was carved up under the Treaty of Trianon in 1920.

Included within the well-labelled collections of agricultural implements, painted furniture and intricate embroidery are numerous unusual exhibits, including etched antler gunpowder horns, ceramic flasks disguised as books, straw and wooden beehives, tools from a hatter's workshop, painted glass icons, expertly woven fish traps, a box of hand puppets used at village fairs and a collection of carved traditional wooden grave markers. There are also inlaid razor boxes exquisitely carved by shepherds and a watch-pole giving a herdsman the necessary elevation from where to observe all his grazing cattle. Of especial interest are the displays of traditional Magyar costumes, including the *suba*, the long sheepskin cloak with shoulder cape worn by nomadic shepherds out on the windswept Great Hungarian Plain (Nagyalföld), known also as the Puszta. This single item of clothing has taken on an almost iconic status, representing the nomadic origins of the early Magyars themselves and lending its shape to the parabolic arch used in Hungarian national architecture in the early 20th century (see no. 67). That such a museum would end up occupying a grand building in such an important location definitely says something about the importance of cultural ancestry in the Hungarian psyche as well as the turbulent history of such institutions.

Hungarian folk art is well-represented in Budapest's Ethnographic Museum

On a more trivial note, film buffs may find the museum familiar since it was used as a location for Alan Parker's 1996 motion picture Evita, its main star Madonna enjoying the luxury of the Kempinski Hotel Corvinus Budapest in Erzsébet tér.

Other places of interest nearby: 35, 37, 38, 39, 41

37 The Statue of Imre Nagy

District V (Lipótváros), the statue of Imre Nagy
on Vértanúk tere
M2 to Kossuth Lajos tér; Tram 2 along the Pest embankment

In a corner of Kossuth Lajos tér, itself named after a prominent leader during the anti-Habsburg Revolution of 1848, can be found a small and leafy square called Vértanúk tere (Martyrs' Square), commemorating thirteen Hungarian generals executed during the same conflict (see no. 48). A century later and Hungary would attempt to rise up once again, only this time against its Communist masters. Again the ringleaders would pay dearly for their actions, none more so than Prime Minister Imre Nagy (1896–1958), whose statue by Tamás Varga, gazing wistfully

A statue of former Prime Minister Imre Nagy looking towards the Parliament

towards the Parliament building (Országház) and away from the Soviet Obelisk in Szabadság tér (see no. 39), can be found in Martyrs' Square today.

Nagy was a so-called Reform Communist, one who dreamt of an independent Hungary free from the compulsory, ultracentralised economic planning of traditional Stalinist Communism (of which the Soviet Union was the main beneficiary), as well as from the overbearing presence of the regime's secret police (the ÁVO). Such thoughts had already seen him removed from office by the Communist Party in 1955.

It was not only Nagy, however, who believed in change but also thousands of workers and students, the latter publishing their *Sixteen Points by the Hungarian Youth* on October 22nd 1956 (a deliberate echo of the *People's Twelve Demands* issued by Hungarian revolutionaries in 1848). Their demands included the withdrawal of Soviet troops, the reinstatement of the moderate Nagy at the head of an enlightened Socialist government, and freedom of the press. The next day, in support of strikes for reforms in Poland, students and workers gathered

 to demand change for Hungary and to demonstrate against the Soviet occupation of Hungary. They congregated symbolically in Petőfi tér, named after the poet revolutionary of the 1848 Revolution (see no. 56) and in Bem tér, named after General Joseph Bem, a Polish general who led the Hungarian army in 1848. They also toppled a statue of Stalin on Dózsa György út near in Heroes' Square (erected on the site of

Bullet holes from the 1956 Uprising on the Agriculture Ministry in Kossuth Lajos tér

a church pulled down for the purpose by Mátyás Rákosi and where an equally controversial monument to the 1956 fighters would be unveiled in 2006) and gathered to demand freedom of the media outside the Magyar Rádió building (the former Esterházy Mansion half way along Pollack Mihály tér). It was at this last location that ÁVO snipers on nearby rooftops started shooting – and the Uprising proper began.

On October 25th thousands gathered outside the Parliament to peaceably voice their anti-Soviet feelings whereupon the Secret Police again opened fire. The tiny bronze balls dotted across the façade of the nearby Agriculture Ministry represent the many bullets fired on what is remembered as 'Bloody Thursday' (the 40th anniversary of which was celebrated by the erection of a basalt column in Kossuth Lajos tér containing an eternal flame).

Following an emergency session held by the Politburo a compromise was reached and Imre Nagy formed a government, political prisoners were freed, the army pledged allegiance to the new government and Soviet troops withdrew from Budapest. At first all went well but when Nagy announced Hungary's secession from the Warsaw Pact in a radio broadcast on November 1st, as well as the abolition of the one-party system, hard-line Communists demanded Soviet assistance. Soviet forces re-entered Hungary and by the November 4th their tanks were on the streets of Budapest. Twenty-two days of bloody street fighting ensued until the uprising was crushed; the statue of a young boy brandishing a rifle outside the old Corvin Theatre at Corvin köz 1 (District VIII), where "the urchins of Pest" fought alongside Hungarian troops from the nearby Kilián barracks, is a poignant reminder of the time.

The Kremlin quickly installed their new General Secretary, a former typewriter repairman named János Kádár (1956–88), while the KGB arrested Nagy and his associates holding them prisoner for two years in Romania. Eventually they were tried secretly in the Military Court of Justice at Fő utca 70–72, condemned to death and executed in June 1958.

Nagy was buried, again secretly, in the now famous Plot 301 of the Kozma utca New Municipal Cemetery, where it would be another three decades, the death of Kádár and the fall of Communism until he and his associates would be given the State Funeral they so justly deserved (see no. 81).

The Museum of Military History (see no. 3) holds an interesting collection devoted to the 1956 Uprising; the Hungarian National Museum (see no. 55) contains various personal effects of Nagy, including his glasses, chess set and even the door of the prison where he was confined.

Other places of interest nearby: 35, 36, 38, 39, 41

38 The Eternal Flame of '48

District V (Lipótváros), the Eternal Flame at the junction of
Báthory utca, Hold utca and Aulich utca
M2 to Kossuth Lajos tér; Tram 2 along the Pest embankment

Szabadság tér (Freedom Square) is one of Budapest's main squares and lies at the heart of a district thrown up rapidly, like so much of modern Pest, in the early 20th century. It was laid out by the architect Antal Pálóczy in 1902 as the city's commercial centre and is still home to the Hungarian National Bank (originally the Dual Monarchy's central bank) at number 9, designed by Ignác Alpár and completed in 1905. The Hungarian Stock Exchange, along one side of the square at number 17, was designed by the same architect and completed the same year; for a long time it housed the headquarters of Hungarian State Television (Magyar Televízió).

An eternal flame for Count
Lajos Batthyány in Lipótváros

Today, it is difficult to imagine that this area was once dominated by slums and factories flooded regularly by the nearby and untamed Danube. Indeed, the so-called Virulj Fountain at the square's southern end marks the former site of the area's rubbish dump, cleaned up by the ever-resourceful Count István Széchenyi (see no. 42). It is equally difficult to picture the huge Habsburg prison-barracks that once occupied much of the square and whose symbolic removal gave rise in part to the square's name. Known as the Új Épület (Neugebäude in German) and meaning 'New Building', the barracks were erected by order of the Austrian Emperor Joseph II (1780–90) as part of the Újváros district ('New City', now Lipótváros). In time the building would come to symbolise Habsburg oppression in Hungary. Most famously it was here on October 6th 1849 that Count Lajos Batthyány (1806–49), Prime Minister of the first modern Hungarian government in 1848, was executed.

The year before had seen civil nationalist uprisings occur across Europe and liberal dissidents in Budapest seized the chance to demand greater autonomy from their Habsburg masters (see nos. 48 & 56). To stem any further trouble the Austrian Emperor Ferdinand I (King Ferdinand V of Hungary) (1835–48) made Batthyány the Prime Minister of a "responsible independent Hungarian Ministry" on April 7th 1848; the Count seemed a good choice bearing in mind he was a firm believer in the notion of an Austro-Hungarian compromise. Although the concessions granted by the Emperor were far-reaching – including emancipation of serfs and freedom of the press – one Ministry member, the lawyer-journalist Lajos Kossuth, went further and proposed the creation of an independent army. This proved too much for Austria, now ruled by the young and strong-willed Emperor Franz Joseph I, who with the help of Russian troops invaded Hungary in June 1849 and put an end to Kossuth's ambitions.

Believing all hope of compromise between Austria and Hungary was now doomed Batthyány resigned his post after only six months and was subsequently arrested by the Habsburgs and tried as a traitor (see no. 65). When his appeal for a pardon failed he attempted to kill himself with his own dagger, an act his captors saw as an honourable one causing them to commute his sentence from hanging to death by firing squad.

The eventual creation of the Dual Monarchy of Austria-Hungary by means of the so-called Compromise Agreement of 1867 showed that Batthyány's original vision of an independent Hungary under the auspices of Habsburg Austria could indeed work. Today, the memory of the unfortunate Count is kept alive in the form of a stone lantern containing a small bronze oil lamp – its flame flickering eternally – to be found at the end of Aulich utca, just off Szabadság tér. His imposing and well-tended mausoleum is located in the Kerepesi Cemetery (see no. 58).

Other places of interest nearby: 35, 36, 37, 39, 41

39 The Soviet Obelisk

District V (Lipótváros), the Soviet obelisk on Szabadság tér
M1 to Kossuth Lajos tér; Tram 2 along the Pest embankment

With the fall of Communism in the late 1980s most of Budapest's overtly Soviet iconography, including street names and statues, was quickly removed. There were a few notable exceptions, however, including the robust sporting statues lining the approach to the old People's Stadium in District XIV, perhaps because they are more Socialist Realist than Stalinist (see no. 79).

There is also the Freedom Monument (Szabadság-szobor) standing 14 metres high on the Citadel ramparts of Gellért Hill and visible from across the city (see no. 13). Designed by sculptor Zsigmond Kisfaludy-Stróbl the statue was erected in 1947 to commemorate the liberation by Soviet troops of Budapest from German forces. The female figure seen today holding a palm frond above her head, however, was originally adorned with a Soviet star on its pedestal and the statue of a gun-toting soldier at its base. Both these appendages were removed in 1992, the soldier ending up in the so-called Statue Park out in District XXII, along with other unwanted Communist iconography (see no. 17). It is worth noting that some commentators believe the Freedom Monument to have been commissioned originally as a memorial to the pilot son of Admiral Miklós Horthy (1920–44), Hungary's inter-war Conservative regent, who died in an air accident engineered by the Germans; the statue's palm frond was intended to be a propeller blade.

Undoubtedly Budapest's most controversial Soviet monument still standing in its original location is the Soviet Obelisk in Szabadság tér. This tall white monument was erected in 1946 by the Soviet army over the last resting place of Russian troops who fell during the liberation of the city. Around its base are reliefs depicting Soviet troops in action and at its top is a golden star. That the obelisk remains perfectly intact is because Hungary signed an agreement stating that the monument would be protected.

Before the Second World War the area now occupied by the obelisk was the site of a symbolic mound topped with a Hungarian flag at half-mast. The mound was made of earth taken from those territories lost by Hungary at the Treaty of Trianon in 1920. It was this loss of two thirds of its land that had helped push Hungary towards an alliance with Nazi Germany in the hopes of reversing the

The Freedom Monument on Gellért Hill commemorating the liberation of Budapest by Soviet troops in 1945

treaty. It is perhaps telling that the Soviets chose this very same spot for their obelisk, a location made even more symbolic by it being directly opposite the American Embassy at number 12. It was in this latter building that Cardinal József Mindszenty, Catholic primate of Hungary and a renowned critic of both Hungary's Fascist and Communist regimes, famously found sanctuary for fifteen long years after the brutal Soviet suppression of the 1956 Uprising (see no. 81).

Even before the First World War Szabadság tér was a sensitive area having been the site of a vast Habsburg barracks that had come to symbolise Austrian oppression of Hungary; the building was eventually pulled down and replaced in 1905 by the Hungarian National Bank and Stock Exchange (see no. 38).

The symbolism of Szabadság tér continues to this day, its very name, meaning Freedom Square, suggesting a deliberate attempt to move away from the traumas of the past. It is no coincidence that the statue of Imre Nagy, Prime Minister of Hungary's brief democratic government in 1956, is within site of the obelisk and yet its head

The Soviet obelisk on Szabadság tér with the Parliament in the background

is turned defiantly *away* from the Soviet monument towards the Hungarian Parliament (Országház) and the democratic ideals that building continues to stand for (see no. 37).

The mood of the area immediately surrounding the Soviet obelisk is lightened by the presence at Honvéd utca 3 of the House of Hungarian Art Nouveau (Magyar Szecesszió Háza). This former private home constructed in 1903 is a colourful paean to the Hungarian Art Nouveau (Secession) Style. It was designed by the architect Emil Vidor – not Ödön Lechner, as is so often the case in Budapest – for the wealthy glue factory owner Béla Bedő. Restored in 2000 after years of neglect the building is today a showcase for its current owner's marvellous collection of Art Nouveau furniture and art, offering a fascinating insight into the lives of the well-to-do a century ago.

Other places of interest nearby: 35, 36, 37, 38, 41

40 The Sacred Right

District V (Lipótváros), St. Stephen's Basilica (Szent István
Bazilika) on Szent István tér
M3 to Arany János utca; M1/M2/M3 to Deák Ferenc tér

On January 1st 1001AD the great grandson of the legendary Magyar
tribal chieftain Árpád became the first King of Hungary (see no. 1).
Born with the name of Vajk in Esztergom 40 miles north of Budapest,
where his father Géza (c.971–997) had transferred the tribal residence
in 972, he was baptised into the Roman Church as István (Stephen).
This was done in order to facilitate the transition of the warring
Magyar tribes into a consolidated Christian nation that would be
acceptable to their powerful neighbour, the Holy Roman Empire.

So it was that the reign of King Stephen I (997–1038) heralded in
some 300 years of difficult and often-violent Hungarian nation building. Stephen's own reign was a turbulent one marked by a serious
revolt of Hungarian pagan chieftains in 1006; it was during this time
that the Venetian missionary Bishop Gellért was famously placed in a
spiked barrel and rolled down Gellért Hill from a spot now marked by
his statue (see no. 13). The king stamped out the revolt and the old
East Asian shamanic beliefs that went with it; he also weakened the
power of the chieftains in favour of a newly created class of nobles,
and minted the first coins.

Although Stephen's son Imre died aged only 24, having been
gored to death by a wild boar, his successors would continue to
develop Stephen's feudal society. Eventually, in 1222 the so-called
'Golden Bull' was issued by the King with provision for an annual
legislative assembly of nobles (known as a Diet) thus enshrining the
constitution of Hungarian feudal society.

Meanwhile, the town of Buda (the name of present day Óbuda
until the 13th century) established itself as the administrative and
geographical centre of the country. Remaining unfortified, Buda
was levelled by a devastating Mongol (Tartar) invasion in 1241 after
which King Béla IV (1235–70) decreed that fortified towns be built
across Hungary, of which his royal residence newly transferred to
Castle Hill (*Várhegy*) would be a very significant example. He ordered
that Hungarians previously living at the foot of the hill, as well as
Germans in Pest, move up to the hilltop, where they settled around
the Church of Mary Magdalene and the Church of Our Lady (later

The twin towers of St. Stephen's Basilica on Szent István tér

Matthias) respectively (see nos. 3 & 7). It is at this time that construction of Castle Hill's famous palace and fortifications also began.

The House of Árpád ended eventually in 1301, when András III (1290–1301) died without leaving an heir, leaving the door open for the Houses of Anjou (King Charles (Károly) I (1308–42) and his son Louis the Great (Nagy Lajos) (1342–82)) and Luxembourg (Sigismund (Zsigmond) (1387–1437)), which ruled for a hundred or so relatively peaceful years before the arrival of the Ottoman Turks (see no. 46).

Looking back at his achievements it is hardly surprising that King Stephen was canonised as early as 1083, indeed as the first Christian monarch of a united Hungary his legacy still resonates in modern Hungary today. Budapest's most tangible tribute is the mighty St. Stephen's Basilica (Szent István Bazilika) designed in 1845 by József Hild in the neo-Classical style; its proximity to the Danube necessitated the excavation of an elaborate three-tiered set of foundations. Destined to be the city's largest church with space for 8,500 worshippers its dome collapsed in 1868 and it was entirely rebuilt by Hungary's foremost Historicist architect Miklós Ybl in the neo-Renaissance style popular in late 19th century Austria-Hungary (it was completed by József Kauser after Ybl's death). The Basilica's twin towers resemble somewhat those of St. Paul's Cathedral in London and the southern one contains Hungary's largest bell, weighing 9 tons. Finally consecrated in 1906 the Basilica would require considerable restoration following serious damage during the Second World War.

Surely the most curious treasure within the Basilica's gilded, barrel-vaulted interior is the so-called 'Sacred Right' (*Szent Jobb*), the mummified clenched right hand of St. Stephen himself. This much-revered relic is housed in its own side chapel inside a lead and glass reliquary shaped like the Matthias Church (Mátyás-templom) on Castle Hill (outside which is a fine equestrian statue of St. Stephen erected in 1906). By dropping a coin in a slot this most revered of Hungarian Catholic relics is illuminated fleetingly like some fairground curiosity; rather more dramatically the hand is paraded around the city each August 20th, the founding father's holy day and a public holiday, marked by a wonderful evening firework display on Gellért Hill. That the relic once held considerable power is witnessed by the Habsburg Empress Maria Theresa (1740–80) returning it to Buda in 1771 in an attempt to placate her Hungarian subjects; the much-travelled hand had previously been kept in Bihar (Transylvania) and Ragusa (Dubrovnik). On the subject of relics notice too the finger bone of Queen Gizella, wife of King Stephen and mother of Imre, in an ornate reliquary monstrance in the Szent Imre Chapel (other religious relics can be found in the Treasury).

Such is the status of the man who helped convert Hungary to Christianity that by special Papal permission a marble statue of St. Stephen by Alajos Stróbl may today be found located on the high altar itself. Another relic of St. Stephen is the crown sent to him by Pope Sylvester II in Rome, which has come to symbolise the

St. Stephen as depicted in a statue alongside the Fishermen's Bastion and Matthias Church on Castle Hill

independent Hungarian state and conveys the authority to rule on whosoever possesses it. So much so that it was smuggled out of Hungary during the Second World War for its own protection and not returned until 1978. In 2000 the post-Communist

Prime Minister Viktor Orbán, keen to rekindle pre-war Christian national values, removed the crown from the Hungarian National Museum to the Parliament (Országház), and in 2001 had it ceremonially floated up the Danube and consecrated in the Cathedral at Esztergom, to coincide with the one thousandth anniversary of King Stephen's coronation there (Budapest lies within the diocese of Esztergom); it was then brought back down the river and re-installed in the Parliament, where it remains to this day. Despite this dramatic action his party was still beaten at the polls by the Socialists two years later.

A stained glass window in the Basilica depicting St. Stephen

Stephen's crown appears elsewhere in the city's iconography, for example held aloft by the Archangel Gabriel on the column in Heroes' Square (it is said that Gabriel appeared to Pope Sylvester in a dream instructing him to send a crown to the new Hungarian king). A representation of St. Stephen's crown can also be seen on the roofline at Bródy Sándor utca 8 (District VIII), Hungary's original House of Representatives after the Compromise Agreement with Austria in 1867.

Other places of interest nearby: 42, 43, 44, 65

41 A Superlative Parliament Building

District V (Lipótváros), the Budapest Parliament (Országház)
at Kossuth Lajos tér 1–3
M2 to Kossuth Lajos tér

Of Budapest's many grand edifices the Hungarian Parliament Building (Országház) on Kossuth Lajos tér is the most recognisable. The seat of the country's National Assembly it is not only the country's largest building but also one of the oldest legislative buildings in Europe.

With daily tours available it has become a popular tourist attraction, too, and warrants a place in every guidebook by virtue of its superlative statistics.

Construction of the Parliament dates back to 1873, when the towns of Buda, Óbuda, and Pest were merged to create the modern city. A new and representative Parliament building was required and an international competition staged to secure a suitable architect. The winner was Imre Steindl (1839–1902) and from the start his design was ambitious.

Work on the building commenced in 1884 and a thousand people were involved. Steindl's plan called for a colossal structure with a symmetrical façade and central dome, set majestically on the Pest side of the Danube so as

The Parliament on the Dabube

to counteract the Royal Palace on the opposite bank. Realised predominantly in the neo-Gothic style (and inspired by London's Houses of Parliament) the work called for 40 million bricks together with half a million precious stones, and no less than 40 kilos of pure gold. Whilst the roofline positively bristles with spires and pinnacles the façade is taken up with 90 statues of Hungarian rulers, Transylvanian leaders, and famous military figures. Over the windows are royal and aristocratic coats of arms, the whole encompassing the city's leading lights both past and present.

The building was inaugurated in 1896 to mark the 1000th anniversary of Hungary's founding. The nation's millennium is permanently memorialised by the Renaissance-style great dome, which soars exactly 96 metres in height. The building's other statistics are almost as impressive, including a length of 268 metres, and the inclusion of 691 rooms, 29 staircases, 27 gates, and 10 courtyards. The staircases alone would measure 20 kilometres if laid end-to-end! Inevitably the Parliament has witnessed numerous milestones in the story of Budapest over the last century. During the Communist era, for example, a large red star was placed on top of the dome. This was removed after President Mátyás Szűrös declared the Hungarian Republic on 23rd October in 1989, from the balcony overlooking Kossuth Lajos tér.

It is from Kossuth Lajos tér that today's visitors gain access to the Parliament – and what treasures await them! Since the Second World War the government has only occupied a small part of the building and so access for the public is extensive. Visitors can walk up the grand staircase, scrutinise the magnificent ceiling paintings by Károly Lotz, admire the glorious stained glass and mosaics by Miksa Róth, and pay homage to the architect himself, Imre Steindl, at his bust displayed in a wall niche.

At the heart of the Parliament is the cavernous hexadecagonal (16-sided) Central Hall. It is here that the Hungarian Coronation Regalia is displayed, including the Holy Crown of Saint Stephen, long a symbol of the independent Hungarian state (see no. 40). Until 1945 the Lower and Upper Houses met here, a function fulfilled today by the National Assembly. Around the hall are ranged several smaller debating chambers, their window sills fitted with numbered cigar-holders so that politicians could deposit their cigars temporarily whilst going in to vote!

Other places of interest nearby: 35, 36, 37, 38, 39

42 A Family of Great Hungarians

District V (Lipótváros), the statue of Count István Széchenyi
in Széchenyi István tér
Tram 2 along the Pest embankment

Standing in Széchenyi István tér with one's back to the palatial Art Nouveau Gresham Palace, named after the London-based insurance company that commissioned its construction in 1907, two less well-known tourist attractions come into view. The first is an elderly acacia tree planted in the 1840s, its boughs now supported on wooden props, said to be the oldest tree in Budapest. The second is a statue of Count István Széchenyi (1791–1860) from 1880, often referred to as the "greatest Hungarian".

Rising up behind the Count's statue is his finest contribution to Budapest, namely the now iconic Chain Bridge (Széchenyi Lánchíd). At the time of his father's death in Vienna in 1820 a united Hungarian capital called Budapest did not exist, the Danube dividing the city firmly in two. Needing to cross from Pest to the west bank to attend to his father's affairs, but there being at that time only a temporary pontoon rendered unusable by ice floes, the young Count vowed to construct a permanent bridge himself and to instigate an Age of Reform.

During the three decades it would take to fulfil his promise the Count would do much to trans-

The statue of Count István Széchenyi in Széchenyi István tér with the Hungarian Academy of Sciences in the background

form Hungary's semi-feudal, agricultural society into an industrialised nation full of civic pride. A great Anglophile he returned from his frequent trips to England with ideas for steamships, steam mills, gas lighting, sports clubs and even flushing toilets. In 1825 he founded and part-financed the Hungarian Academy of Sciences (Magyar Tudományos Akadémia), also in Széchenyi István tér, causing quite a stir when he gave his inaugural speech in Hungarian instead of Habsburg-approved Latin. Even the Count's wife did her bit by planting the first trees in Szabadság tér in 1846, previously a refuse tip, where today stands the Virulj (Flourish) Fountain.

The Count's famous Chain Bridge, designed in neo-Classical style by Englishman William Tierney Clark (his only other surviving work crosses the Thames at Marlow in England) and built by the unrelated Scots engineer Adam Clark, was eventually opened in November 1849 thus linking permanently Buda and Pest (a tunnel would continue the route below Castle Hill a few years later). Unfortunately, the unveiling coincided with the Habsburg suppression of the 1848 Hungarian Revolution and although the first carriage across the nearly finished bridge carried the Hungarian crown from Buda to safety in Debrecen to the east, the first men to cross the bridge were victorious Austrian troops.

Looking towards Castle Hill across Budapest's famous Chain Bridge

As a result Count Széchenyi, who believed that the creation of a modern national state was only possible by working within the confines of the Habsburg Empire, became increasingly disillusioned, succumbing eventually to a total breakdown. Despite a partial recovery the Count's later political manifestos brought the unwelcome attentions of the Habsburg secret police and in 1860 this greatest of Hungarians committed suicide in Vienna, after being told he would be sent to an asylum.

It should not be forgotten that Széchenyi's father, Count Ferenc Széchenyi, also did much to consolidate Hungary's nationhood, especially in the field of the arts. Since 1786 he had built up a vast personal collection of literature and other artefacts relating to the country's history. In 1802 with the approval of Emperor Francis II (1792–1835) he founded the National Széchenyi Library (Országos Széchenyi Könyvtár), donating his collection of 15,000 books and 2,000 manuscripts to the state. The library was eventually transferred to Wing F of the Buda Royal Palace where today it boasts two million books and five million documents. Most importantly it contains the world's greatest collection of works pertaining to all things Hungarian (known collectively as *Hungarica*) including some precious volumes (*Corviniani*) from the lost library of Renaissance King Matthias (Mátyás) 'Corvinus' Hunyadi. The count's collection of 20,000 coins and other archaeological artefacts eventually formed the basis of the Hungarian National Museum (see no. 55).

Count István's son, Ödön, also continued the family tradition by instigating the construction of the funicular railway from Clark Ádám tér up to the Royal Palace (see no. 2), as well as importing Hungary's first motorised fire engine from England in 1870 (see no. 80).

Other places of interest nearby: 2, 40, 41, 43, 44

43 Pubs in Ruins

District VII (Erzsébétvaros), Szimpla kert ruin pub
at Kazinczy utca 14
M2 to Astoria

From Castle Hill to Heroes' Square, Budapest is a city beloved by visitors for its architectural diversity. Splendid palaces, ancient churches, bath buildings, and imposing arcades all contribute to the feel of the place, even though some of them are crying out for restoration. That is the reality of Budapest in modern times: Vienna it is not. But how many visitors would actually go out of their way to visit a badly dilapidated apartment house, especially if it was of little apparent historical interest? The answer, surprisingly, is quite a few! Moreover, they are not looking for art and history but rather drink and entertainment, in one of Budapest's so-called Ruin Pubs (Romkocsma).

The phenomenon of the Ruin Pub originated in the run-down Jewish Quarter of Pest in District VII, where lack of money, neglect, and an absence of gentrification has created an abundance of crumbling and sometimes abandoned late nineteenth century apartment buildings. The cost of restoring such huge structures remains prohibitive but this hasn't deterred a new type of Budapest entrepreneur. Leaving the buildings almost exactly as they are, potential landlords of Ruin Pubs acquire a lease – and move straight in. All that's needed is a makeshift bar, a sound system, and some battered furniture from the local flea market and a Ruin Pub is born!

Against this unexpected but friendly backdrop the city's youth are coming together to revel in the ruins, a beer in one hand and an opinion in the other – and visitors are more than welcome, too. The granddaddy of Ruin Pubs, Szimpla Kert at Kazinczy utca 14 (District VII), was the first to be opened and remains arguably the best of them all. Typically the building's façade has been shorn almost entirely of its plaster exterior, victim to the elements and decades of little or no maintenance. Similarly, its once imposing balustrading and wall brackets are slowly crumbling away. And yet this building remains a joyful and lively place. A row of bicycles are parked neatly outside, troughs of flowers are hanging from the rickety old balcony, and cheerful signs inviting passers-by to step across the threshold.

Inside, the Szimpla consists of several rooms, as well as a large open-air garden, which together can accommodate hundreds of people.

Szimpla kert is the granddaddy of Budapest's ruin pubs

They come here to party well into the night, fuelled by a broad selection of beers, wines, and cocktails. It's another world, and little wonder that a reader survey conducted by respected travel publisher Lonely Planet placed Szimpla amongst the Top 5 best bars in the world. Only the A38 Bar on-board a converted river barge moored on the city's Danube embankment proved more popular (see no. 13).

The Ruin Pub movement has subsequently expanded beyond the borders of District VII, taking the city's increasingly popular new Bohemian culture with it (for a list of those currently in operation visit www.ruinpubs.com). Nor does the burgeoning movement encompass only vacant lots. These days it includes other intriguing spaces such as rooftops, a great example of which is the Corvintető at Blaha Lujza tér 1 (District VIII), which promotes itself as an underground club in the open air. And it probably needs to since much prime Ruin Pub real estate in District VIII, the former Roma Quarter (Nyócker) out beyond the József körút, is in the process of being levelled and replaced with anonymous office blocks, displacing the local community in the process (see no. 57). To participate in a fascinating tour of what's left visit www.beyondbudapest.hu.

Other places of interest nearby: 62, 63, 64

44 Continental Europe's Oldest Underground Railway

District V (Belváros), the Underground Railway Museum (Földalatti Vasúti Múzeum) in the underpass by the Károly körút entrance to the Deák Ferenc tér Metró station M1/M2/M3 to Deák Ferenc tér; Tram 47, 49 around the Kiskörút

Budapest's public transport authority, the BKV, boasts no less than 10 different forms of vehicle on its extensive citywide network. These include both the conventional (tram, trolleybus (introduced in 1949 to honour Stalin's seventieth birthday, explaining why they are numbered from 70 upwards!), bus, suburban railway and riverboat) as well as the more unusual (the Cogwheel and Children's Railways (see no. 21), the funicular (see no. 2) and the chairlift (see no. 22)).

However, Budapest's oldest and most venerable mode of transport is undoubtedly its underground railway, reaching out from Deák Ferenc tér in the centre of Pest to the Széchenyi Baths in City Park; indeed it was the first in continental Europe and is the second oldest in the world (the first being London's Metropolitan 'Tube' line; the third was the Paris Metro).

Although rendered on street plans as the Yellow M1, locals know the railway as the *Földalatti*, meaning literally 'under the earth'. Tucked away in busy Deák Ferenc tér (the only point where all Budapest's Metró lines intersect) can be found the tiny but fascinating Underground Railway Museum, which tells the full story of this historic railway line. Its fascinating collection of models, old tickets, architects' plans and two antique carriages are displayed to great effect in a short stretch of disused tunnel.

A wrought iron sign marks the entrance to the world's second oldest underground railway

Thoroughly renovated and restored to its original appearance in 1996, the M1 was completed originally in 1896 by a Swiss firm as a novel means of transporting visitors to the city's Millennium Exhibition in City Park. One of its first passengers was the Habsburg

A vintage railway carriage in the Underground Railway Museum at Deák Ferenc tér

Emperor Franz Joseph I (1848–1916), a man famous for his distrust of modern inventions! He somewhat condescendingly permitted the railway to call itself the József Ferenc Underground Electric Railway Corporation (FJFVV Rt.), a name it retained until 1923 when it became a part of the Budapest Capital Town Transport Corporation (BSZK Rt.) (it is today a part of the Budapest Transport Enterprise (BKV Rt.)). The line ran along the full 2.5-kilometre length of Andrássy út, itself a dead-straight French-style boulevard laid out in the 1870s and named after Count Gyula Andrássy, Hungary's Prime Minister after the Compromise Agreement with Austria.

The boulevard's grand mansions, State Opera House (Magyar Állami Operaház) and special lane reserved for gentlemen 'out riding' made it one of the finest streets in Europe. Not wishing to alter this renowned urban landscape with a traditional tramway, and eager to promote Budapest as a modern European capital, the idea of an underground railway proved popular with the authorities. Unlike the London Underground, however, the line would not run through a tunnel but rather a 'cut-and-cover' trench, squeezed in above the main sewer and directly below the road surface (this accounts for its characteristically low ceiling height of just 2.85 metres). Each of the ten stations were identified originally at pavement level by ornate pavilions but these were pulled down in the 1920s and replaced by today's distinctive yellow-painted iron balustrading. The stairways and platforms are uniformly clad in burgundy and white tiles, a style mimicked perfectly by the Millennium Restaurant at Andrássy út 76.

Very different from the old carriages displayed in the museum are those that run along the M1 today, being tripartite articulated railcars built by Hungary's renowned Ganz Electrical Works and the engineering company Ganz-MÁVAG, and capable of transporting 190 passengers at 60 kilometres per hour. During the 1970s and 80s the Budapest Metró was supplemented by the more workaday red M2 and blue M3 lines constructed with Soviet financial assistance and using distinctive blue Russian rolling stock.

Today, the historic M1 has eleven stations, which afford easy access to some of Pest's most historic buildings. The stations (together with the buildings and their architects) are as follows: 1) Vörösmarty tér (Vigadó Concert Hall by Frigyes Feszl on Vigadó tér); 2) Deák Ferenc tér (Lutheran Church by Mihály Pollack on Deák Ferenc tér); 3) Bajcsy-Zsilinszky út (St. Stephen's Basilica by József Hild on Szent István tér); 4) Opera (Opera House by Miklós Ybl on Andrássy út); 5) Oktogon (Franz Liszt Music Academy by Flóris Korb and Kálmán Giergl on Liszt Ferenc tér); 6) Vörösmarty utca (note the original tiled station name here) (the 'Nagykörút' thoroughfare by Alajos Hauszmann); 7) Kodály körönd (Calvinist Church by Aladár Árkay on Városligeti fasor); 8) Bajza utca (elegant villas by various architects on Városligeti fasor); 9) Hősök tere (Millenary Monument by Albert Schickedanz on Hősök tere); 10) Széchenyi fürdő (Széchenyi Thermal Baths by Győző Czigler on Állatkerti körút); 11) Mexikói út (Institute for the Blind on Mexikói út by Béla Lajta).

Other places of interest nearby: 40, 41, 43, 65, 66

45 The Parisian Arcade

District V (Belváros), the Parisian Arcade (Párizsi udvar) at
Ferenciek tere 10–11/Petőfi Sándor utca 2–8
M3 to Ferenciek tere

One of the little-known delights of Pest is to stumble upon its hidden
courtyards (*udvar*) and passageways sprinkled across Districts V, VI
and VII (see no. 65). Now in varying states of decay and restoration, they quickly transport the visitor fortunate enough to discover
them away from busy streets and into more peaceful and mysterious
worlds.

Surely one of Pest's most splendid passages is the so-called
Parisian Arcade on Ferenciek tere – a square named after the nearby
Franciscan church – in the downtown district of Belváros. It is part
of a beautiful building designed by architect Henrik Schmahl in 1909
as the Inner City Savings Bank. The style employed is known as
Eclecticism and it reflects the late 19th century tradition of architects
in Austria-Hungary to draw on Gothic, Renaissance and Baroque

The former Inner City Savings Bank on Ferenciek tere

elements when designing public buildings and to incorporate them on the *same* façade (another splendid example is the New York Palace with its famous café at Erzsébet körút 9–11, built as the head office for an American insurance company and with a riot of spires, windows, balconies and columns across its façade). However, the most interesting feature of the Savings Bank is the Parisian Arcade, completed in 1913 and so named because it is based on those popular in Paris in the late 19th and early 20th century. This architectural gem combines a wonderfully eclectic mix of Moorish and Venetian architectural elements. Memories remain of the building's original banking function in the recurring motif of the bee, a longstanding symbol of thrift, found on the exterior and in the Arcade's gloriously vaulted stained glass ceiling by Miksa Róth. With its riot of dark wood panelling, period shop fronts and mosaic flooring, this arcade truly represents *fin de siècle* Pest at its most exuberant.

Just one road away to the west, running down through the Belváros area from Vörösmarty tér in the north to Vámház körút in the south, is the famous shopping street of Váci utca. Now largely pedestrianised, and catering predominantly for tourists, it too retains examples of Pest architecture from a century ago. Worth looking out for is the Secessionist (Hungarian Art Nouveau) facade and interior of the Philanthia florist at number 9, the ornate angel-topped façade from the same period at number 8, as well as the Thonet House at number 11A; the latter is by Ödön Lechner, the pioneer of Hungary's Secessionist movement (see nos. 54 & 78). The streets running off Váci utca are interesting too, especially Régiposta utca, Kigyó

The entance to the Parisian Arcade

The cupola and main passageway of the Parisian Arcade

utca and Párizsi utca. On Szervita tér is a former Turkish Bank undertaken in 1906 by Ármin Hegedűs and Henrik Böhm in a characteristic blend of backward-looking Historicist together with contemporary Secessionist styles, dominated on the outside by a magnificent mosaic of *Hungaria*, the symbolic representation of Hungary.

Since the 1950s the Jégbüfé has looked out from the ground floor of the Parisian Arcade over Ferenciek tere. This classic Communist-era stand-up café is typically modest, with a series of chrome display cabinets filled with reliable pastries and cakes made daily in the huge basement bakery. The cherry slice (meggyes pite) and poppy-seed pastry (mákos briós) are both highly recommended!

Other places of interest nearby: 43, 46, 47, 48

46 From Turkish Mosque to Baroque Masterpiece

District V (Belváros), the Inner City Parish Church (Belvárosi plébánia templom) on Március 15 tér
M3 to Ferenciek tere; Tram 2 along the Pest embankment

With the end of the legendary House of Árpád and the crowning of Charles Robert of Anjou as Charles (Károly) I in 1308 (1308–42), Hungary enjoyed one and a half centuries of relative stability (see no. 1). During this time the new Angevin king, together with his son Louis the Great (Nagy Lajos) (1342–82), made Hungary into one of the most important nations of medieval Europe. In turn their successor, Sigismund (Zsigmond) of Luxembourg (1387–1437), became Holy Roman Emperor in 1433 and transformed Buda's Castle Hill into a splendid permanent royal residence (see no. 9).

Meanwhile, however, a growing and menacing threat lay to the south, namely the burgeoning empire of the Ottoman Turks. Their expansion was initially checked by the poweful noble János Hunyadi, whose son Mátyás (the Renaissance King Matthias 'Corvinus' Hunyadi) was crowned King of Hungary in 1458 (see no. 7). Buda's first Golden Age ensued with much embellishment of the palace on Castle Hill. The death of Matthias in 1490, however, and the resultant dispersal of the powerful Black Army of mercenaries that had helped him conquer Vienna in 1485, together with a peasant revolt in 1514, did much to destabilise the land.

On August 29th 1526 the Turks led by Suleyman the Magnificent, Sultan of the Ottoman Empire, routed the Hungarians at the Battle of Mohács in southern Hungary. They went on to plunder Buda of its royal treasure and to ransack Pest. Tragically, the young king Lajos II (1506–26) died on the battlefield. Fifteen years later in 1541 the Turks returned and occupied Castle Hill, making Buda the permanent seat of Ottoman Hungary for the next 150 years.

In the meantime, most of the local population had fled to Pozsony (present-day Bratislava), which became the capital of the north and west parts of the country that fell to the Habsburg Ferdinand I (1526–64) (brother of Holy Roman Emperor Charles V). Buda effectively became a provincial Ottoman town, Castle Hill and its surroundings as developed by King Matthias being transformed to suit the needs of its new occupiers. Now essentially a Muslim settlement, repopulated with trustworthy subjects including Bosnian Muslims, Sephardic Jews, Italian merchants and loyal Serbs, all existing religious buildings were either destroyed (e.g. the Budaszentlőrinc Monastery, see no. 23) or else converted into mosques (e.g. the Matthias Church (Mátyás-templom)) (see no. 7). Only one church, namely that of Mary Magdalene, received special dispensation to continue as a Christian place of worship, although this too proved a temporary gesture (see no. 3).

The bell towers of the Inner City Parish Church in Belváros

Not until the Siege of Vienna in 1683 were the Ottomans eventually defeated, the armies of a Christian European alliance under Holy Roman Emperor Leopold I proceeding to attack Buda Castle in 1686, reducing it to ruins in the process. Following another resounding defeat by Prince Eugène of Savoy at the Battle of Zenta in 1697 the Turks relinquished their hold on Hungary at the Peace of Karlowitz in 1699. From the ruins of Buda would eventually emerge a triumphantly Baroque city without a minaret in sight, whilst Pest would develop as a commercial centre handling grain and livestock from the Great Hungarian Plain (Nagyalföld).

With the above in mind it is unsurprising that so little Ottoman architecture remains in Budapest beyond the famous thermal baths (see no. 12) and a handful of turban-topped tombs (see no. 28). However, in a Baroque church on Március 15 tér, pressed up incongruously against a modern flyover from the Elisabeth Bridge (Erzsébet híd), is a further unusual reminder of the age of the Ottomans. The Inner City Parish Church is the oldest church in Pest and was constructed originally in the Romanesque style of the 12th century, on the supposed grave of the martyr St. Gellért (see no. 13). It was

A Turkish mihrab preserved inside the Inner City Parish Church

refurbished in the Gothic style in the 14th century (hence the Gothic arched *sedilias* behind the altar) and then in the Renaissance style in the 16th century. Then, during the Ottoman period in the 17th century, the Turks converted the church into a mosque. One of the changes they made was to add a characteristic prayer alcove (*Mihrab*) in the eastern wall of the chancel, facing in the direction of Mecca. It is this alcove that can still be seen today, positioned to the right of the high altar and inscribed with Koranic texts. Eventually, following a fire in 1723 the building's nave and façade were largely rebuilt, accounting for the typical white-plastered Baroque façade that dominates the building today.

Although little Ottoman architecture remains in Budapest, the city's Turkish legacy still manifests itself in several other ways, namely cuisine (paprika (see nos. 47 & 52), coffee (see no. 6) and sweet cakes (see no. 10)), language (the words kukorica and dohány, meaning 'corn' and 'tobacco' respectively, are Turkish) and the fig trees that still grow along Ménesi út on the southern slope of Gellért Hill.

Other places of interest nearby: 45, 47, 48, 49

47 Heathen Pepper and Herdsmen's Soup

District V (Belváros), a selection of restaurants serving Hungarian food including the Kárpátia Restaurant at Ferenciek tere 7–8
M3 to Ferenciek tere

Hungarian cooking is without doubt one of the great cuisines of Europe, a fact obscured to some degree by the global success of the country's signature dish – goulash (*gulyás*). Even this dish is often misunderstood, being in reality a hearty beef and onion soup rather than a stew, spiced with paprika that can be sweet and fragrant rather than hot.

Meaning 'herdsman' in Hungarian, goulash was first made in the 9th century by Magyar nomads out on the windswept Great Hungarian Plain (Nagyalföld). Before setting out the shepherds would cook cubes of meat together with onions in a traditional iron kettle known as a *bogrács*.

The Kárpátia Restaurant at Ferenciek tere serves traditional Hungarian cuisine in a historic setting

The resulting stew was then sun-dried and packed, ready to be rehydrated when required.

Paprika probably arrived into Hungary with the Ottomans in the 16th century (although some commentators suggest India or even America as its origin) and was originally referred to as 'Heathen Pepper'. The Christians admired it for its appearance only and used it as a bedding plant in their gardens. However, when trade embargos resulting from the Napoleonic Wars in the 18th century made pepper scarce, paprika came into its own as a source of seasoning.

Cabbages for sale in a Budapest market hall

It was now that paprika was used to add flavour and colour to goulash (see no. 52).

Traditional Hungarian cooking remains essentially peasant cooking – despite the popularity of French and Austrian cooking at the royal court from the late 17th century onwards – designed to satisfy the hearty appetites of farm labourers.

At the heart of most Hungarian meat dishes is the use of pork fat, onions, and paprika, the finished dishes invariably served with gnocchi-like *galuska* or shorter *csipetke*. Although lighter, Mediterranean-influenced dishes are now ousting such wholesome fare in the city's restaurants, the classic paprika dishes still remain: in addition to Goulash there is *pörkölt* (a stew of meat and onions cooked in paprika-flavoured pork fat, not to be confused with goulash), *csirke paprikás* (chicken *pörkölt* stewed with paprika, onions, and sour cream), and *tokány* (a stew of beef or veal, sometimes with cream, plus mushrooms, asparagus, peas, goose liver and parsley). Other favourites include goulash soup with beans (*babgulyás*), chunky carp broth seasoned with paprika (*halászlé*), delicate pike-perch from Lake Balaton (*fogas*), cold sliced goose liver with toast and red onion rings (*hideg libamáj*), and Savoy cabbage stuffed with rice and minced pork on a bed of sauerkraut with a twist of pork fat and sour cream (*töltött káposzta*). For a snack there is always the famous Hungarian salami, eaten traditionally at breakfast and teatime, as well as an assortment of spicy sausages (*kolbász*).

Excellent wine is also produced in Hungary with short hot summers and long cold winters favouring full-bodied red wines with a few whites. These include excellent reds from Villány and Szekszárd, strong Bull's Blood (*Bikavér*) from

Paprika-infused Hungarian sausages (kolbász)

Eger, white wines from the volcanic shore of Lake Balaton, light rosés from Sopron and, of course, the famous Tokaj wine. *Tokaji aszú* dessert wine is pressed from over-ripe (hence very sweet) grapes that have been touched by *botrytis cinerea* ("noble rot") then added to the base wine in baskets known as *puttony* (the latter is still used on the label to signify the wine's sweetness).

For a traditional Hungarian dining experience book a table at the historic Kárpátia at Ferenciek tere 7–8 (District V), its neo-Gothic vaulted ceiling painted to look like the Matthias Church on Castle Hill. In business since 1877 it is famous for its paprika chicken, Transylvanian stuffed cabbage, and live Gypsy music. During the summer months diners spill out into the courtyard of the neighbouring church (for other restaurants in Budapest with an ecclesiastical connection see nos. 8 & 65). Good Hungarian food is also served in the Alabárdos Restaurant occupying an ancient cellar at Országház utca 2 (District 1) and the centuries-old Margitkert Restaurant at Margit utca 15 (District 2). For fish dishes Hungarian-style try the rustic Horgásztanya Vendéglő at Fő utca 27 (District 1), which offers catfish, carp, and pike-perch.

For equally good Hungarian food but in an altogether more humble – and perhaps more authentic – setting visit Kádár Étkezde at Klauzal tér 9 (District VII), with its chequered tablecloths and cheerful service.

Budapest has numerous restaurants that occupy unusual locations. In Buda (District II), for example, there is the Matteo at Pasaréti tér inserted into a 1930s bus shelter, and the Remiz Kávéház és Étterem at Budakeszi út 5, which incorporates ironwork from an old tramway (for other transport-themed restaurants see nos. 44 & 60). Other idiosyncratic restaurants include the antique-filled Légrádi Antique at Bárczy István utca 3–5 (District V), the intimate French Restaurant M at Kertész utca 48 (District VII), its plain papered walls bearing pen sketches of illusory fixtures and fittings, and the aptly-named Restaurant Robinson on the edge of a lake at Állatkerti körút 3 in City Park (District XIV) (for other maritime-themed restaurants see no. 16).

Other places of interest nearby: 45, 46, 48, 49

48 The Coffee House Revolutionaries

District V (Belváros), the Pilvax Hotel and Restaurant at
Pilvax köz 1–3
M3 to Ferenciek tere

Public holidays in Hungary tend to be national affairs dominated by three important dates: August 20th (St. Stephen's Day celebrating the foundation of the Hungarian state), October 23rd (marking the anniversary of the first spontaneous demonstration against the Soviets and the subsequent 1956 national uprising) and March 15th (celebrating the beginning of the 1848 Revolution against the Habsburgs). All three events have thrown up their fair share of heroes but probably none more so than that of 1848.

Following the expulsion of the Ottomans from Buda's Castle Hill by Austrian troops in 1686 the Habsburgs imposed harsh rule on Hungary. Vienna became the centre of power and Hungarian affairs were orchestrated from Pozsony, present-day Bratislava. Despite nearly a decade of Hungarian rebellion under Transylvanian Prince Ferenc Rákóczi II (1703–11) peace eventually took hold, Hungarian nobles recognising Habsburg rule under the Szatmár Accord, the Habsburgs in return recognising Hungary's feudal Diet (a legislative assembly of nobles). Gradually, over the next century, Buda was re-built as a German-speaking Baroque town and its ruined palace symbolically restored by Empress Maria Theresa (1740–80) and her son Emperor Joseph II (1780–90). Meanwhile, Pest became a commercial hub handling grain and livestock from the Great Hungarian Plain (Nagyalföld).

However, this period of enlightened Habsburg despotism would be shortlived and at the turn of the century the first signs of trouble appeared. Inspired by the French Revolution of the 1790s a group of Hungarian Jacobins (promulgators of extreme revolutionary opinion) were uncovered by the Habsburg secret police, its leaders executed near Déli Station on land still known as Vérmező (Field of Blood). The development of Buda and Pest continued but so did anti-Habsburg sentiment, now voiced increasingly through the Hungarian language itself, which became the country's national language of both literature and rebellion. The loudest voice was undoubtedly that

A military band commemorates the beginning of the 1848 Revolution beneath the statue of Sándor Petőfi in Petőfi tér

of nationalist Lajos Kossuth (1802–94), an eloquent lawyer-journalist and minor noble. In 1839 a reform-oriented liberal Diet convened under the shrewd politician Ferenc Deák (1803–76) – and Kossuth took the opportunity to criticise sharply the Austrian administration. Then, in 1848, civil nationalist uprisings exploded across Europe threatening the old monarchical orders. On March 3rd Kossuth seized his chance by demanding in Parliament a separate ministry for Hungary and an end to tax privileges for land-owning nobles. On March 15th, with news arriving of an uprising in Vienna, dissident liberals met in the Pilvax Café in downtown Pest to plan their own strategy for revolution.

Pest's coffee houses had long provided an open forum for liberals and intellectuals and, although the original Pilvax is long gone, its namesake, now a hotel and restaurant, stands nearby and makes for a good location to imagine the revolution unfolding (patriots can be seen doing just this every March 15th). It lies just off Petőfi Sándor utca, named after one of the rebels – the poet Sándor Petőfi – who, according to a tenacious urban legend, read his *National Song* from the steps of the National Museum later the same day, encouraging Hungarians to rise up against their Habsburg masters (see no. 56). Also on this day the dissident Táncsics Mihály, a former weaver, was freed from the old city jail on what is now called Táncsics Mihály utca 9, on Castle Hill.

Frightened by the *People's Twelve Demands* calling for a liberal-ised constitution, Austrian Emperor Ferdinand I (King Ferdinand V of Hungary) (1835–48) sanctioned a Hungarian Ministry on April 7th under Count Lajos Batthyány (1806-49), an advocate of Austro-Hungarian compromise, which included both Kossuth and Deák (see no. 38). The reforms were far-reaching: the press were freed, the peasants were emancipated and the privileges of the nobility were reduced. For Kossuth, though, this was still not enough and he encouraged the new Diet to recommend the creation of an independ-ent Hungarian army. For the Habsburgs this was too much, prompt-ing the incoming Emperor Franz Joseph I (1848–1916) to encourage a Croatian invasion to force a compromise, the Croats being just one of numerous minorities within Hungary who made up half the population and were unhappy with the dominance of the Hungarian language.

The region soon descended into war and the Hungarian gov-ernment withdrew to Debrecen in the east, where they ceased to recognise Habsburg auhority over Hungary; in August 1849 with the help of Russian troops, the Emperor crushed the revolution with little mercy. Habsburg rule was again imposed and it would not be until 1867 that a workable Austro-Hungarian Compromise (*Ausgleich*) was brokered by Ferenc Deák, facilitated in part by Austrian military defeat in Italy in 1859.

Opposed to violence and often remembered as the "Wise Man of the Nation" Deák was the only senior member of the 1848 government to survive with a political career. By contrast, the poet Petőfi died in 1849 aged just 26 at the Battle of Segesvár in Transylvania and is remembered by a statue in Petőfi tér, where flags and flowers are placed each March 15th; his body was never found. Batthyány was branded a traitor and faced a firing squad, his memory being kept alive by an eternal flame just off Szabadság tér (see no. 38), and Lajos Kossuth fled into exile, his name unforgettable courtesy of a huge statue outside the Parliament building (Országház).

Not surprisingly Deák, Batthyány and Kossuth all have suitably grand and well-maintained tombs in the Kerepesi Cemetery (see no. 58). The many other fighters of the 1848 Revolution to die for their cause are celebrated in a heroic monument on Castle Hill as well as numerous street names across the city, including Március 15 tér and Vértanúk tere (Martyrs' Square), the latter in memory of thirteen Hungarian generals executed during Habsburg reprisals (see no. 37).

The Hungarian National Museum (see no. 55) and the Museum of Military History (see no. 3) both hold fascinating collections of artefacts relating to the 1848 Revolution.

Other places of interest nearby: 45, 46, 47, 49

49 The Legendary Hotel Astoria

District V (Belváros), the Danubius Hotel Astoria
at Kossuth Lajos utca 19–21
M2 to Astoria; Tram 47, 49 around the Kiskörút

Budapest is a city peppered with unusual hotels whose grand facades and opulent public rooms all have tales to tell. Amongst this number is the Hilton on Castle Hill, its walls incorporating ghostly Gothic remains (see no. 8), the Gellért with its glorious Art Nouveau baths (see no. 15), the 1930s-styled Hotel Andrássy designed by a former Olympic swimming gold medallist (see no. 24) and the Gresham Palace at the Pest end of the Chain Bridge, once the headquarters of a London-based insurance company (see no. 42). There is also the Corinthia Grand Hotel Royal on Erzsébet körút, recently rebuilt in the style of the 1896 original that had been erected as part of the city's Millennium celebrations. Bartók once performed in its ballroom, Hollywood stars enjoyed soirées there and it was the venue for a screening of one of the Lumière Brothers early films.

Historic too is the Hotel Astoria on Kossuth Lajos utca, opened in March 1914 during the period known as the *Belle Époque*, a Golden Age just prior to the First World War. The hotel replaced the Zrínyi Coffee Shop (1824), a popular haunt of revolutionary poet Sándor Petőfi, before which a blacksmith had occupied the site. By contrast, the new hotel in French Empire Style had an entrance hall with all the charm of a private mansion, embellished with green marble columns, gilt-edged mirrors and mahogany panelling picked out in brass and copper. It even boasted elevators and a centralised vacuum-cleaning system! Incidentally, it was so-named because its first General Manager had worked at New York's Waldorf Astoria. The faded elegance spills over into the adjoining Mirror Café too, where today people go to chat, play cards or just read a good book below the twinkling chandeliers.

However, as well as many happy occasions over the years, it should not be forgotten that the Astoria has also witnessed several turbulent episodes in the city's history. Shortly after its opening it was the venue for the meeting of the country's first democratic government for the newly independent First Hungarian Republic, following the collapse of the Austro-Hungarian Empire in 1918. Unfortunately, its Prime Minister Count Mihály Károlyi would not last and a year later the hotel witnessed a get-together of a shortlived Hungarian Soviet Republic under Béla Kun (see no. 17). Following the country's tragic slide towards Fascism the Astoria saw its darkest years when it became a favourite with Gestapo officials during the Second World War (the Dohány utca Jewish ghetto could be seen from its upper windows) (see no. 69). Coincidentally, one of the hotel's architects, Emil Ágoston, was designer of the former Hungária Baths at Dohány utca 44, its empty pools rumoured to have been the scene of Nazi attrocities. As if that was not enough, in 1948 the old hotel was forcibly nationalised, its former

Old fashioned opulence in the Hotel Astoria on Kossuth Lajos utca

owner Dr. István Unger emigrating to England with nothing more than a pair of Champagne glasses. Within a few years the Astoria would become the makeshift headquarters for the Red Army during the 1956 Uprising (see no. 37). Since then things have quietened down for the Astoria and today it welcomes those in search of how things were in Budapest before two World Wars changed everything forever.

Other places of interest nearby: 46, 47, 48, 49

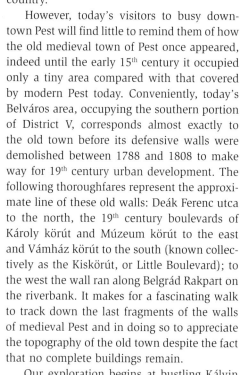

50 The Old Walls of Pest

District V (Belváros), Ferenczy István utca
M2 to Astoria; Tram 47, 49 around the Kiskörút

Comprising a flat open swathe of land on the eastern bank of the Danube the area known as Pest had been settled sporadically since before Roman times. In 1406 Pest was granted the status of 'free town' and it soon became the second largest settlement in the country.

However, today's visitors to busy downtown Pest will find little to remind them of how the old medieval town of Pest once appeared, indeed until the early 15th century it occupied only a tiny area compared with that covered by modern Pest today. Conveniently, today's Belváros area, occupying the southern portion of District V, corresponds almost exactly to the old town before its defensive walls were demolished between 1788 and 1808 to make way for 19th century urban development. The following thoroughfares represent the approximate line of these old walls: Deák Ferenc utca to the north, the 19th century boulevards of Károly körút and Múzeum körút to the east and Vámház körút to the south (known collectively as the Kiskörút, or Little Boulevard); to the west the wall ran along Belgrád Rakpart on the riverbank. It makes for a fascinating walk to track down the last fragments of the walls of medieval Pest and in doing so to appreciate the topography of the old town despite the fact that no complete buildings remain.

Our exploration begins at bustling Kálvin tér, where the red marble relief of a knight, just beyond the modern archway of the Hotel Mercure Korona straddling Kecskeméti utca, marks the former site of one of the medieval town's three gateways. Until c.1800 the area outside the gate was still a rural suburb of vine-

A knight in armour marks the former site of one of Pest's medieval gateways

yards and fields, of which a few steep-roofed houses remain, clustered next to the Inner City Calvinist Church; inside the gate was a warren of narrow winding alleyways that are still followed by today's streets. On the lefthand side runs Bástya utca where, at the junction with Veres Pálné utca, a stretch of the old southern wall can be found in a children's playground.

Retracing one's steps leads onto Magyar utca along which the old east wall once ran, just inside today's Múzeum körút. Fragments of walling can just be made out inside the hotel's carpark and catering entrances. Farther along on the righthand side can be found a further chunk of wall on Ferenczy István utca. Unfortunately, the most impressive remains, including some with their original crenelations, are now hidden away inside the courtyards of 19th century apartment houses at Múzeum körút 21–29; tantalising glimpses may be snatched through the peepholes in their front doors!

At today's Astoria Metró station once stood medieval Pest's eastern gateway, the Hatvani Kapu (see the wall plaque at Kossuth Lajos utca 20), the last gate to be demolished in 1808. It was guarded by a rondella depicted on a wall plaque in the underpass. Beyond this point the eastern wall continued northwards along what is now Károly körút, where further wall fragments remain in the courtyards opposite Dohány utca. Of the northern and western walls of old Pest nothing now remains to be explored although it is known that there were once round bastions along the riverbank. There is also a wall plaque at Váci utca 3 marking the spot where the third town gate once stood.

A fragment of medieval
town wall hidden away
in a courtyard on the Kiskörút

The oldest existing parts of the walls date from before the Mongol (Tartar) invasion of 1241 but despite being strengthened they did not prevent Pest from being destroyed. With the Danube frozen the Mongols continued across the river on foot and sacked Óbuda as well. After the Mongol retreat King Béla IV (1235–70) relocated his people from the unprotected Danube floodplain of Pest and Óbuda up to the security of the newly fortified Castle Hill – until this time probably uninhabited.

Nearly 300 years later history was cruelly repeated when the walls of Pest, rebuilt during the early 15th century, fell once again, only this time to Ottoman Turks. They ransacked Pest in 1526 and then returned in 1541 to occupy Buda for 150 years. In time Pest would pick itself up once again, handling grain and livestock from the Great Hungarian Plain (Nagyalföld) and shipping it out along the Danube.

In 1686 the Habsburgs eventually expelled the Ottomans from Buda but the walls of Pest were never again rebuilt, indeed following a Hungarian revolt against the Habsburgs in 1701 the Austrians ordered all fortifications in Hungary to be rendered ineffective. Despite this the ruined walls of Pest continued to exert an influence on the town's layout, especially in defining what was termed the 'Old City', inside which only Catholics were permitted to erect places of worship. This explains why Pest's Jewish Quarter was established just outside the Károly körút (see no. 62).

By the late 19th century old Pest would be unrecognisable, with its reinforced riverbank to reduce flooding, a series of three concentric boulevards to handle increased traffic and new railway stations and other grand buildings.

Other places of interest nearby: 49, 51

51 The Garden Church of St. George

District V (Belváros), the Serbian Orthodox Church of St. George
(Pesti Szerb orthodox templom) at Szerb utca 2–4
M3 to Kálvin tér; Tram 2 along the Pest embankment

Before the First World War Budapest was the second city of the Habsburg Empire. As such it attracted people from all over the crown lands, including Austria, Bohemia (now the Czech Republic), Croatia, Galicia (now Southern Poland and Western Ukraine) and Slovenia. Serbian merchants, too, had been trading in the city since the Middle Ages but their first large-scale immigration occurred when the Ottoman Turks invaded Serbian lands in the early 16th century.

As a result Serbians fled into neighbouring Catholic Habsburg territories, large numbers of them sailing up the Danube to Budapest (some settled in the town of Keve on Csepel Island, which was re-named Ráckeve, 'Rác' being Hungarian for Serb; it is interesting to note that during the Balkan crisis of the 1990s Budapest again provided a safe haven for fleeing Serbs).

A depiction of St. George and the dragon outside the Serbian Orthodox Church on Szerb utca

Within a few decades of arriving the Serbs had built their own church in the Pest area, the successor to which can be found today in a quiet and leafy corner on Szerb utca. Erected in c.1750 and surrounded by its own little garden the church is dedicated to St. George, a mosaic of whom, depicted in characteristic equestrian pose slaying a blue, red-eyed dragon, can be seen in a niche outside. The choice of St. George is an interesting one in that despite being reduced to an optional memorial day in the Roman Catholic calendar, this 4th century martyr is still honored as a saint of major importance by the Eastern Orthodox Church, of which the Serbian Orthodox Church is a part. Christian mythology relates how George happened upon a city-state whose water supply was in the lair of a dragon. In order to get water the inhabitants daily lured the beast away by the gift of a sacrificial maiden. In killing the dragon George freed the people from their pagan habits leaving them free to be baptised as Christians *en masse*.

Serbians were first converted to Eastern Orthodox Christianity – a modern name applied to those churches claiming to be the historical church established by Jesus and his apostles 2,000 years ago – when they migrated to the Balkans in the 7th century. Later, during the Byzantine period, they fell under the authority of the Orthodox Church of Constantinople at a time when Eastern Orthodoxy was experiencing its Golden Age (it would continue to flourish in Russia and Greece after Constantinople's fall).

Also adhering to the tenets of the Eastern Orthodox Church are the Greeks, whose church (Görögkeleti templom) on Petőfi tér in District V is Budapest's great orthodox structure. It was built by the city's once thriving Greek trading community, in the wake of Emperor Joseph II's Edict of Tolerance (1781). The church was belatedly consecrated in 1801 on the Sunday before the Feast of the Assumption, hence its dedication to the Virgin Mary. It boasts a late 18th century Rococo façade redesigned by Opera House architect Miklós Ybl in 1872, when it was also given a pair of spires (the southern one was damaged in the Second World War and never rebuilt). Undoubtedly, its most magnificent feature is a beautiful, 17 metre-high, painted wooden *iconostasis* created in 1797 by the renowned altar-piece workshop of Miklós Jankovics; the painting and gilding were undertaken by craftsmen from Vienna.

The iconostasis inside the Greek Orthodox Church on Petőfi tér

From the medieval Greek for 'standing shrine' or 'icon stand' an *iconostasis* is a screen decorated with icons that mimicks the original curtained pillars of the Temple in Jerusalem. Its function is to divide the nave of an Eastern Orthodox Church from the Holy of Holies, where the mysterious processes of the Divine Liturgy (including the Transubstantiation) remain deliberately concealed from the parishioners. In keeping with the stringent rules of icon painting, the Budapest *iconostasis* comprises four rows of icons with eleven icons on each row (a smaller but no less impressive *iconostasis* can be found in the Church of St. George described above). Today, the Orthodox Church of Greece is one of sixteen so-called 'autocephalous' Eastern Orthodox Churches that go to make up the Eastern Orthodox Church as a whole. Like the Serbian Church it too was formerly a part of the Orthodox Church of Constantinople but became autocephalous in 1833, that is it was no longer subject to any higher ecclesiastical authority yet remained "in full communion" with other Eastern Orthodox churches (the Serbian church became autocephalous in 1766).

At Fő utca 90 in Buda's District II can be found a chapel built in 1760 dedicated to St. Florian, patron saint of firefighters. In 1920 it was given to the so-called Uniate (Greek Catholic) Church who unusually use the Greek Orthodox liturgy but recognise the Pope (rather than the Patriarch) as supreme pontiff. To the left of the entranceway is a shrine to the Madonna of Máriapócs (a village in Hungary) by whose divine intervention Prince Eugène of Savoy is said to have repelled the Turks at the decisive Battle of Zenta in 1697. The Prince commissioned a Baroque palace for himself in the town of Ráckeve on Csepel Island to the south of Budapest, where another fine Eastern Orthodox Church is located.

Other places of interest nearby: 49, 50, 52

52 The Market Halls of Pest

District IX (Ferencváros), the Central Market Hall (Központi Vásárcsarnok) at Vámház körút 1–3
Tram 2 along the Pest embankment, 47, 49 around the Kiskörút

Hungary's two main culinary exports are undoubtedly paprika and goulash (*gulyás*), the former going a long way to giving the latter its distinctive colour and taste. The bushy paprika shrub (more correctly *Capsicum annuum*) probably arrived into Hungary with the Ottomans in the 16th century but was not commonly used as a spice until the time of the Napoleonic Wars two centuries later (see no. 47). It continues to thrive around the Southern Hungarian towns of Szeged and Kalocsa, where images of its cheery red fruits drying in the sun are a favourite with photographers. Once ground into powder,

Pest's Central Market Hall on Vámház körút

or paprika, it can be hot or mild depending on the variety used and the ratio of seeds to pulp. The fruits are also eaten raw, the slender green ones being fiery, the plump yellow ones mild. It was the Hungarian 1937 Nobel Prize-winning chemist Albert Szent-Györgyi (1893–1986) who first isolated Vitamin C whilst chewing raw green Capsicum, noting that it contained the plant world's highest concentration of that particular vitamin.

One of the many culinary uses for

paprika is in goulash and most of Budapest's myriad restaurants will offer it on their menus (see no. 47). However, a different way to sample traditional Hungarian food, and especially to see its ingredients in their raw state, is to visit the city's traditional market halls (*Vásárcsarnok*). Chief amongst these is the recently renovated Central Market Hall on Vámház körút. Built in 1896 this lofty covered market, made from decorated brick, glass and iron girders,

A ram's head decorating the Hold utca market hall

was designed by Samu Pecz, Hungarian winner of an international competition to design the hall. The building was originally connected to the nearby Danube by a subterranean canal along which barges once brought fresh goods, the neighbouring University of Economic Science having once been the Main Customs Office.

Today, the hall is an ideal place to see Hungary's natural and manmade produce as well as to sample traditional Hungarian fast food along the upstairs balconies. There are entire stalls selling paprika in a bewidering array of types, including *csemege* (extra sweet), *féledes* (semi-sweet), *rózsa* (pink), *erős* (strong) and *pfefferoni* (very strong).

Other atmospheric 19th century market halls, of which most older districts once had one, can be found at Hold utca 13 (District V), Hunyadi tér (District VI), its crumbling façade dotted with bulls' and boars' heads, Klauzál tér (District VII) and Rákóczi tér (District VIII). The markets of Budapest are also good hunting grounds for lángos, the nation's favourite fast food, consisting of a disc of fried potato batter topped with garlic, sour cream or grated cheese. They include the market hall on Lehel tér (District XIII) in the lee of the vast St. Margaret's Church (Szent Margit-templom), itself a 1930s copy of the now ruined 13th century Romanesque collegiate church of Zsámbék.

Other places of interest nearby: 51

53 A Powerful Centre for the Arts

District IX (Ferencváros), the Trafó House of Contemporary Arts (Trafó Kortárs Művészetek Háza) at corner of Liliom utca 41 and Tűzoltó utca
M3 to Ferenc körút; Tram 4, 6 around the Nagykörút

Like other cities across Europe, Budapest over the last decades has broken with tradition when erecting new centres for the arts. Rather than building grand made-to-measure edifices, as was prevalent at the end of the 19th century, the trend has been towards the conversion of industrial-era structures. A fine example is the A38, a former Ukrainian river barge now moored permanently on the banks of the Danube and re-fitted as a cultural centre (see no. 16). Another is a converted ceramic pipe factory at Horánszky utca 5 (District VIII), now used as artists' studios, a gallery, and café-bar.

Equally original has been the Trafó, another self-styled House of Contemporary Arts on a side street just inside District IX (Ferencváros). Opened in 1998 during the Budapest Spring Festival it occupies one of the city's first electricity substations, built in 1909 to supply southern Pest; *Trafó* means 'transformer'. The station had been abandoned for some fifty years by the time it was re-discovered in the early 1990s by a French anarchistic art group, who staged a series of concerts there. However, it wasn't long before the building came to the attention of the Budapest City Council, who purchased the site using

A converted power station in Ferencváros is home to the Trafó House of Contemporary Arts

funds leftover from a failed bid for the World Expo. As a result it was converted into a well-equipped, multi-functional centre for the arts that provided a legitimate successor to the legendary but defunct Young Performers' Club (Fiatal Művészek Klubja, or FMK), whose dilapidated villa on Andrássy út was sold to raise further funds. The Club had inspired Budapest's *avant-garde* artistic movement in the 1980s and the villa had been the venue for legendary underground music events.

Today, the Trafó complex includes a 312 square-metre Performing Hall, which can be either a seated auditorium for 300 or else a 500-person concert hall, the adjacent Trafó Coffee House, where literary evenings are held, and the Studio, reserved for rehearsals and modern dance workshops. In the basement can be found the columned Trafó Gallery as well as the atmospheric Trafó Bár Tangó restaurant and lounge, its name taken from the briefly famous Tütü Tango Club on Hajós utca where numerous cultural initiatives were pioneered during the 1980s; the Trafó Bár Tangó continues this tradition with its jazz concerts and discussion evenings. The cellar also hosts the eponymous Pince Club where the spirit of the FMK is continued by means of regular underground DJ sessions.

The key to the ongoing success of the Trafó is the attention it gives to a wide variety of both Hungarian and international contemporary artistic and cultural genres, namely contemporary dance, modern theatre, current trends in graphic arts and regular modern music concerts (including twice-yearly festivals). The centre also boasts an impressive commitment to the discovery of budding young artists and their encouragement through the provision of contemporary arts training. As Trafó's own website declares: "Trafó is an institution, a building, a place, a medium, vibrating, an intellectual adventure, risk, possibility…A place where life speaks about dance, theatre, visual arts, literature, music…A place where emotion is allowed more space than the usual…"

Other places of interest nearby: 54

54 Buildings for the Birds!

**District IX (Ferencváros), the Applied Arts Museum
(Iparművészeti Múzeum) at Üllői út 33–37
M3 to Ferenc körút; Tram 4, 6 around the Nagykörút**

Like Paris and Vienna, the architectural landscape of Budapest still bears the unmistakeable stamp of the European Art Nouveau. Across the Austro-Hungarian Empire this radically new and innovative style, known as the Secession, was especially controversial because it broke away so sharply from the staid and backwards-looking Historicist tradition favoured by the Habsburg authorities. In Hungary its main practitioner was the architect Ödön Lechner (1845–1914), who used the Secession as an opportunity to create a distinctly national Hungarian style, one that would not only reflect the colourful and mythical past of a country celebrating a thousand years of nationhood but also utilise radical new materials and design principles (see no. 78). Most striking in this respect is Lechner's insistent use of colourful glazed ceramics for the roof tiles and decorative surfaces of his buildings.

To achieve this, he turned to the Zsolnay ceramic factory in Pécs, Southern Hungary. Originally a producer of earthenware and stoneware, Vilmos Zsolnay together with his son and two daughters had transformed the company in the late 19th century with sales of its hugely popular tea services and vases. Most importantly for Lechner the Zsolnays also pioneered a frost and heat resistant architectural ceramic, known as pyrogranite, which could be moulded into intricate designs and coated with exotically coloured iridescent eosin glazes. An early use by Lechner of pyrogranite is the blue-tiled Thonet House at Váci utca 11A (1888–89) (see nos. 45 & 78). A glance at the stunning blue roof of his later Hungarian State Geological Institute (1899) (see nos. 30 & 78), as well as the green and yellow tiles and other ceramic ornaments on his former Royal Post Office Savings Bank (1899–1901) (see no. 78), illustrate vividly the desired effect. Not everyone was so ennamoured, however, and when one observer suggested to Lechner that it was impossible to see his profusion of rooftop decoration from the street, the architect replied, "The birds will see them"!

Undoubtedly, Budapest's Secessionist beacon when viewed from afar is the Zsolnay-tiled dome of Lechner's Applied Arts Museum

Zsolnay tiles on the roof of the Applied Arts Museum on Üllői út

Inside the Franz Liszt Music Akademy

(1893–96), wherein together with his colleague Gyula Pártos he combines Moorish and Indian designs with Hungarian folk motifs. The use of Zsolnay glazed bricks outside and swirling majolica handrails in the foyer is not to be missed. Needless to say, the staid and conservative Emperor Franz Joseph I was unimpressed when he opened it as part of the city's millennial celebrations. Designed deliberately to reflect the eastern origins of the Magyars rather than the western origins of the Renaissance it remains one of Europe's most extraordinary museum buildings.

Other architects in Budapest also used Zsolnay's patented weatherproof tiles, as witnessed by the polychrome roof of the Matthias Church (Mátyás-templom) (1896) on Castle Hill (see no. 7), the blue-tiled domes of City Park's elephant house (1912) (see no. 73) and the Central Market Hall (1896, re-roofed 1994) on Vámház körút (see no. 52). There were also other more specialised uses of Zsolnay products, for instance in the blue ceramic tomb of Sándor Schmidl (1903) by Béla Lajta, a pupil of Lechner, in the Kozma utca Jewish Cemetery (see no. 59), the sea-green steam-resistant tiling of the Gellért Baths (1912) (see no. 15) and the opulent, gold-glazed interior of the Franz Liszt Music Academy (1907).

Although the Zsolnay firm spent much of the Communist era churning out insulators for power lines they are now producing fine ceramics again, which can be purchased in the Zsolnay Porcelain shop at Kígyó utca 4 (District V); antique Zsolnay ceramics are available in the Virág Judit Gallery at Falk Miksa utca 30 (District V) and the Zsolnay Café in the Radisson Blu Béke Hotel at Teréz körút 43 (District VI) serves tea in Zsolnay porcelain.

Other places of interest nearby: 53

55 Brass Screws, Propaganda and the Monk's Brick

District VIII (Józsefváros), the Hungarian National Museum
(Magyar Nemzeti Múzeum) at Múzeum körút 14–16
M3 to Kálvin tér; Tram 47, 49 around the Kiskörút

In the pantheon of great Hungarians who have helped shape modern Budapest the name of Széchenyi ranks high (see no. 42). It was Count Ferenc Széchenyi whose great penchant for collecting books and other historical items led not only to the founding of the Széchenyi National Library (Országos Széchenyi Könyvtár) but also the Hungarian National Museum (his son István would later build the city's iconic Chain Bridge). After the count's death in 1820 his personal collection of 20,000 coins and archaeological artefacts, relating to the history of Hungary found a permanent home in a custom-built neo-Classical building (1846) by Mihály Pollack, on the aptly named Múzeum körút. At the

An inscribed medieval brick in the Hungarian National Museum

time it opened the building was so far out of town that grazing cattle occasionally wandered in!

The collection has been added to continually ever since producing one of Europe's greatest, and it could be said quirkiest, national museums. Thus, alongside traditional exhibits such as prehistoric tools, fossilised bones, Roman sculptures and medieval metalwork, can be found some real oddities. These mostly reside in the second floor collections that illustrate Hungary's history from its founding up to and beyond the fall of Communism.

Room 1 for instance, devoted to the Árpádian dynasty, contains a brick from a 13th century monk's tomb inscribed thus: "Why are you staring at me? You'll be the same as I am. Better say the Lord's Prayer"! Rooms 3 and 4, covering the 14th and 15th century houses of Anjou and Luxembourg, have on display an unusual pair of ivory saddles as well as fragments of surprisingly ornate medieval ceramic stoves. Room 12 is devoted to the revolutionary events of 1848 and includes a printing press once owned by the firm that printed the

A Communist-era living room in the Hungarian National Museum

People's Twelve Demands from that tumultuous time (see no. 56). In Room 14 is a huge collection of screws and bolts representing the entire range once manufactured by a successful 19th century Budapest firm. Meanwhile, Room 19 contains artefacts from the Second World War including samples of the Swedish diplomat Raoul Wallenberg's Jewish protective passes (see no. 63). This part of the collection concludes with Room 20 illustrating the Communist era in Hungary and including a fully furnished council flat, propaganda posters and some typically downbeat shop windows. Most poignant of all are the *pince-nez* glasses and travelling chess set of the Communist moderate Imre Nagy, executed for his part in the 1956 Uprising against the Soviets (see no. 37).

For a feel of how the streets of Budapest appeared in the 50s and 60s there are still a few old Communist-era shop fronts along Király utca, filled with plastic trinkets, lamp shades and electrical components. Probably most illuminating are the café-cum-bars known as Presszó, for example the Bambi at Frankel Leó út 2–4 (District II), its kitschy and outmoded 1960s fittings evoking an era and a lifestyle that is fast becoming a thing of the past.

Other places of interest nearby: 50, 56, 61

56 Hungarian History in Paper and Stone

District VIII (Józsefváros), the Hungarian National Museum
(Magyar Nemzeti Múzeum) at Múzeum körút 14–16
M3 to Kálvin tér; Tram 47, 49 around the Kiskörút

The Hungarian National Museum in Budapest is not only the country's largest museum (8,000 square metres) but also undoubtedly one of Europe's greatest (see no. 55). Unlike its counterparts in other European cities, however, the museum building itself has played a significant role in the city's turbulent history.

From the 1820s onwards Hungary entered a period of prosperity known as the Reform Age. During this time Buda and Pest were developed quickly, Hungarian became the national language (1844) and rural feudalism gave way to the creation of an industrialised nation-state. Most noticeably, following the Great Flood of 1838 (see the wall plaque on the Franciscan Church on Ferenciek tere), Pest was given adequate river defences and redesigned as the city's commercial and cultural heart, laid out around a series of concentric boulevards lined with grand public buildings.

A printing press in the Hungarian National Museum similar to that used to produce the People's Twelve Demands in 1848

The previous Baroque idiom was abandoned in favour of a majestic neo-Classical style, which reflected the commercial aspirations of a new *bourgeoisie* wanting an architecturally homogeneous city. Although much of it was lost during the Second World War (notably Pest's glorious neo-Classical waterfront), the style is still represented by Pest County Hall (Pest Megyei Önkormányzati Hivatal) (1838–41) at Váci utca 6, the Gyürki Mansion (1855) at Apáczai Csere János utca 5 and the piers of the Chain Bridge (1839–49) (see no. 42). Budapest's most important neo-Classical building, however, is the Hungarian National Museum (1837–46), designed by Mihály Pollack, who was also responsible for finishing the neo-Classical Lutheran Church in Deák Ferenc tér.

Completed during a time when civil nationalist uprisings were occurring across Europe, the museum's overt republican symbolism, in the form of motifs derived from Classical Greece and Rome, found great favour with Budapest's liberal dissidents (see no. 55). Little wonder then that a persistent urban legend relates how on March 15th 1848 the Hungarian revolutionary poet Sándor Petőfi (1823–49) chose the museum's steps to recite his patriotic poem *Nemzeti Dal* (*National Song*), with its famous line *"Talpra Magyar"* (*"Rise up, Hungarians"*), as a call to arms against the Habsburgs (see no. 48).

The revolutionary poet Sándor Petőfi commemorated on the steps of the Hungarian National Museum

Inside the museum today there is a room devoted to the events of 1848, pride of place going to a printing press once owned by the company that printed the *People's Twelve Demands*, which were circulated around the city and dispatched to Vienna. Although wide-ranging concessions were forthcoming from the Habsburgs, and an independent Hungarian Ministry formed, the incoming Austrian Emperor Franz Joseph I (1848–1916) eventually snuffed out the uprising following misguided attempts to create an independent Hungarian army.

The offices that once housed the printing press were located just around the corner on Kossuth Lajos utca, where there is also a plaque marking Petőfi's former lodgings. Today, the museum steps are the setting for patriotic songs and speeches each March 15th in memory of the start of the ill-fated revolution. The Petőfi Museum of Literature (Petőfi Irodalmi Múzeum) can be found at Károlyi utca 16 (District V).

The Kiscelli Museum in Óbuda (District III) has a collection relating to the history of printing in Budapest (see no. 31). Hungary's first printed work was the Chronicle of Buda produced by a printer from Nuremberg called András Hess during the reign of the Renaissance King Matthias (Mátyás) Corvinus Hunyadi (1458–90). The square where his Castle Hill workshop operated from 1472 onwards is now called Hess András tér. Bibliophiles should also track down the little-known 4th floor reading room at Szabó Ervin tér 1 (District VIII), built inside the former neo-Rococo mansion (1887) of the Wenckheim family, accounting for its grand stuccoed rooms decorated with mosaics and chandeliers. It is known today as the Ervin Szabó Library (Szabó Ervin Könyvtár) after a vociferous advocate of the Workers' Movement. Another grand residence in the same district to suffer a similar fate was the former town house of Count István Károlyi at Múzeum utca 17, converted into a library by the Communists after the Second World War but retaining its superb wood panelling and spiral staircase. Fascinating too are the city's wonderful antiquarian bookshops (antikvárium), for example Központi Antikvárium at Múzeum körút 15, founded in 1881 and filled to bursting with old books, prints and maps. Book lovers will also appreciate the Writers' Bookshop (Irók Boltja), formerly the Café Japan, at Andrássy út 45, replete with armchairs and tea urn, and Treehugger Dan's Bookstore & Café, the "Local Bookstore with a Global Conscience", at Csengery utca 48 (District VI).

Other places of interest nearby: 50, 55, 61

57 The Roma Quarter

District VIII (Józsefváros), the Roma Parliament
at Tavaszmező utca 6
Tram 4, 6

Most guidebooks to Budapest list District VIII (Józsefváros) as being home to the Hungarian National Museum and the Kerepesi Cemetery with little else besides. However, sandwiched between the two is a fascinating, run-down and little-visited area that has long been home to the city's gypsy, or more correctly Roma, population.

Gypsies were once supposed to have come from Egypt, hence their name, but probably began their wanderings from India. Their language, known as Romanes (or sometimes Romany), is related to the north Indian tongues of Hindi and Punjabi. With their distinctive art and mysterious traditions they arrived in Europe by caravan in the 11th century, reputedly consoling the Hungarians with their musicianship after the latter's defeat by the Turks at the battle of Mohács in 1526.

Today, Hungary's half a million Roma are a part of a distinct European nationality that lacks its own nation. The majority of those living in Budapest are called Romungros. Although they are far from being fully assimilated into Budapest's working class they no longer speak Romanes and have foregone most of their ancient traditions. It is from this culturally diluted group that many of Budapest's 'Gypsy bands' hail, peddling their folksy bittersweet melodies and drinking

The Roma Quarter of Józsefváros was once filled with communal courtyards like this

songs around the city's traditional restaurants since the 19th century (for example the Margitkert in Buda and the Kárpátia in Pest (see no. 47)). Most distinctive to the outsider's ear will be the *csárdás*, with its slow opening section and breakneck second, played on the fiddle and the hammered Zimbalon and supposed by 19th century nobility to have been performed originally in country inns (*csárda*) by peasants. Whilst such performances may delight the tourists, little of it hails from the true Roma tradition or from real Magyar folk music (see no. 70).

The doorway of the Roma Parliament

The Oláh, or Vlach, are a second smaller Roma group who arrived in Budapest during the 19th century. Still practising several Roma dialects they are proud to continue Roma traditions. A sub-group is the Boyash, living mostly in Southern Hungary having arrived from Croatia.

Budapest's Roma quarter lies just beyond József körút. Many of its streets are extremely dilapidated with more than their fair share of murky beer cellars, car workshops and near-abandoned apartment buildings; such features, however, are what sets the area apart and it should be explored with care and sensitivity before it is swept away forever.

At Tavaszmező utca 6, not far from the district's Baroque parish church (see no. 26), is the so-called Roma Parliament. This shabby old apartment block is home to the Roma Assembly, dedicated to the preservation of the Roma identity and to giving its people a political voice. The building is crammed with Roma art and its concert hall sometimes comes alive with Roma music both traditional and modern. With entry into the European Union it is to be hoped that the lot of the previously downtrodden Hungarian Roma will get a little better.

Whilst Budapest's Roma Quarter may now be largely in ruins, elsewhere in the city conscious efforts are being made to promote Roma cultural traditions to a new audience. Notably, Romani Design at Szent István tér 3 (District V) is an innovative design shop doing much to reinvent Roma culture. Dresses and jewellery for women, shirts and ties for men are all imbued with floral Roma motifs. Roma fine art and cooking is also available.

58 Monuments and Mausolea, Poets and Politicians

District VIII (Józsefváros), the Kerepesi Cemetery (Kerepesi temető) at Fiumei út 16
M2 to Keleti Pályaudvar, then Tram 24 or walk; a useful map is available from the gatehouse or florist at the main gate

To the south of Budapest's glorious Eastern Railway Station (see no. 60) can be found the Kerepesi Municipal Cemetery. Of Budapest's three main cemeteries (*temető*) this one is the most important, the others being the pretty Farkasréti Public Cemetery in District XII (see no. 19) and the workaday New Municipal Cemetery at Kozma utca in District X (see no. 81).

The tomb of Ferenc Deák in the Kerepesi Cemetery

Like all great urban cemeteries, Kerepesi fulfils a dual role within the city, namely as an impressive last resting place for its great, good and not so good, and as a leafy and peaceful park where people can escape the bustle of modern life. Laid out on a monumental scale in 1874 its wide boulevards direct the visitor effortlessly and deliberately towards the most imposing of the cemetery's many mausolea. Their present state of preservation together with the numbers of fresh flowers placed upon them can often be telling in a city where so many regimes have ruled. Thus, the trio of exuberant, well-maintained monuments to Hungarian heroes Lajos Kossuth (1802–94) (Plot 23), Count Lajos Batthyány (1806–49) (Plot 19) and Ferenc Deák (1803–76) (Plot 37/1) still rise triumphantly above everything else. It is hardly surprising that these men continue to be held in such high esteem: Kossuth was a vociferous prime-mover during the anti-Habsburg struggle of the late 1840s; Batthyány was Prime Minister of a briefly independent Hungary after the abortive 1848 Revolution and was executed as a result; and Deák engineered the famous 1867 Compromise Agreement with Austria acknowledging Hungary as a part of a Dual Monarchy with its own Parliament in Budapest. Similarly, at Plot 21 can be found a well-maintained garden dedicated to those who opposed the Soviets during the 1956 Uprising; equally well kept is the nearby linen-draped equestrian monument to József Antall (1932–93) (Plot 28), the first Prime Minister of a democratic Hungary who died in 1993.

By contrast, the relatively unfrequented plot to the left of the main entrance contains the urns of those who fought on behalf of the Soviets. Equally unloved is the crumbling Pantheon to the Workers' Movement (Munkásmozgalmi mauzóleum) between Plots 12 and 14. These forlorn monuments were erected during the 1950s when the cemetery had been closed and reserved for Communist ceremonial burials only. Another is the grave of chess master Géza Maróczy (1870–1951), chess players enjoying state support and a special status during the Communist era. That's not to say that the Communist era in Budapest did not have its adherents, for the grave of János Kádár (1912–89) in Plot 12, Hungary's last Communist General Secretary, is still well-tended, although it was vandalised in 2007. History remembers him as the Communist who took swift and bloody revenge on the 1956 revolutionaries but then offered amnesties in 1963 to those imprisoned in an attempt to appease the population. His new economic reforms broke with traditional Communist thinking to some extent but by the time of his death in 1989 the writing was on the wall for traditional Communism in Hungary. His epitaph reads: "I lived for Communism and the People".

Away from the monuments of important political figures are the equally interesting graves of Budapest's poets, singers and other creatives from the last hundred years. These include the novelist Mór Jókai (1825–1904) (Plot 18), outspoken during the 1848 Revolution and still causing a stir aged 74 by marrying a young actress, rebellious poet Attila József (1905–37) (Plot 36), who was thrown out of the Communist party and later committed suicide, Endre Ady (1877–1919) (Plot 19/1), the "Founder of Modern Hungarian Lyric Poetry", and music hall performer Lujza Blaha (1850–1926) (Plot 18/1), known as 'the Nation's Nightingale', whose grave takes the form of a carved four-poster bed! Also worth tracking down is

The four-poster bed tomb of singer Lujza Blaha in the Kerepesi Cemetery

renowned confectioner Emil Gerbeaud (1854–1919) (Plot 26), the "Saviour of Mothers" Ignác Semmelweis (1818–91) (Plot 34/1) (see no. 10), scientist Leó Szilárd (1898–1964) (Plot 27), who together with Einstein invented a refrigerator without moving parts, and the architects Miklós Ybl (1814–91) (Plot 34/1) and Ödön Lechner (1845–1914) (Plot 28). By contrast, plots 38–40 are now largely abandoned, their headstones to long forgotten Hungarian commoners just visible amongst the undergrowth.

For those wishing to delve further into the history and traditions of Budapest's burial customs there is a small Funeral Museum inside the Main Gate of the Kerepesi Cemetery – and don't forget All Saints' Day (November 1st) and All Souls' Day (November 2nd), when thousands of locals visit the cemeteries leaving flowers and flickering candles for the dead.

Other places of interest nearby: 59, 60

59 The Forgotten Jewish Cemetery

District VIII (Józsefváros), the Kerepesi Jewish Cemetery (Kerepesi zsidó temető) at Salgótarjáni utca
M2 to Keleti Pályaudvar, then Tram 24 and 37 or walk

That the Jews have played a vital and long-standing role in the development of Budapest is obvious, not only from the historical record but also from the surviving Jewish fabric of the city. This includes numerous synagogues, prayer houses and more than a dozen small Jewish cemeteries in former villages that now make up the city's suburbs (see nos. 9, 32 & 62). However, in order to appreciate the size, prestige and prosperity of Budapest's pre-Second World War Jewish community one should visit the two main Jewish cemeteries, containing both the overblown mausolea of the industrial elite as well as the graves of ordinary Jewish citizens.

Nearest to the city centre is the extraordinary Kerepesi Jewish Cemetery (Kerepesi zsidó temető) on Salgótarjáni utca, laid out in 1874 as a distinct burial ground to the east of the Kerepesi Municipal Cemetery (see no. 58). Although now all but abandoned the cemetery once served numerous well-to-do Jewish families whose ornate tombs jostle for space just inside the main entrance. There are at least nine magnificent family vaults undertaken for successful industrialists by architect Béla Lajta, a pupil of the famous Ödön Lechner. These include Baron Manfréd Weiss, owner of the Csepel steel works, the Hatvany-Deutsch family, sugar

Abandoned mausolea
in the Kerepesi Jewish Cemetery

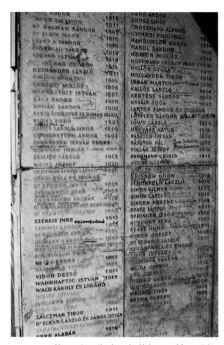

Names inscribed on the Holocaust Memorial in the Kozma utca Jewish Cemetery

millers and patrons of the arts, and the Goldbergers, whose Óbuda textile factory supplied the Habsburg monarchy (see no. 30). Lajta also designed the Sváb family crypt protected by a pair of striking black marble hawks. Also worth looking out for are tombs bearing coats of arms signifying ennobled families, as well as the grave of the renowned Hungarian-Jewish poet József Kiss. By contrast, towards the rear of the cemetery are the plain and weed-choked headstones of those who lost their lives in the Budapest ghetto or else were shot and thrown into the Danube by the Fascist Arrow Cross, the Nazis' Hungarian collaborators. Lajta is also responsible for the cemetery's partly ruined turreted gateway (1908) and now roofless Mesopotamian-style Ceremonial Hall, where pre-burial rites once occurred.

Continuing eastwards into District X, at the end of tram route 37, lies Budapest's main Jewish Cemetery (Kozma utcai zsidó temető), appended to the north-west corner of the Kozma utca New Municipal Cemetery (see no. 81) and accessible at Kozma utca 6. Established in 1868 it contains the remains of some 300,000 Hungarian Jews. Again the visitor will discover many beautiful abandoned tombs here, including grand mausolea ranged around the perimeter wall (for example the lion-fronted Zsigmond Brüll tomb with its glorious mosaics, and the temple-like Redlich mausoleum by Ignác Alpár, designer of the Parliament (Országház) building). These are only slowly being restored after decades of neglect. Béla Lajta's work is again in evidence, most extraordinary of all being his cerulean blue, glazed and gilded ceramic tomb for the wealthy Pest grocer Sándor Schmidl. Its tunnel-like shape is based on the *suba*, the sheepskin cloak worn by Magyar shepherds out on the windswept Great Hungarian Plain (Nagyalföld) (the Wellisch family tomb takes a simi-

Béla Lajta's ceramic tomb for wealthy Pest grocer Sándor Schmidl in the Kozma utca Jewish Cemetery

lar form) (see no. 67). Erected in 1903 the ceramics were produced by the renowned Zsolnay factory (see no. 54).

The cemetery's focal point today is undoubtedly the 1949 Holocaust Memorial made up of connected vertical stone slabs and columns bearing the names of thousands of Jews who lost their lives during the Second World War; relatives have subsequently added by hand the names of those unwittingly omitted.

Hidden away along a nearby dirt track (Harangláb-Csucsor utca) is the little-known Gránátos utca Orthodox Cemetery used by Hassidic Jews. Established in 1922 and last used in 1993 it has 5,000 headstones with men, women and rabbis laid out in distinct zones. It replaced the old walled Orthodox Cemetery to be found at Csörsz utca 55 across the Danube in Buda (District XII). The latter, founded in 1860, is one of Budapest's oldest surviving Jewish cemeteries.

Also on the west bank of the Danube is Óbuda's Orthodox Cemetery at Külső Bécsi út 369 (District III), opened in 1922 by a 31-year old rabbi whose death three days later in a car accident meant he was the first to be interred there. Monuments include one to the 149 patients, doctors and nurses of the Maros utca hospital murdered by the Nazis on January 21st 1945, and another to victims of Adolf Eichmann's enforced labour march to Vienna.

A further Jewish cemetery of note is part of the Farkasréti Public Cemetery (Farkasréti temető) accessible from Érdi út (District XII) (see no. 19). Established in 1885 it contains graves inscribed in Hebrew, Hungarian and German, one of which is that of Dr. Gyula Képes, a member of the Austro-Hungarian North Pole Expedition of 1872.

Other places of interest nearby: 58, 60

60 Railway Stations and Steam Trains

District VIII (Józsefváros), the Eastern Railway Station
(Keleti Pályaudvar) at Baross tér
M2 to Keleti Pályaudvar

Unlike the magnificent 19th century railway stations of Vienna, which were heavily bombed during the Second World War in order to reduce their ability to service Germany's military fronts, those of Budapest (*pályaudvar*, or *pu* for short) have survived intact, continuing to exude a little of the romance of the golden age of steam. Admittedly the so-called Southern Railway Station (Déli Pályaudvar) on Alkotás út (District I) (serving south-east Hungary and Lake Balaton, the former Yugoslavia, Croatia, Slovenia and the Adriatic) is modern, but the old Eastern and Western Railway Stations are architectural gems.

The Eastern Railway Station (Keleti Pályaudvar) at Baross tér is Budapest's main railway terminus and serves trains to north-west Hungary, Vienna, Bucharest, Warsaw, Bulgaria and Turkey. The station was constructed in 1884 as part of a great, late 19th century expansion of Hungary's railways and was at the heart of an imperial

The grand façade of Budapest's Eastern Railway Station (Keleti pályaudvar)

rail network fanning out across this part of the Austro-Hungarian Empire. Some 6,850 miles of track were laid between 1890 and 1914 – nearly 50% of the country's total permanent way – largely as a result of the economic policies of Gábor Baross, Minister for Transport, after whom the square containing the station is named. All lines were directed through Pest making the empire's dependents reliant on the city; this explains why today there is still no direct Vienna-Zagreb line. Despite some recent renovations, the dramatic architecture and old columned buffet at Keleti still have the power to transport the visitor back to a more elegant age of rail travel.

Only a year before Keleti's construction the famous Orient Express route had been launched, taking passengers from Paris eastwards through Budapest and on to Istanbul. Despite its world famous name the Orient Express service was eventually scrapped in December 2009. It is recalled in the Orient Express Restaurant, which occupies a converted railway carriage outside Déli Railway Station on Krisztina körút (District I).

To the west of Keleti Station runs the grand boulevard known as the Nagykörút (Great Boulevard) opened in 1896 to commemorate the 1000th anniversary of the conquest by Prince Árpád of the Carpathian Basin (it is Budapest's longest thoroughfare and actually

comprises several roads, namely Szent István körút, Teréz körút, Erzsébet körút, József körút and Ferenc körút). The most imposing architectural statement on the boulevard is undoubtedly the Western Railway Station (Nyugati Pályaudvar) at Nyugati tér (District VI), saved from destruction by a group of vociferous conservationists. It is actually built on the site of Pest's first station from where a train departed for Vác on July 15th 1846. The present station is the point of departure for those travelling to north and east Hungary, Romania (Transylvania) and Bratislava.

The station was constructed in 1874–77 by August de Serres on behalf of Gustav Eiffel's famous company in Paris, accounting for the stations's

The former Habsburg imperial waiting room at the Western Railway Station (Nyugati pályaudvar)

distinctive steel-framed construction, similar to the French capital's Gare du Nord. Behind the enormous colonnaded glass façade, through which trains arriving and departing can be seen from the street, is a 25,000 square metre concourse across which an out-of-control steam engine once skidded onto the street! Towards the rear of the hall can be found a locked door that once led to the Habsburg royal family's private waiting room. Above it is a marble lintel carved with their famous motto *"Viribus Unitis"* (Strength through Unity). Finally, to the right of the main façade, there is the old railway buffet, still a grand dining room with ornate stucco work, frescoes and period light fittings despite having been converted recently into a fast food restaurant.

A Budapest railway ticket office unchanged for a century

It seems fitting that an authentic steam train, known as the Nostalgia Train (Nosztalgia vonat), should leave Nyugati every Saturday morning from May to September heading north to Szob on the Danube Bend (Dunakanyar). For real devotees of the iron horse there are a hundred or so locomotives on display at the Hungarian Railway History Park (Magyar Vasúttörténeti Park) at Tatai út 95 (District XIV). There are also wonderful scale models at the Transport Museum in City Park (see no. 77).

Other places of interest nearby: 58, 59

61 Silver Screen Budapest

District VIII (Józsefváros), the Uránia National Film Theatre
(Uránia Nemzeti Filmszínház) at Rákóczi út 21
M2 to Astoria, then Bus 7 for one stop or walk

It remains something of a mystery why so many influential photographers have hailed from Hungary. Some commentators have suggested that a country known for its *avant-garde* intellectual and artistic tendencies used visual imagery to speak to the wider world in a way not possible through the unexportable Magyar language (see no. 68). Whatever the reason the same is true regarding the art of cinematography in which Hungarians have also traditionally excelled.

As with Hungarian photographers it has been those actors and filmmakers working abroad, often changing their names to work in Hollywood, who became internationally famous: producer Sándor Korda (Alexander Korda) (*The Third Man*), director Mihály Kertész (Michael Curtiz) (*Casablanca*) and actors Béla Blaskó (Béla Lugosi) (*Dracula*) and László Löwenstein (Peter Lorre) (*The Maltese Falcon*). Before leaving Hungary after the First World War never to return, Korda had established the renowned Corvin Stúdió, Kertész had directed no less than 38 films, Blaskó (as Arisztid Olt) had been a star of silent films and Löwenstein had made a name for himself on the stage. They left not only an indelible mark on Hungarian filmmaking but also a country that could boast some 270 permanent cinema houses.

In order to experience something of this early and exciting period of cinema a trip to the Uránia National Film Theatre in District VII is highly recommended. The building was originally constructed in the mid-1890s as a music and dance hall at the instigation of an entrepreneur called Kálmán Rimanóczy. Its architect Henrik Schmal chose an exotic style that fused Venetian Gothic and Moorish-Mughal in equal measure. By the turn of the century, however, the Hungarian Academy of Sciences had earmarked the building for conversion into a theatre, where the Uránia Scientific Society could stage lectures illustrated by moving pictures. So it was that from 1899 onwards the building became the Uránia Hungarian Scientific Theatre.

Although not finally converted into a commercial cinema until 1917, the building did enter the history books in spring 1901 when it became the setting for Hungary's legendary first feature film. Called

The Uránia National Film Theatre on Rákóczi út

simply *Dance* and directed by Béla Zitkovszky it featured the famous Hungarian actress Lujza Blaha dancing the *csárdás* (see no. 58); tragically, the film was later lost in a fire.

In 2002 the Uránia National Film Theatre was restored back to the original comfort and splendour of its 1930s heyday whilst its audio and visual technology were brought into the 21st century. The interior is quite magnificent, notably the cusped Moorish arches and alcoves of the foyer in whose ceiling is an oculus opening through the floor of the café above. The auditorium itself is a riot of gilded vaulting, elegant balconies and sumptuous furnishings.

The bond of affection that exists between Budapest's cinemagoers and the Uránia cinema reflects the survival not only of modern filmmaking in Hungary, albeit at a more modest pace than in its 1960s-70s heyday (István Szabó's *Mephisto* won an Oscar for Best Foreign Film in 1980), but also the continuing popularity of cinemagoing in general. Indeed, going to the cinema in Budapest can mean more than just watching a film: it can be both a social and an educational experience. The Corvin Cinema at Corvin köz 1 (District VIII), for example, built as a theatre in 1923 and used as a stronghold during

Neo-Baroque details adorn the Corvin Cinema on Corvin köz

the 1956 Uprising, is today a modern multi-screen complex with café and gallery (see no. 37). Similarly, the Örökmozgó Filmmúzeum at Erzsébet körút 39 in the same district offers not only works from the Hungarian Film Institute to which it is linked but also a bookshop and café. Additionally, there are several arthouse cinemas providing further extras, such as the Toldi that sells CDs and books.

It should not be forgotten too that Budapest has provided the backdrop for several international motion pictures, including Gérard Depardieu's *Cyrano de Bergerac* (the Cyrano restaurant at Kristóf tér 7–8 (District V) lent its chandelier!), Madonna's *Evita* (the Ethnographic Museum (see no. 36)), Szabó's *Sunshine* starring Ralph Fiennes (the Serbian Orthodox Church (see no. 51) and Király Thermal Baths (see no. 12)), *Being Julia* starring Jeremy Irons and Annette Bening (the Hotel Astoria (see no. 49)), and the football filmw *Escape to Victory* (the MTK football ground at Salgótarjáni út 12–14 (District VIII)).

Other places of interest nearby: 55, 56, 62, 63

62 In the Ghetto

District VII (Erzsébetváros), the Jewish Quarter
(Zsidó negyed) on Dohány utca
M2 to Astoria; Tram 47, 49 around the Kiskörút

During the mid-13th century AD King Béla IV (1235–70) issued a charter allowing Jews to live safely on Castle Hill, where they managed the court's finances as well as the state mint. Following a brief expulsion under the over zealous King Lajos I (1342–82) in 1350 they soon returned, this time settling around Táncsics Mihály utca (known originally as Zsidó utca, or Jew Street), where their synagogue lies buried at number 23. Interestingly, most of these early Jewish settlers were German Ashkenazi Jews fleeing less tolerant European countries.

Following the Ottoman invasion of 1541 the Jews remained in Buda, as a result of which Suleyman the Magnificent resettled many of them in Turkey and the Balkans, where their trading skills were highly valued. In time Jews filtered back to Buda again, only this time they were mostly Sephardic; their medieval Prayer House, or *Bethel*, can be seen at Táncsics Mihály utca 26 (see no. 9). In return for the freedom to trade and worship they fought alongside their Ottoman rulers in 1686 when a Habsburg Christian army arrived to capture the city. When the Turks were eventually vanquished most Jews were either executed or taken

The Orthodox Synagogue on Kazinczy utca in the Jewish Quarter of Pest

Inside the Orthodox Synagogue on Kazinczy utca

prisoner, thus closing ignominiously the first chapter of Budapest's Jewish history.

Within a century Jewish traders had been enticed back yet again to work their commercial magic in the city, this time under the aegis of the wealthy Zichy Counts in Óbuda to the north of Castle Hill, where their imposing synagogue still stands (see no. 32). Meanwhile, across the river in Pest, predominantly Ashkenazi Jewish merchants and innkeepers were congregating around Király utca in what is now called Erzsébetváros (District VII), creating what would become the

Jewish Quarter of Budapest. Its location was dictated by Emperor Joseph II's Edict of Tolerance (1781), which stipulated that whilst non-Catholic places of worship were acceptable they must remain *outside* the old city walls (see no. 50).

In 1867 Jews were granted civic and legal equality and the resultant flood of immigrants into the city fuelled a manufacturing boom that created Budapest's prosperity – and made many Jews very wealthy (e.g. the Csepel Island munitions factory of Baron Weiss (see no. 84), the Goldberger textile factory in Óbuda (see no. 30) and the leather works of the Lőwy family at Berzeviczy utca (District IV), founders of the nearby Újpest synagogue). Budapest rapidly became Europe's largest financial centre east of Vienna – only Chicago grew more quickly at the time – and by 1930 Jews accounted for a quarter of the city's population (approximately 200,000).

Yet by the outbreak of the Second World War Hungary had not only passed proscriptive anti-Jewish legislation but entered the war on the side of Nazi Germany (see no. 69). By early December 1944, 70,000 of an estimated 140,000 Jews still living in Budapest had been rounded up and placed inside a fenced-off ghetto in District VII on the orders of Adolf Eichmann, self-styled "Transport Administrator" of what the Nazi's called their Final Solution of the Jewish Problem. The fence ran along Dohány utca, Károly körút, Király utca and Kertész utca. That so many Jews still existed in Budapest at this time, as compared to other urban areas within Nazi-occupied Europe, was due to the relatively benign Hungarian policies regarding the Jews prior to the German occupation of Hungary in March 1944. It was also because several international legations were hard at work trying to slow down the deportations that had already emptied the countryside of its Jewish inhabitants (see no. 63). Consequently, when the Red Army liberated the city some 100,000 Jews were found still alive, compared with only 175,000 (from an original 625,000) remaining elsewhere in Hungary; almost 550,000 Hungarian Jews – from a total population of 825,000 in 1939 – had lost their lives at the hands of the Nazis (the Holocaust Memorial Centre (Holokauszt Emlékközpont) at Páva utca 39 (District IX) tells the full story).

Some of the dead are commemorated by the Holocaust Memorial in Raoul Wallenberg Park, behind the mighty Central Synagogue (Zsinagóga) at Dohány utca 2–8; nearby was once the site of one of the ghetto gates. The memorial takes the form of a metallic willow tree designed by celebrated sculptor Imre Varga. Visible from Wesselényi utca its leaves are inscribed with the names of Jewish "martyrs" Also visible from the street is the domed Heroes' Temple

(Hősök temploma), dedicated to Jewish soldiers lost in the Great War, as well as a colonnaded Garden of Remembrance, its ivy-covered headstones marking the resting place of those buried here during the ghetto. The synagogue itself, completed in 1862 by Viennese architect Ludwig Förster in Byzantine-Moorish style and capable of holding 3,000 worshippers, is the World's second largest after New York's Temple Emmanuel, its twin towers rising 43 metres into the air. To the left of the main entrance can be found the National Jewish Museum (Országos Zsidó Múzeum) founded in 1931, which according to a plaque on its façade occupies the site of the birthplace of Theodor Herzl, Father of Zionism.

Hungary's Jewish community today numbers 100,000 (the largest in Central Europe), of which 80,000 or more reside in Budapest. Thankfully, the city's Jewish Quarter is buzzing once again as witnessed by the thriving Orthodox Synagogue (1910) at Kazinczy utca 29–31, the Jewish Community Centre at Síp utca 12, the Biblical World Gallery at Wesselényi utca 13 and numerous kosher restaurants, butchers and bakers. Also within the Jewish Quarter is a magnificent but crumbling synagogue at Rumbach Sebestyén utca 11, designed by Vienna's Otto Wagner (1872), and an intimate Hasidic synagogue hidden in a courtyard behind the Lubavitch Yeshiva (Talmudic college) at Vasváry Pál utca 5. Other less well-known synagogues dotted around the city (only twenty from an original 125 have survived) include the Kőbánya Synagogue at Cserkész utca (District X), now a Christian church (see no.80), a well-concealed one at Frankel Leó utca 49 (District II), and the tiny Pesti Súl modern Orthodox synagogue at Visegrádi utca 3 (District XIII).

It is a little-known fact that the world famous escapologist Harry Houdini was born Ehrich Weiss on Dohány utca on March 24th, 1874. Son of a local rabbi his family emigrated to Wisconsin in America when he was four years old. The family's pet name for young Ehrich was 'Ehrie' from where the name Harry would later be corrupted; the name Houdini was in tribute to French magician Jean Eugène Robert-Houdin.

Other places of interest nearby: 61, 63, 64

63 The Mystery of Raoul Wallenberg

District VII (Erzsébetváros), Raoul Wallenberg Park behind the
Central Synagogue at Dohány utca 2
M2 to Astoria; Tram 47, 49 around the Kiskörút

An enduring mystery to have risen from the ashes of the Second World War is that concerning the Swedish diplomat Raoul Wallenberg (1912–?), after whom the cobblestoned park behind the Dohány utca Central Synagogue in Pest's Jewish Quarter is named (see no. 62). In July 1944 the young Wallenberg, destined originally for a career in business, was dispatched to Budapest under the aegis of Swedish, American and Jewish refugee organizations and charged with the task of saving Jews threatened with deportation. Nazi Germany had invaded Hungary in the previous March and had already deported 400,000 Jews, mostly from the countryside, since May (see no. 69). Wallenberg

A statue of Raoul Wallenberg
on Nagyajtai utca in Buda

empathised with the Jews having encountered many of them fleeing Hitler's Germany whilst he worked for a bank in Palestine in 1936.

Wallenberg used his country's neutrality to offer diplomatic immunity to Jewish families in Budapest by issuing protective passes known as 'Wallenberg Passports', examples of which are today displayed in the Hungarian National Museum (see no. 55). With such passes Jews were not obliged to wear the yellow Star of David. Things became more difficult, however, in October 1944 when regent Miklós Horthy's government, at that time effectively a German puppet cabinet, was toppled and the openly Fascist Arrow Cross party seized control under Ferenc Szálasi. By December, 70,000 out of an estimated 140,000 Jews still remaining in the city had been placed in a fenced-off ghetto on Dohány utca awaiting deportation (see no. 62).

Wallenberg's response was to hang the Swedish flag above thirty or so selected buildings – many in Újlipótváros, hence there being a street named Raoul Wallenberg utca there today – thus rendering them neutral 'safe houses', where 15,000 Jews were afforded a measure of protection. As the situation worsened Wallenberg became a common sight on the streets, handing out food and medicine to Jews being marched out of the country towards Austria, bribing officials and brazenly halting trains bound for the concentration camp at Auschwitz-Birkenau in Southern Poland in order to hand out his protective passes.

When the Russian army eventually entered Budapest in January 1945 Wallenberg was waiting for them, eager to explain his post-war support plan for Budapest's remaining Jews (275,000 survived in total throughout Hungary from an original population of 825,000). Granted permission to drive to the Soviet military headquarters at Debrecen Raoul Wallenberg then disappeared from the historical record forever. Subsequent Soviet reports suggest that his attempt to collaborate with the Russians led to his mistaken arrest by the NKVD (later the KGB), on suspicion of him being a spy for the Americans. The official Soviet statement remains that he died of natural causes in the KGB's Lubyanka prison near Moscow on July 17th, 1947. A persistent rumour, however, is that Wallenberg survived in Russian hands long after the war and reports of his sighting by other Gulag survivors are reported right up to the 1970s. Whatever his fate the achievements of the brave young Swede, who may well have helped up to 100,000 Jews avoid the concentration camps, are still remembered in Budapest today, not only in the naming of Raoul Wallenberg Park but also by a monument in Szent István Park (District XIII) and a statue erected in 1987 on Nagyajtai utca in Buda's District II.

Returning to Wallenberg Park there can be found a statue commemorating another "righteous gentile" who strove to save the Jews. It

A detail of the memorial to Carl Lutz on Dohany utca

is that of Italian businessman Giorgio Perlasca, who masqueraded as a Spanish diplomat in order to issue false papers. Likewise, on a wall at Dob utca 11 there is a monument to Carl Lutz, a Swiss consul who began the war getting German citizens out of British Palestine. Using his contacts he helped organise safe passage into Palestine for many Budapest Jews, a task he continued to pursue even after December 1944 when most other diplomats left the city. Like Wallenberg he established many safe houses in Budapest.

Also of interest, at Nyáry Pál utca 11 in the southern part of Belváros (District V), is a wall plaque to Katalin Karády, the Hungarian Marlene Dietrich, who sheltered persecuted Jews during 1944. Despite being arrested and beaten by the Gestapo, she survived the war and left after the Communist takeover to live in Brazil. Her ashes were repatriated to Budapest in 1991 (see no. 19).

One final character in the story of saving Hungary's Jews is Rezső Kasztner, founder of the Jewish Help and Rescue Committee. He remains a controversial figure in that he saved Jews by making deals with top-ranking Nazis. Most famously he attempted to broker negotiations between the allies and Adolf Eichmann in which a million Jews would be released in return for trucks. Behind the scenes was the pragmatist Heinrich Himmler looking for ways to open up peace talks in the face of inevitable German military defeat and the growing Bolshevik threat. The British quickly rejected the deal as "monstrous" but Kastner managed to convince Himmler, via an SS intermediary named Kurt Becher who was living on Andrássy út, that the Americans would be more amenable. During these tense times Kasztner fought to keep the lure of trucks and a truce dangling under the noses of the Nazis, and in return he secured the release of 1,700 Jews, including many from his hometown of Kolozsvár, now in Romania. Although they were taken initially to Bergen-Belsen, Himmler was persuaded to release them at the Swiss border as a gesture to the Americans. The fact that so many Jews were still alive when the Red Army took Budapest is in part because of the continued diplomatic pressure Kasztner placed on Himmler to release his Jews and to postpone further Jewish deportations so as not to jeopardise possible peace talks. After the war Kasztner moved to Palestine where his dealings with the Gestapo, and friendship with Becher, overshadowed the many lives he saved. He was gunned down by an extreme nationalist in 1957 then exonerated by the Israeli Supreme Court a year later. There is now a memorial to Kasztner at Váci utca 12.

Other places of interest nearby: 61, 62, 64

64 Bright Sparks

District VII (Erzsébetváros), the Hungarian Museum of
Electrical Engineering (Magyar Elektrotechnikai Múzeum)
at Kazinczy utca 21
M2 to Astoria

Occupying an imposing 1930s-era electricity sub-station on Kazinczy
utca the Hungarian Museum of Electrical Engineering is fittingly
located. It is a little-known fact that Hungary holds an important
place in the early history of electricity, indeed it should not be forgotten that the first electric train was built in Budapest's Ganz Electrical
Works (see no. 27) and that it was a Hungarian monk, one István
Jedlik, who invented the world's first electric motor.

Jedlik was born in Szimő (now modern Slovakia) in 1800 but
changed his first name to Ányos when he joined the Benedictine
order in 1817. Always a keen amateur engineer and physicist, in
1828–9 he constructed the first rotating machine based on electromagnetic impulses (a predecessor of the DC motor). That Jedlik is
rarely credited with this important invention is said to be due to his
religious background, preventing him from either selling or patenting
his invention. Not until 1861 did he eventually write about his discovery, as a result of which he became Rector of Budapest's University of
Sciences (1863) and eventually an honorary member
of the Hungarian Academy
of Sciences (1873). His journals relate how he discovered the so-called principle
of self-ignition, something
he exploited in his "single-pole electric starter", thus
formulating the principle
of the dynamo (when electricity is connected to a
dynamo it then becomes
an electric motor). Jedlik
achieved all this at least
six years before German
engineer Siemens produced

The façade of the Hungarian Museum of Electrical
Engineering on Kazinczy utca

a near identical motor for commercial purposes resulting in him being credited erroneously with its invention. Jedlik, the true "Father of the Dynamo", then went on to discover the possibility of voltage mutiplication, a process he demonstrated successfully with his "Tubular Voltage Generator" at the Vienna Exhibition of 1873. Jedlik died aged 95 and is buried in Győr in northwest Hungary.

With all this in mind it is indeed fitting that Budapest should have a museum illustrating the history of electricity, from its generation, through its distribution and eventual consumption. Of far greater interest than it may at first appear, the museum not only contains Jedlik's dynamo but also a great array

A sign outside the Telephone Museum on Castle Hill

of motors, generators and transformers that spark into life at the flick of a switch. The collection of old lamps is especially illuminating!

A collection of similar interest is the Telephone Museum (Telefónia Múzeum) at Úri utca 49 in Buda's Castle District (District I). It is located in a former telephone exchange – itself once a priory that later became the King's Court and the Ministry of the Interior – established in 1928 as a sub-exchange of the Krisztinaváros telephone exchange. Its now antique 'Rotary 7A1-type sub-exchange with crossbar switchboard', which was used until 1985, was the country's first automatic exchange. Hungary's own Tivadar Puskás, who later collaborated on the improvement of the telephone with prolific inventor Thomas Alva Edison, is responsible for inventing the telephone exchange itself in 1881, as well as the Telephonograph in 1894.

The technically minded might also wish to explore the Radio and Television Museum (Rádió- és Televíziótörténeti Múzeum) at Pollack Mihály tér 8–10 (District VIII). It is an interesting notion that Hungary's pre-eminence in all things technical could in part be because of the logical nature of the Hungarian language: as such it works well as a language of technology.

Other places of interest nearby: 62, 63, 65

65 The Secret Courtyards of Pest

District VII (Erzsébetváros), Gozsdu udvar between
Király utca 16 and Dob utca
M1/M2/M3 to Deák Ferenc tér

Despite Pest being the commercial heart of Budapest, and as such the noisiest and most populous part of town, it is also the location for one of the city's least known features: its secret courtyards (*udvar*). Within a very few steps these portals to the past can transport the visitor almost immediately from bustling streets to peaceful, historical and sometimes mysterious havens. It should not be forgotten that the courtyards of Pest are in effect an urban version of those found in traditional farms out on the Hungarian Plain: a practical and secure arrangement whereby living and working areas are ranged around a courtyard, accessed by a gated entrance off the street.

The Gozsdu udvar courtyards between
Király utca and Dob utca

A tour of some of these courtyards, with their ornate ironwork balconies, stairwells and gardens, makes for a fascinating thematic journey. The following examples are dotted around Districts V, VI and VII – along streets mostly thrown up in the eclectic late 19th century Historicist style – and are sometimes made all the more tantalising for being visible only through peepholes in the heavy doors fronting the street.

Running between Király utca 16 and Dob utca in District VII can be found the so-called Gozsdu udvar, an elaborate series of seven interconnecting courtyards once owned by Transylvanian Romanian entrepreneur Manó Gozsdu and built in

A magnificent courtyard at Dohány utca 20 in Erzsébetváros

1904 by Győző Czigler. Lying within Pest's old Jewish quarter this warren of rooms and passageways was originally home to numerous Jewish family businesses and was a model project in its day. The courtyards have recently been renovated and are now bustling with life once more.

Close-by, on Király utca itself, can be found a series of traditional early 19th century Pest townhouses and apartment buildings. The street was Pest's original main thoroughfare before Andrássy út was constructed and it still retains a certain buzz from former times. Numbers 27 and 29, unusual in that they are visitable, are splendidly decaying apartment buildings, their balconies strung out with pot plants and washing lines. By contrast, numbers 25 and 28 are grander, their Habsburg-yellow paintwork fresh and gardens well tended.

Staying within District VII's Jewish quarter are several more interesting courtyards, at Klauzál utca 15, Síp utca 13, Dob utca 14 and 20, and a magnificent example with Tuscan-style balustrading at Dohány utca 20. There is also a sumptuous Venetian-style courtyard at Rákóczi út 80, its triple-tiered balconies a riot of ironwork, stucco and window boxes.

Farther north in District VI there is another magnificent courtyard at Teréz körút 33, noteworthy for its porticoed balconies (several other courtyards around number 6 have been converted into shopping arcades and consequently lost their charm). Grandest of all, however, are the courtyards within the mansions on Andrássy út, notably at numbers 79 and 83–5, built for the wealthy during the late 19th century.

Moving southwards now into District V there are similarly grand courtyards at Múzeum körút 7 and 35, the former still retaining its wooden cobbles to dampen the noise generated by horses' hooves and carriage wheels. The building itself, a grand balconied home built in 1852 for the Unger family, is an early work by the architect Miklós Ybl, famous for designing the Andrássy út Opera House.

Running parallel to Múzeum körút is Magyar utca where lies the Károlyi Park (Károlyi kert), once the garden for the now magnificently restored Károlyi Mansion, home to one of Hungary's great patrician families (their chateau-style town house on Pollack Mihály tér has fared less well having been gutted by fire in 1945). In the mansion's pretty inner courtyard is the Károlyi Étterem és Kávéház accessible at Károlyi utca 16. A respite here offers pause to think about Hungary's first Prime Minister Count Lajos Batthyány, dragged from the building in 1849 as a traitor by the Habsburgs (see no. 38), as well as Count Mihály Károlyi himself, Prime Minister of the newly independent First Hungarian Republic after the collapse of the Austro-Hungarian Empire in 1918 (his statue stands to the north of the Parliament building). This was his townhouse until his resignation in 1919 when Hungary briefly declared itself a Hungarian Soviet Republic under Béla Kun (see no. 17).

Not far away, at Ferenciek tere 7–8, is the Kárpátia, another restaurant occupying an unusual location, namely the courtyard of the 18th century Italian Baroque-style Franciscan Church (Ferences templom) (see no. 47). Even more unusual is the so-called Parisian arcade (Párizsi udvar) on Párizsi utca with its cavernous interior of dark wood and stained glass (see no. 45).

Of course, for each of these documented courtyards there are myriad others that remain concealed and silent, their facades crumbling and sooty, their fountains long dried up and choked with ivy. It is said that during the liberation of Budapest from the Nazis in 1944-5, some of the 25,000 citizens and Soviet soldiers who perished were buried in these courtyards, it being too dangerous to venture with their bodies out onto the streets. To this day their graves remain unmarked.

Other places of interest nearby: 40, 44, 64, 66, 67

66 The Mineral Water Millionaire

District VI (Terézváros), mansion at Andrássy út 3
M1 to Bajcsy-Zsilinszky út

The house at Andrássy út 3, Budapest's most elegant 19th century street, contains several secrets. From 1972 until 2012 it was home to Budapest's Postal Museum, although it now serves the more mundane function of office building. A closer look at the building's grand doorway reveals the cryptic initials "AS" and "ES". Long before it became a museum this grand mansion built in 1886 was home to Andreas Saxlehner and his opera-singing wife, Emma. A peep inside the entrance hall reveals wonderful ceiling and staircase frescoes by the period's fore-most practitioner, the romanticist painter Károly Lotz. The theme of the paintings is water, Andreas Saxlehner's wealth having come from bottling mineral water sourced from the thermal springs of Kelenföld in south Buda. One particular scene depicts the god Mercury sending bottles of the life-saving elixir down to earth. The offices of the mineral water company were located in the courtyard at the back of the building, where inci-

Stairs leading up to the former apartment of Andreas Saxlehner at Andrássy út 3

Water-themed frescoes in the entrance hall at Andrássy út 3

dentally there is a subterranean stream that once supplied a Jewish ritual bath.

As a result of his commercial success Mr. and Mrs. Saxlehners' seven-room apartment on the first floor is truly sumptuous, with Carrara marble fireplaces, English silk wallpaper, Murano crystal chandeliers and etched glass mirrors. Of particular note is the stained glass by Miksa Róth, a master craftsman to rival Tiffany, whose own little museum at Nefelejcs ("Forget-me-not") utca 26 (District VII) is worth finding.

Budapest Postal Museum currently resides at Benczúr utca 27 (District VI) where exhibits include a reconstructed 19th century post office, part of a pneumatic postal exchange, and an old post office lightning conductor battered by the weather. Diehard philatelists should head to the Stamp Museum (Bélyegmúzeum) at Hársfa utca 47 (District VII), containing a mind-boggling collection of over 12 million stamps from around the world, including the Hungarian "reserve Madonna", Hawaiian missionary stamps, a very rare Tuscan 3-lira stamp, superlative issues such as the largest and the smallest, as well as a fascinating collection of forgeries. Collectors will also enjoy the Banknote and Coin Collection in the Hungarian National Bank at Szabadság tér 8 (District V), illustrating the history of Hungarian coins and banknotes from the country's oldest (a Denarius issued by Hungary's first king, St. Stephen (István)) right up to the present, and including a special display on the monetary history of Transylvania. It is Budapest's second largest coin collection after that of the Hungarian National Museum (see no. 55).

Other places of interest nearby: 40, 44, 65, 67

67 Monkeys, Angels and All Things Modern

**District VI (Terézváros), the New Theatre (Új Színház),
at the junction of Dalszínház utca and Paulay Ede utca 35
M1 to Opera**

The architects Ödön Lechner and Otto Wagner dominated showpiece architecture in *fin de siècle* Budapest and Vienna respectively (see no. 78). They pioneered their own individual brands of European Art Nouveau in an attempt to escape the stolid, backwards-looking Historicist style favoured by many architects in late 19th century Austria-Hungary.

Known as the Secession this brief and extraordinary love affair with colour, texture and new materials would not outlive the Great War – and neither would Lechner and Wagner. In Vienna it mutated swiftly into austere Modernism and Bauhaus-style Functionalism: in Hungary the story was somewhat different.

What set Lechner apart from Wagner was that he used the Secession to develop Hungary's first truly national architectural style, infusing swirling organic Art Nouveau decoration with distinctly Hungarian folk motifs; the latter using the Orient for inspiration,

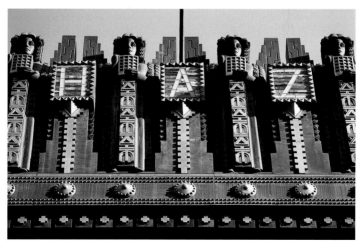

Béla Lajta's unusual New Theatre on Paulay Ede utca

whence the ancient Magyars were believed to have originated (see no. 1). Lechner's architecture is thus as much about *le Style Moderne* as it is about celebrating his country's gradual shift away from the Habsburg yoke and the re-assertion of its national cultural identity.

Exotic ornament on the New Theatre

During the troubled years of the early 20th century, an unusual and idiosyncratic architectural style emerged in Hungary that managed to fuse the folk-inspired elements of the Secession together with the functionalist demands of international Modernism that would eventually dominate Europe in the 1920s. This unique transitional style is best expressed in the works of Károly Kós (see no. 82) and especially in those of one of Lechner's students, the architect Béla Lajta (1873–1920).

Lajta's use of the Hungarian folk motif is well illustrated in his incredible ceramic tomb for Sándor Schmidl (1903) in the Kozma utca Jewish Cemetery, its tunnel-like shape based on the *suba*, the sheepskin cloak worn by Magyar shepherds on the Great Hungarian Plain (Nagyalföld) (see no. 59). The architectural corollary of the *suba* was the catenary, or parabolic arch, which Lajta used in the entranceway to his Institute for the Blind (1905–7) at Mexikói út 60 (District XIV), replete with folkloric motifs and biblical scenes to reaffirm national identity. He used another for the porch of the Hospital of Neurosurgery (1908–11), only this time smothering it in Hebraic motifs and Old Testament scenes symbolizing Hungary's presumed biblical ancestry (see no. 1). The architect Aladár Árkay also borrowed the parabolic arch for the massive ochre and gold tiled porch of his Art Nouveau Calvinist Church (1911–13) at Városligeti fasor 5–7 (District VII).

Lajta's work gradually took on a more streamlined, modernistic approach with a strongly Semitic (Near/Middle Eastern) influence. This work is best exemplified by his Parisiana nightclub (1908–09) in District VI, re-named the János Arany Theatre (Arany János Színház) after the famous Hungarian Romantic poet, and subsequently the New Theatre. Along the roofline are nine ceramic angels acting as crenelations, each separated by turquoise plaques bearing the words 'Új Színház' (New Theatre), which hark back to the flamboyance of Art Nouveau. By contrast the plain marble façade punctuated only by sculpted grey monkeys seems more like Mesopotamian *adobe* architecture and foreshadows the pared-down Functionalism that would come into vogue in Hungary over the next two decades.

Lajta's later works are conspicuous for their use of strong horizontal and vertical elements – both constructional and decorative – and a willingness to reveal the actual structure of the buildings themselves. Most important in this respect is his Széchenyi School at Vas utca 11 (District VIII) and the Rózsavölgyi Building (1912) at Szervita tér 5 (District V). Some historians view the latter as a landmark of European architecture in the way it anticipates the *avant-garde* Modernist style, Lajta's works representing the first manifestation of what would become the dominant architectural style of the West in the 20th century.

Another distinctive theatre building, just one street away from the Új Színház, is the Tivoli (Tivoli Színház) at Nagymező utca 8; designed by Gyula Fodor in 1911 it has a beautifully restored Art Deco lobby by Ferenc Flau. Nagymező utca itself is sometimes referred to as the "Broadway of Budapest" because of the proximity of two further theatres, namely the pink neo-Rococo Operetta Theatre (Fővárosi Operettszínház) (1898) at number 17 and the Thália Theatre (Thalia Színház) just opposite at 22–24.

Other places of interest nearby: 64, 65, 66, 68

68 The Magyar House of Photographers

District VI (Terézváros), the Hungarian House of Photographers in the Manó Mai House (Magyar Fotográfusok Háza a Mai Manó Házban) at Nagymező utca 20
M1 to Opera

Gyula Halász (known as 'Brassaï'; *Paris by Night*), Lucien Hervé (photographer to Le Corbusier), Endre Ernő Friedmann (known as Robert Capa; the D-Day landings and co-founder of the Magnum Photographic Agency), André Kertész (combat photographer in the Great War and later *Vogue*), László Moholy-Nagy (*avant-garde* photographic artist): the roll call of influential and internationally recognised Hungarian photographers is indeed an impressive one and an unusual building in Budapest has been recently converted into a shrine to their endeavours.

The Manó Mai House on Nagymező utca

It seems fitting that the location chosen is the unique building at Nagymező utca 20, erected in 1894 at the instigation of Imperial and Royal Court Photographer Manó Mai (1855–1917). Apprenticed at the early age of fourteen to photographer Péter Kalmár on Andrássy út, Mai became an independent photographer in his early twenties. Soon famous for his portrait photography, especially that of children, and winner of numerous awards for photography (including eventually a gold medal at the Paris World Exhibition in 1900) he went on to become a founder of the National Association of Hungarian Photographers, whose periodical A *Fény* (*The Light*) had its editorial office here.

The building itself is in the neo-

Renaissance style in order to impress illustrious clients – who were photographed in the 2nd Floor Daylight Studio – and to stress the artistic merit of photography as an art form (note the yellow majolica *putti* clutching box cameras on the facade!).

Mai died in 1917 and in 1932 the house was sold to the Jewish musical impresario Sándor Rozsnyai and his wife Mici, known in the world of showbusiness as Miss Arizona. Together they created the legendary Arizona nightclub on the premises, famous for its extravagant floorshows and boasting numerous European nobles amongst its clientele. However, in 1944 the Gestapo closed the club down and its proprietors sent to their untimely deaths. A less colourful change of usage occurred in the early 1960s when the building became the Budapest branch of the Hungarian Automobile Association.

Things came full circle, however, when the Hungarian Association of Photographers began purchasing the property piecemeal and opened the Mai Manó Gallery on the mezzanine floor in 1995. This was followed in March 1999 by the unveiling of the Hungarian House of Photographers on the first and second floors, created by the Museum of Hungarian Photography in Kecskemét, the country's largest photographic museum, 50 miles south of Budapest. The excellent galleries and exhibitions now contained within the Mai Manó House showcase the work of both contemporary and classic Hungarian photographers across a broad range of formats, from reportage and sociological photography to *avant-garde* art.

A question that remains unanswered is why Hungary produced so many significant photographers (and film makers for that matter), from the early days right up to the present, with Budapest boasting more than 300 studios by the early 20th century? Perhaps the medium of still and motion pictures provided a mouthpiece to the wider world that the distinctly non-European Hungarian language was unable to offer? Whatever the answer, the photographers listed above, to which can be added Paul Almásy, Emeric Fehér, Martin Munkácsi, Rosie Ney and Rogie André, were all Hungarian by birth. They all developed their own individual styles and by leaving Hungary to pursue their work became international talents.

Other places of interest nearby: 67, 69

69 The House of Terror

District VI (Terézváros), the House of Terror Museum
(Terror Háza Múzeum) at Andrássy út 60
M1 to Oktogon or Vörösmarty utca; Tram 4, 6 around the
Nagykörút;

For many people the grand late-19th Century Boulevard called Andrássy út represents the very pinnacle of refined city living. Certainly its grand mansions, opera house and cafés still lend an air of comfort and elegance from a bygone age. However, there is one building, at number 60, where this could not be further from the truth: it is the so-called House of Terror and it catalogues the worst excesses of the Nazi and Communist regimes.

Hungary's slide into the hands of Nazi Germany is well documented, prompted in part by the crash of 1929 and the labour discontent that followed, during which time Hungary's Conservative regent Admiral Miklós Horthy (1920–44) appointed the right-wing Gyula Gömbös as Prime Minister (see no. 3). Gömbös sought closer ties with the Nazis in the hope of reversing the Treaty of Trianon under which Hungary had lost two thirds of its territory. As in Vienna anti-Semitism became rife (see no. 63) and by 1938 Hungary was allied with Germany. However, with the rout of the Hungarian 2nd Army on the Russian front, German troops, fearing an impending Soviet attack, invaded Hungary on March 19th 1944. Despite Hungarian protestations a Jewish ghetto was quickly established in Budapest and the daily deportation of Jews to Auschwitz-Birkenau in Southern Poland began (400,000 between May 14th and July 8th).

In October 1944 Admiral Horthy made a desperate plea for

The unmistakeable House of Terror on Andrássy út

an armistice resulting in his removal by the SS. In the meantime, the Hungarian Fascist Arrow Cross party lead by Nazi puppet Ferenc Szálasi seized control of Hungary. Whilst high-ranking Nazi officers drank coffee in the elegant surroundings of the Astoria Hotel (see no. 49), overlooking Adolf Eichmann's fenced ghetto that was now home to 70,000 Jews (see no. 62), it was the Arrow Cross who roamed the streets in search of more Jews and other political opponents. They executed hundreds of them in the basement of their headquarters at Andrássy út 60, whilst herding others down to the Danube to be shot or drowned (see the wall plaque at Szilágy Dezső tér (District I) and the poignant sculpture of a row of empty shoes on the quayside south of the Parliament building (Országház) opposite Zoltán utca (District V)).

A window in the House of Terror

As if this was not enough, following the defeat of Germany in April 1945, history then cruelly repeated itself. The incoming Hungarian Communist party, fronted by hardline Stalinist Hungarian General Secretary Mátyás Rákosi (1945–56), simply took over Andrássy út 60 and made it the headquarters for their own secret police, the much-feared ÁVO (later the ÁVH). Rákosi's henchmen terrorised, deported or executed anyone branded an enemy of the state; in their leisure time they took coffee in the Lukács café a few doors away at Andrássy út 70.

With the eventual collapse of Communism the building at Andrássy út 60 remained locked until February 2002, when it reopened as the House of Terror Museum. Its conversion by the then Christian Conservative government (FIDESZ-MDF) was not without controversy, some criticising the fact that Communist crimes were

Empty shoes on the quayside: a sculpture
opposite Zoltán utca

being focussed on more sharply than those inflicted by the Nazis.

The building's four floors illustrate the horrors inflicted by both Fascists and Communists, the walls plastered with hundred of photographs of victims looking down onto a Soviet tank, a symbol of Communist military might. Most chilling of all is the elevator ride that takes visitors down into the prison basement, restored as it appeared in 1955 where countless interrogations and acts of torture took place. The poignant Hall of Tears recalls the 25,000 people who lost their lives when the Soviets brutally repressed the anti-Communist Uprising of 1956. Before leaving the museum the visitor passes through two final rooms that eventually lift the spirit somewhat, depicting the unfettered joy felt by Hungarians with the collapse of Communism in 1989.

Other places of interest nearby: 67, 68, 70

70 Remembering Zoltán and Béla

District VI (Terézváros), the Zoltán Kodály Memorial Museum
and Archives (Kodály Zoltán Emlékmúzeum és Archívum)
at Andrássy út 89, Kodály körönd 1
M1 to Kodály körönd

On the 25th anniversary of the 1867 Compromise Agreement, which created the Dual Austro-Hungarian Monarchy and gave Budapest its own Parliamant, the Habsburg Emperor Franz Joseph I decreed that Budapest should become a capital equal to Vienna. With the millennial anniversary of Prince Árpád's conquest of the Carpathian Basin on the horizon too, a Golden Age was ushered in. Architecture, literature and photography all flourished as a result.

Another channel through which this newfound confidence and sense of nationhood manifested itself was classical music, especially the work of Zoltán Kodály (1882–1967) and Béla Bartók (1881–1945). In the early 20th century the major influences on music in Budapest were German, especially the work of the two great Richards, Strauss and Wagner. However, from 1905 onwards a new and distinctly Hungarian school was created as Kodály and Bartók began exploring the roots of traditional Hungarian music and its essentially oriental characteristics (a study known as 'ethnomusicology'). As a result they were able to create masterpieces of modern music that at the same time were suffused with Magyar folk traditions, creating a uniquely Hungarian-sounding form of classical music that is still popular and influential today (their works are permanent fixtures on the repertoire of Budapest's seven symphony orchestras). This symbolic freeing of Hungarian music from German and Viennese influence was just as

A wall plaque marking the former apartment of composer Zoltán Kodály on the Kodály körönd

The Franz Liszt Music Academy on Liszt Ferenc tér

important in asserting Hungarian nationhood as any contemporaneous building, writing or political act.

In order to document the disappearing folk music of Greater Hungary Kodály began in 1905 to compile a vast corpus of traditional music using a phonograph. In time he would create a revolutionary method of music training based on the folk songs he discovered thereby engendering an innate appreciation of classical music in Budapesters that is still found to today. His first taste of commercial success came with the stirring *Psalmus Hungaricus* premiered in 1923 at a concert to mark the 50th anniversary of the union of Buda, Óbuda and Pest; similarly, his *Budavári Te Deum* was premiered in the Matthias Church (Mátyás-templom) in 1936 as part of the 250th anniversary of the regaining of Castle Hill from the Ottomans. This author's favourite remains the lushly orchestrated *Dances of Galánta*, evoking the area currently in Slovakia where Kodály spent much of his childhood.

From 1924 until his death in 1967 Kodály occupied a ground floor apartment on the körönd, or Circus, a still grand if crumbling architectural punctuation mark along Andrássy út. The composer's cosy rooms are now a museum, his books and folk art preserved just as he left them.

In 1906 Béla Bartók joined Kodály in his ethnomusicological quest and together they travelled far and wide making field recordings of Magyar peasant music, which they believed to be Hungary's true folk music. Bartók's achievement was to synthesise the East European folk melodies and dance rhythms he encountered with the compositional stylings of the Western *avant garde* (for example those of Stravinsky): the results, from simple piano pieces through string quartets to grand orchestral works, are both modern and Magyar – and made to last.

A listen to his *Three Village Scenes* with their ecstatic Slovak female voices will not quickly be forgotten.

Bartók's former villa at Csalán út 29 in the Buda Hills (District II) is now the Bartók Memorial House (Bartók Béla Emlékház) and contains some fascinating artefacts from his Transylvanian wanderings. Meanwhile, the Bartók archives are held in the former town palace of the Erdődy family at Táncsics Mihály utca 7 (District I), now the Music History Museum (Zenetörténeti Múzeum) with its delightful back garden. The Erdődys had been patrons of Beethoven, who visited here in 1800.

Today, Bartók and Kodály lie buried in the Farkasréti Public Cemetery, the liberal-minded Bartók (witness the sentiments expressed in his only opera, *Duke Bluebeard's Castle*, as well as in his ballet *The Miraculous Mandarin*) having died in exile in New York in 1945, appalled that his country had slipped into the grip of Nazism. His remains did not return to Hungary until the fall of Communism in 1988, when he was given a well-deserved state funeral (see no. 19).

It is interesting to note that before meeting Kodály, Bartók's idea of Hungarian folk music had been based on supposed gypsy melodies found in the works of Franz Liszt (1811–86). Despite drawing predominantly on Italian and French influences, Liszt had famously incorporated elements of the csárdás, a peasant dance presumed by the nobility to be danced at country inns, and the verbunkos, a rousing gypsy-style recruiting song created for the aristocracy during the Napoleonic wars, into his Hungarian Rhapsodies (see no. 57). For an insight into this other great Hungarian composer's life (whose surname means 'flour'!) visit the Franz Liszt Museum (Liszt Ferenc Múzeum) in the composer's last house at Vörösmarty utca 35 (District VI). Liszt's Coronation Mass accompanied the crowning of the Habsburg Emperor Franz Joseph I as King of Hungary in the Matthias Church (Mátyás-templom) following the Austro-Hungarian Compromise Agreement of 1867, and his statue flanks one side of the entrance to the Opera House (on the other side is Ferenc Erkel, composer of the Hungarian national anthem, the Himnusz); another statue of Liszt, in bronze, near the Liszt Music Academy in Liszt Ferenc tér (where Kodály taught composition and Bartók taught piano), depicts the composer in full keyboard-playing flight.

Other places of interest nearby: 69, 71

71 Where East Meets East

District VI (Terézváros), the Ferenc Hopp Museum of Eastern Asiatic Arts (Hopp Ferenc Kelet-Ázsiai Művészeti Múzeum) in the György Ráth Villa at Városligeti fasor 12
M1 to Kodály körönd

It was the Irish author Bram Stoker who, on the first page of his novel Dracula, so evocatively described Budapest as "...a wonderful place...The impression I had was that we were leaving the West and entering the East". As if to emphasise this, the city boasts not one but two museums devoted to the art of East Asia, within a stone's throw of each other in District VI.

The reason Budapest can boast *two* museums of Asian art is because at the heart of both collections is one man: the Hungarian businessman, traveller and art collector Ferenc Hopp (1833–1919). One

of the museums, at Andrássy út 103 in District VI, is Hopp's former holiday villa, now home to temporary exhibitions, a library and the remains of his Oriental garden based on one he visited in West Java (the Chinese Moon Gate and *Tirthankara* shrine are still extant). The other museum, around the corner on Városligeti fasor, was the home of György Ráth, first Director General of the Museum of Applied Arts, wherein the Ferenc Hopp Museum of Eastern Asiatic Arts now resides.

Born in Moravia (today the Czech Republic) Ferenc Hopp came to Pest to work as an apprentice for the opti-

The Chinese Moon Gate in the garden of Ferenc Hopp's former villa on Andrássy út

cal appliance manufacturer, Calderoni. After undertaking part of this in Vienna and the United States he returned to Budapest and eventually became owner of the company.

So financially successful was Hopp that by the age of fifty he was able to embark on a series of five trips around the globe until the outbreak of war in 1914. Although his travels took him to the Mediterranean as well as West Africa, where he visited the Congo railway, his true love was East Asia. Whilst travelling in these areas he amassed an enormous collection of some 4,000 or so souvenirs and genuine works of art. On returning from these journeys Hopp would give illustrated lectures detailing his adventures although curiously he never kept a diary. Telling us as much about the obsessive and eccentric character of Hopp himself as

Buddha and pagoda in front of the Hopp villa on Andrássy út

about Asian Art in general, his huge collection was bequeathed to the Hungarian State on his death and has been added to ever since: it now contains nearly 20,000 objects.

The visitor to the Ferenc Hopp Museum of Eastern Asiatic Arts will today discover an exotic and heady mix of objects collected by both Hopp as well as numerous other Asia specialists, the majority acquired in China and Japan, but also including items from India, Tibet and Nepal, Indonesia and Buddhist Mongolia. Thus, the room devoted to Hopp himself contains Japanese ivories and Chinese woodcarvings not to mention his very first acquisition, namely an Ostrich egg from Aden! Meanwhile, the Károly Csapek Memorial Room contains some fascinating *thangkas* from Inner Mongolia, a *thangka* being a religious painting on fabric usually portraying the Buddha or Buddhist monks (*lamas*) in stereotypical poses. The word *thangka* means 'rolled up' because these painted banners could be stored and transported like scrolls.

Not to be missed is the collection of around 250 pieces of *netsuke* to be found in the room devoted to Japanese Art. Now highly collectable, these miniature sculptures in ivory, wood or metal had an intriguing practical use. Traditional Japanese garments (*kimono or kosode*) were without pockets and so personal possessions, such as pipes and tobacco pouches (*tabako-ire*), writing utensils, money, seals and medicines, were placed in containers called *sagemono*, hung by a cord from the kimono's sash (*obi*). These containers were sometimes beautifully crafted (*inro*) and held shut by sliding beads threaded onto the cord. And the fastener that secured the cord to the sash was the carved, toggle-like *netsuke*. The same room contains some intricately detailed lacquered combs, one of which is decorated with crayfish. The ceramics collection upstairs should also be seen if only for its wildly ornate ceramic roof tiles.

Needless to say, the long-standing Hungarian tradition of academic interest in the East has been in part because Hungarians believe themselves to be of Eastern origin (see no. 1).

Other places of interest nearby: 70, 75

72 The Ruins on Rabbit Island

District XIII (Margitsziget), Margaret Island (Margitsziget)
between Árpád and Margit Bridges
Tram 4, 6 around the Nagykörút to Margit híd

A traditional way for Budapesters and tourists alike to escape the bustle of city life is to spend a couple of hours on Margaret Island (Margitsziget), a hundred hectare green oasis effectively sealed off to private vehicles. Moored like a great ship in the middle of the Danube (*Duna*), between the Árpád and Margit Bridges, the island offers abundant leisure opportunities in the form of gardens (English, French and Japanese), wooded areas, extensive lawns, paths, cycleways and a reproduction 1820s bandstand. Additionally, there is the 1930s-styled Palatinus Swimming Pool (Palatinus Strandfürdő) fed by thermal springs (it is Budapest's largest open air pool with room for 10,000!), the Alfréd Hajós National Sports Pool (Hajós Alfréd Nemzeti Sportuszoda), designed by and named after Hungary's swimming gold medallist at the first modern Olympics in Athens in 1896, and a fine outdoor theatre. There is also the

The rebuilt Chapel of St. Michael on Margaret Island

elegant late 19th century Danubius Grand Hotel Margitsziget (designed in neo-Renaissance style by Opera architect Miklós Ybl) and its sister the modern Danubius Health Spa Resort Margitsziget. The latter draws on the island's renowned thermal waters for the cure of locomotive and other disorders. Even the pools of the nearby Japanese Garden are artesian-fed, the warm water being home to terrapins.

Relaxing aside, Margaret Island can also boast a long and interesting history from which several fascinating fragments still remain. Originally there were three islands in the river here, named Spa, Pictor and Rabbit. The first record of human activity on them is in the Roman period when the Danube marked the eastern frontier of the Roman Province of Pannonia (now Transdanubia). Although nothing remains today it is known that the Romans built villas and fortifications here, as well as the first bridge connecting the islands with Buda on the west bank (see no. 34).

In the Middle Ages the Archbishop of Esztergom built a palace here and the kings of the ruling Árpádian dynasty favoured the islands as a royal hunting reserve, hence the name Rabbit Island. It was also during this period that the name Margaret Island finds its origin, Margaret being the daughter of King Béla IV (1235–70). The King had promised that if Hungary emerged safely from the Mongol (Tartar) invasion of 1241 he would thank God by building a convent on the islands and have his daughter raised there as a nun. Thus, following the withdrawal of the Mongols, a Dominican Convent (Domonkos kolostor) was constructed and in 1251 the nine-year-old Princess Margaret began her training there. Living a famously ascetic existence she died just twenty years later having refused a marriage proposal from King Ottokar of Bohemia. It is said that each year on February 15th, the day of her death, the island takes on a special light. Margaret was buried on the island together with her brother Stephen V (1270–72) and father King Béla IV, a red marble slab marking the spot amongst the wooded Convent ruins excavated in 1838. A statue of Saint Margaret, who was canonised in 1943, can be found near the altar of St. Stephen's Basilica.

In addition to the Dominicans, the Premonstratensian (Augustinian) and Franciscan orders also used the islands, as a place of refuge and retreat. Although soon overshadowed by the powerful Dominicans there are still remains from these establishments. They include the original bell from the Chapel of St. Michael (Szent Mihály-kápolna), which is all that remains from the 12th century Augustinian monastery and is now rehung in a rebuilt chapel, and some walls of the 13th century Franciscan priory (Ferences kolostor).

With the Ottoman occuption of 1541 the island's religious life ended abruptly: all religious buildings were razed, the nuns fled to Pozsony (Bratislava) taking Margaret's remains with them and the islands became a *harem* for the Pasha. Following the departure of the Turks the islands were abandoned until 1796, when the Palatine Archduke Joseph of Habsburg (one of the sons of Emperor Leopold II

(1790–92)) erected a summer villa on the site of the old Franciscan priory, surrounded by a huge English-style garden (the *Palatine* was the imperial representative in Hungary). The villa eventually became a hotel but was irreparably damaged during World War Two: its demolition revealed the priory ruins once again.

As part of river regulation works in the 19th century the separate islands were finally joined together by the construction of a common embankment. The resulting single large island, now 2.5 kilometres in length, became a popular strolling ground for the well-heeled, who enjoyed walking amongst the 10,000 trees, mostly planes and oaks, planted by Habsburg gardeners. It was under these trees that the romantic poet János Arany found literary inspiration.

The island was eventually purchased from the Habsburgs, landscaped and opened to the public as a park in 1908 (an admission charge would deter the poor until its abolition in 1945). A new arm was built from the Margaret Bridge enabling pedestrians to pass directly onto the southern tip of the island, although not until 1950 was the Árpád Bridge opened at the north end. Also constructed around this time was the

An ornate water tower on Margaret Island

ornate and now UNESCO-protected concrete water tower (1909–11) that doubles as the Office of Weights and Measures.

A final point of interest is the Centenary Monument (Centenáriumi emlékmű) by István Kiss, erected for the hundredth anniversary of the unification of Buda, Pest and Óbuda in 1873, and containing iconic objects from the city's turbulent past, such as telephones, munitions and railway lines, all rendered in bronze.

With such a long and illustrious history it is not surprising that Budapesters claim Margaret Island to be one of Europe's first and finest parks. Little wonder too that languorous afternoons spent amongst the fountains, roses and ruins have given rise to an old proverb that says love begins – and love dies – on Margaret Island.

Before the Danube was regulated fish swam here all the way from the Black Sea, including the much-prized Viza, a type of Sturgeon, accounting for the name of the Vizafogó ('Viza catcher') area on the eastern riverbank in District XIII.

73 The Art Nouveau Elephant House

District XIV (Városliget), the Budapest Zoo and Botanical Gardens (Fővárosi Állat- és Növénykert) at Állatkerti körút 6–12 in City Park (Városliget)
M1 to Széchenyi fürdő

Budapest's first zoo opened its doors as a private institution in 1866 under the guidance of the noted scientist János Xantus. Although it is sometimes claimed as one of the world's oldest zoos it is actually relatively young: London Zoo was founded much earlier in 1828, whereas Vienna's collection at Schloss Schönbrunn was actually the first having been founded as early as 1752. However, the Budapest Zoological and Botanical Garden still ranks as one of the world's most historic. Much of its present form was established in the early 1900s when it became a municipal property, as a result of which a large-scale redevelopment was undertaken. Since that time it has become one of Central Europe's leading animal collections and an enduring favourite with both locals and visitors alike, warranting a further programme of renovations in the mid-1990s that is still ongoing today.

The reason for the latest round of works is twofold: firstly, to ensure an

The extraordinary elephant house at Budapest Zoo in City Park

Sculpted animal heads adorn the elephant house in Budapest Zoo

appropriate and healthy environment for the zoo's important collection of 500 species of animals and 4,000 types of plants – representing ecosystems as diverse as the African Savanna and the Arctic – and secondly, to preserve the zoo's numerous historic buildings dating back almost a century. Consequently, among the modern enclosures and state-of-the-art interpretation centres can be found some gems of Secession (Hungarian Art Nouveau) architecture shot through with a characteristic streak of the Oriental, designed to show the creatures off against a suitably exotic backdrop.

The first to be encountered is the monumental entrance to the zoo itself, held aloft by a troupe of elephants and topped off with a ring of polar bears, their paws placed obediently on blocks in front of them. Running around the portal itself is a beautifully coloured frieze of exotic tropical birds and plants. Even the perimeter fence of the zoo to the right of the entrance, with its wrought iron tree motifs and etched birds, is worth a quick look.

Once inside the zoo proper look out for the graceful Palm House erected in 1912 by the famous Eiffel Company of Paris, its lofty halls containing squirrel monkeys, free-flying birds and butterflies. There is also the Bird House (*madárház*) built in 1911 by Károly Kós, an architect who created a distinctly Hungarian style of architecture based on the country's medieval folk past as well as the village architecture of his native Transylvania (see no. 82).

Most extraordinary, however, is Neuschloss-Knüsli's incredible Elephant House (1912), its domes clad in blue Zsolnay ceramic tiles giving more the impression of a mosque than an animal house (see no. 54). Built at the same time as the Palm House its meticulous renovation warranted a European Union *Europa Nostra* prize in 2000. Attached to the building is a 70-metre high minaret rebuilt in 1998 offering visitors a spectacular vista across the tree canopy of City Park in which the zoo is located.

Other unusual highlights of the zoo include a Japanese Bonsai garden as well as a reconstructed peasant farm from the Upper Tisza region, stocked with a variety of historic Hungarian breeds (e.g. Swallow-bellied Woolly pigs, Bald-necked hens, Spotted cattle, Mudi dogs, Cikta sheep and Hucul horses).

The zoo gained fleeting celluloid fame in 1933 when the undeservedly little-known American film *Zoo in Budapest* was released to little acclaim. Starring Loretta Young and Gene Raymond it concerns an unusual young man who has spent his life in the zoo where his only friends are the animals, that is until he meets a young orphan girl on a zoo visit with her carers. The film remains charmingly naïve in both its plot and characterisation whilst also affording a fascinating glimpse of the old zoo itself.

For a further look at the development of wildlife on earth, as well as in Hungary and the Carpathian Basin in particular, visit the Hungarian Natural History Museum (Magyar Természettudományi Múzeum) at Ludovika tér 2 (District VIII), as well as the Tropicarium-Oceanarium in the Campona Shopping Centre at Nagytétényi út 37–45 (District XXII), where alligators, sharks and rays swim freely in Central Europe's largest marine aquarium.

Other places of interest nearby: 74, 75, 76, 77, 78

74 Budapest's Answer to Coney Island

District XIV (Városliget), the Amusement Park (Vidámpark)
at Állatkerti körút 14-16 in City Park (Városliget)
M1 to Széchenyi fürdő

Squeezed into the far northern corner of Budapest's City Park (Városliget), the site of the city's millenial celebrations of 1896 (see no. 76), can be found Vidámpark. Meaning literally 'Amusement Park' its 6.5 acres occupy a corner between the zoo (see no.73), the municipal circus and the Széchenyi Baths (see no. 15), where there is a station for the world's second oldest underground railway line (see no.44). Needless to say, being an attraction that has had to justify its existence commercially, it has kept up to date by replacing many of its older rides with newer, noisier and more thrilling ones. However, here and there can still be found a few colourful reminders from the park's Golden Age, now protected as historic structures.

Pride of place goes to its original merry-go-round carousel (*Körhinta*) constructed in 1906 and so well restored in 1996 that

Europe's longest wooden rollercoaster in Budapest's Amusement Park

it garnered a European Union *Europa Nostra* prize. Its wooden horses are carved superbly, fixed onto mechanisms that make them gallop gently. Of the same vintage is the *János Vitéz Barlangvasút*, an artificial cave railway that consists of carriages pulled along a track by an electric engine disguised as a dragon (it was originally called the Dragon Railway). Along the way are a series of quaint dioramas peopled by wooden figures including Hungarian and Turkish soldiers fighting with swords. The scenes are lifted from the epic Hungarian folklore poem *János Vitéz* (*John the Valiant*) written in 1846 by Hungary's most celebrated romantic poet

All the fun of the fair in Budapest's Amusement Park

and freedom fighter Sándor Petőfi (see nos. 48 & 56). Extracts from the poem are played through loud speakers as the ride takes place.

Two other popular rides from the past are the Caterpillar (*Hernyó*), so-named because its carriages have been clattering up and down its wavy track since 1930, and the Whip (*Kanyargó*), sending its passengers skidding around a noisy metal trackway.

Another survivor is the park's huge timber-built rollercoaster (*Hullámvasút*), reminiscent of the historic Coney Island funfair in the New York district of Brooklyn. Built in 1922, and with a length of one kilometre forming nine "waves", it remains Europe's longest wooden rollercoaster. The carriages climb to a height of 28 metres and take 5 minutes (at a maximum speed of 50 kilometres per hour) to complete the circuit. Access to the ride is made through an entrance building that contains a small museum detailing the park's fascinating history. Finally, flowing beneath the timber struts of the old rollercoaster there runs a stream carrying Fairy Tale Boats (*Mesecsónak*) that travel through a series of artificial caves constructed before the Second World War.

Other places of interest nearby: 73, 75, 76, 77, 78

75 The Art of Socialist Realism

District XIV (Városliget), the MÉMOSZ Architects' Trades' Union building at the corner of Dózsa György út 84a and Városligeti fasor
M1 to Hősök tere

After the Second World War the Yalta Conference placed Hungary firmly within the Eastern Bloc, under the ever-watchful eye of the Soviet Union. It was a situation that would endure until the collapse of Hungarian Communism in 1989. The first task of Budapest's architects during this period was to reconstruct bomb-damaged buildings and to undertake necessary public housing projects quickly and cheaply. Not surprisingly the results were basic and practical in the extreme, an inevitable if uninspired extension of the city's pre-war brush with Functionalism. However, gradually there grew a national architectural style that managed to modify the stultifying guidelines imposed by the Soviet architectural model. The effect may only have been a subtle one when compared with the exuberance of the anti-Habsburg Secession (Hungarian Art Nouveau) but it was a beacon of hope for a nation that craved independence (see no. 78).

So it was that during the late 1940s, Hungarian architects managed to continue erecting buildings in the International Modernist style pio-

Socialist Realism reliefs adorn a Communist-era building on Dózsa György út

neered in the twenties and thirties (see no. 24). Typical is the bus station (1949) in Erzsébet tér (now a protected building) by István Nyíri, with its strikingly inclined roof, and the MÉMOSZ Architects' Trades' Union building (1947–50) on Dózsa György út, on the west side of City Park. The latter, designed by the MATI group that included Lajos Gádoros has a striking Le Corbusier-like glass façade. As a taste of things to come, this was Budapest's first building to contain an example of the Communist art form known as Socialist Realism, in this case reliefs depicting proud construction workers laying bricks and carry-

Soviet-era sportsmen at the former People's Stadium, now the Ferenc Puskás Stadium

ing planks. Such works, although obviously propagandist, are by turns muted and accomplished when compared to the brutish giant Stalins and other revolutionary heroes that would be erected in the city's streets and squares during the same period, most of which were torn down after the fall of Communism in 1989 (see no. 17).

By the early 1950s, however, the Communist authorities had condemned Modernism as an embodiment of Western decadence and replaced it with a stripped-down neo-Classical style, which they felt harked back to a purer and less troublesome age. Thus, the stolid Town Hall (1952) by József Körner on Mechwart tér (District II) is a good example of what was now deemed acceptable, as was the School of Applied Arts (1953) by Zoltán Farkasdy at Zugligeti út 9 (District XII), its portico like that of a Greek temple. The style reached something of an apogee in 1955 with the Budapest Technical University (1955) by Gyula Rimanóczy, its façade adorned with reliefs depicting

An agricultural worker outside
the Agriculture Ministry

manual workers that have the feel of sculptures from ancient Greece, a feeling emphasised by the Greek-style frieze and tympanum. Hungarian architects had stealthily managed to work within the confines of the Socialist Realism ideal, whilst also conveying the feeling of the democratic ideals of Classical Greece!

With the death of Stalin and the dawn of the 1960s the architecture of Budapest once again began to reflect the ideals of Modernism and its attention to the needs of people rather than politics; in doing so an architectural process that had begun forty years previously was re-awakened.

Further examples of the Socialist Realism aesthetic include the sculpted sportsmen outside the Ferenc Puskás Stadium (see no. 79), the worker's statue on Csepel Island (see no. 84) and the pair of young agricultural workers ensconced outside the Agriculture Ministry near the Parliament building (Országház). See also the salvaged shop windows in the Hungarian National Museum, the last few remaining Soviet-era shopfronts and bars dotted around the suburban streets of Pest (see no. 55) and the neon sign above a doorway at Nagymező utca 28 announcing the presence of the 18th Lawyers' Work Collective (18. sz. Ügyvédi Munkaközösség).

Other places of interest nearby: 71, 76, 77, 78

76 A Fairytale Castle and the Mulberry Garden

District XIV (Városliget), Vajdahunyad Castle (Vajdahunyad Vára) in City Park (Városliget)
M1 to Hősök tere

In 1896 Budapest went all out to celebrate the thousandth anniversary of legendary chieftain Prince Árpád leading the seven Magyar tribes down onto the Great Plain, thus establishing the Hungarian nation (see no. 1). With newfound confidence resulting from the so-called Compromise Agreement with Habsburg Austria, together with capital generated by the thriving commercial centre of Pest, the city exploded in an architectural celebration of the country's mythical origins and sense of nationhood. Nowhere was this better manifested that in the exuberant setpiece of Heroes' Square (Hősök tere) and City Park (Városliget), the former acting as a grand portal to the latter. Heroes' Square is Budapest's most symbolic public space and lies at the end of the Andrássy út boulevard. It contains Hungary's two most important commemorative monuments reflecting the nation's history, namely the Millenary Monument and the Heroes' Monument (the latter known

Vajdahunyad Castle in City Park

originally as the Tomb of the Unknown Soldier). Around the base of the former can be seen statues of Árpád and the six other Magyar chiefs, whilst above them rises a column surmounted by the Archangel Gabriel clutching the golden crown of King Stephen (István) (see no. 40). The monument's designer, Albert Schickedanz, was also responsible for the Fine Arts Museum (Szépművészeti Múzeum) to the left, as well as the Hall of Art-Kunsthalle (Műcsarnok) on the right.

However, since the square was not finally completed until 1929, it was the park beyond that played host to the actual millennial celebrations of 1896. Originally a royal hunting domain the land was drained and planted out as an English-style park, designed in part to act as a filter for dust blowing in off the Great Plain to the east. The architect Ignác Alpár was selected to decorate it with a number of temporary symbolic structures that would form a suitable backdrop for the festivities. Chief amongst these was the fairytale Vajdahunyad Castle, proving so popular with visitors that it was not dismantled at the end of the celebrations as had been planned but rather re-built as a permanent feature.

The castle stands on Széchenyi Island at the centre of the park and was designed to represent all the major historical styles of Hungarian

Modern sculpture surrounds the former villa of Alajos Stróbl in the Mulberry Garden on Bajza utca

architecture in a single structure. Thus, in the main courtyard there is a cloistered Romanesque chapel based on the 13th century abbey church of Ják near Szombathely in Western Hungary. Similarly, the Gothic tower to the right was inspired by Segesvár Castle (now Sighisoara) in Transylvania (Romania). Nearby is a wing in the Baroque style resembling the façade of the famous Esterházy Palace in Fertőd near Sopron and now containing the Museum of Hungarian Agriculture (see no. 77). Meanwhile, the castle's main façade, overlooking the lake, is a copy of the early Gothic 13th century castle of the Hunyadi family at Vajdahunyad (now Hunedoara) in Transylvania. A member of this influential family was Matthias (Mátyás) 'Corvinus' Hunyadi, crowned King of Hungary in 1458 (see no. 7).

Modern art in the Mulberry Garden

Not too far away, at the corner of Bajza utca and Lendvay utca, is another repository for various sculptural fragments, namely the little-known Mulberry Garden artists' colony. It was founded in the 1880s in support of the newly established Hungarian Academy of Fine Art. Artists such as fresco painter Károly Lotz and sculptor Alajos Stróbl not only had their workshops here but also highly individual villas, Stróbl's being notable for its distinctive colonnaded frontage. The surrounding garden is filled with copies of Classical, medieval and Renaissance sculptures, whilst in the centre is a genuine Baroque Calvary rescued from Józsefváros. Authentic, too, are the medieval fragments removed from the Matthias Church (Mátyás-templom) during Frigyes Schulek's purist reconstruction of that building. So renowned was the Mulberry Garden in its day that even the Habsburg Emperor Franz Joseph I paid a visit.

Other places of interest nearby: 73, 74, 75, 77, 78

77 "Nothing is Worthier to a Free Man than Agriculture"

District XIV (Városliget), the Museum of Hungarian Agriculture (Mezőgazdasági Múzeum) in Vajdahunyad Castle in City Park (Városliget)
M1 to Hősök tere

A little-known fact about Budapest's Museum of Hungarian Agriculture is that it is the largest museum of its type in Europe. Founded in 1896 it was opened to the public in 1897 in the Baroque and Gothic wings of Vajdahunyad Castle in City Park (see no. 76). Inside the museum, above one of the grand stuccoed stairways, are the well-chosen words of the Roman author Cicero: "Nihil Melius, Nihil Homine Libero Dignius, quam Agricultura" (Nothing is better, nothing is worthier to a free man than agriculture).

The collections themselves encompass a wildly eclectic array of subjects, from the history of pig breeding on the ground floor, to traditional fishing techniques on the first floor, and the development of Hungarian viticulture in the cellars. Worth looking out for is the splendid Lake Balaton canoe hewn from a single treetrunk, the huge wooden wine presses, and the reconstructed grape-picker's cottage with its rope bed. Pride of place goes to Hungary's first agricultural steam engine imported all the way from Lincoln in England in 1852. Of considerable political interest are the Communist-era propaganda posters depicting happy peasants and healthy farm labourers working the land. A further highlight of the museum is the colourfully decorated hunting hall with its painted ceiling and stained glass windows, at one end of which can be found an unusual fossilised antler.

Upon leaving the museum glance at Miklós Ligeti's statue opposite the entrance enti-

Old brewing apparatus in the Museum of Hungarian Agriculture in City Park

tled *Anonymous*, depicting the so-called "unknown chronicler" of the Magyars. According to the statue's inscription he may have been a clerk in the 12th century court of King Béla III (1172–96). Signing himself as "P. dictus magister", or "Master P.", he most notably penned the Latin *Gesta Hungarorum*, the first known written account of Hungarian history.

A statue of Anonymous, author of Hungary's first history

Also located in City Park is the fascinating but little written about Transport Museum (Közlekedési Múzeum) at Városligeti körút 11, one of the oldest museums of its type in Europe. Affording an excellent overview of Budapest's extraordinarily varied modes of transport the many displays include the history of Hungarian shipping (see nos. 16 & 33), the development of horsedrawn transport through to the motorcar and motorcycle, the history of Hungarian railways, including some magnificent model steam engines, and even the space capsule of Hungary's first and only cosmonaut. Best of all is the museum's model railway, its trains speeding through a miniaturised Hungarian landscape every hour. Even the museum café is set inside an old railway dining car! The museum also features model aeroplanes, a theme taken up in the Transport Museum's Historic Aircraft & Spacecraft Exhibition (Repüléstörténeti és Űrhajózási Kiállítás) just across the park in the Petőfi Csarnok at Zichy Mihály út 14 (District XIV).

Other places of interest nearby: 73, 74, 75, 76, 78

District XIV (Városliget), Villa Sipek-Balázs at Hermina út 47
M1 to Széchenyi fürdő

Tucked away on a side street looking westwards across City Park can be found the delightful, and often overlooked, Villa Sipek-Balázs. With its pastel pink stuccoed walls, tapering chimney and graceful winter garden it is a late work by the architect Ödön Lechner (1845–1914), the so-called Gaudí of Budapest. This epithet is well deserved since by the time the little pink villa was constructed in 1905 Budapest's skyline had been indelibly stamped with Lechner's highly distinctive architecture, much like Antonio Gaudí was doing in Barcelona.

The charming Villa Sipek-Balázs on Hermina út

As a young man one of Lechner's formative influences was undoubtedly visiting the family brickworks; his first commission, the former State Railway Pensioners' Building (1881–84) at Andrássy út 25 (District V), would use plenty of visible brickwork within the confines of a traditional neo-Renaissance structure. His interest in fired clay would also lead him to the Zsolnay family, pioneers of a frost and heat resistant architectural ceramic they called pyrogranite, which could be intricately moulded and finished with coloured glazes. Used by Lechner on the façade of the neo-Gothic Thonet House at Váci utca 11A (1888–89) (see no. 45), Zsolnay ceramics would soon feature highly in his signature buildings.

However, like his counterpart Otto Wagner in Vienna, looking to the past for inspiration was not enough for Lechner and within fifteen years he would be hailed as the creator of the Hungarian Art Nouveau. Known as the Secession throughout the Austro-Hungarian Empire, the Art Nouveau of Central Europe strove to secede, or break away, from the unimaginative and stolid Historicist style favoured by Habsburg Emperor Franz Joseph I (1848–1916). In Budapest the ever-patriotic Lechner went one step further than his counterparts in Paris and Vienna by using the Secession to create a truly national Hungarian style, one that would befit a country about to celebrate a thousand years of nationhood. Thus, in addition to the writhing organic forms, gilded maidens and novel

A detail of the former Royal Post Office Savings Bank on Hold utca

construction techniques seen elsewhere in Europe, Lechner also included both Hungarian folkloric motifs as well as blatantly Oriental themes reflecting the supposed eastern origins of the Magyars.

His first fully-fledged work in this medium was the Applied Arts Museum (1893–96) (see no. 54), revoutionary in that it was erected on a steel frame. His critics unfairly tagged it "the Gypsy Palace" for its controversial profusion of non-traditional decoration. A statue of the architect sits unperturbed in the museum's forecourt. Next came the Hungarian State Geological Institute (1899) (see no. 29) roofed with bright blue tiles and topped with four Atlas figures supporting a globe. Lechner's crowning glory, however, is considered by many to be his former Royal Post Office Savings Bank (Postatakarékpénztár) (1899–1901) at Hold utca 4 (District V), with its combination of polychrome roof tiles, stuccoed facade decorated with folk motifs edged in visible wavy brickwork, and a riot of pretzel-like Zsolnay pyrogranite ceramic ornaments. Chief amongst the latter are winged

Hungarian State Geology Institute

serpents on the finials (signifying renewal), honey-coloured bee-hives on the pilasters towards which lines of glazed bees are crawling (symbols of thrift), and even skylights in the form of cockerels. Sadly for Lechner it was just too much for some and the Minister for Culture stopped government funding for any more public buildings in the new style.

So it was that the architect who more than any other had defined his country's nationhood in bricks and mortar never received another major commission.

However, Lechner continued to work, albeit unoficially, with various students and followers, producing amongst other things the little villa on the edge of City Park and a wholly unexpected primary school with Ármin Hegedűs at Dob utca 85 (District VII). His influence was lasting, too, moreso perhaps than his Seccesionist contemporaries elsewhere, since Hungary's need to express its national spirit against a backdrop of centuries of suppression would continue well into the 1980s. Architects such as Béla Lajta (see no. 67), Károly Kós (see no. 82) and Imre Makovecz (see no. 19) would all endeavour to build on Lechner's notion of a national Hungarian style, albeit in very different ways.

Ödön Lechner died in 1914 and is buried in Budapest's Kerepesi Cemetery (see no. 58), not far from the grave of Miklós Ybl, Hungary's foremost Historicist architect.

Similar in design to the Villa Sipek-Balázs is the Art Nouveau Villa Egger (1902) by Emil Vidor at nearby Városligeti fasor 24 in District VI. On a far grander scale the Gresham Palace (1905–07) by Zsigmond Quittner and the brothers Vágó at the Pest end of the Chain Bridge is typical Hungarian Art Nouveau too, especially in its tiling and wrought iron work.

Other places of interest nearby: 73, 74, 75, 76, 77

79 The People's Stadium

District XIV (Istvánmező), the Ferenc Puskás Stadium (Puskás
Ferenc Stadion), formerly the People's Stadium (Népstadion),
on Stefánia út
M2 to Stadionok (Népstadion) then walk along Ifjúság utca

Tucked away just outside the
Kiskörút at Lónyai utca 62
(District IX) is a modest wine
bar called the Hat-három (6:3)
Borozó (a Borozó is a traditional
wine bar, *bor* being Hungarian
for wine; a Söröző is a similar
establishment selling *sör*, or
beer). This Borozó's unusual
name refers to Hungary's greatest footballing victory, namely
the legendary 6–3 triumph over
England at the old Wembley

The Hat-három (6:3) Borozó on Lónyai utca

Stadium in 1953; the bar's walls are hung with nostalgic photos
depicting ecstatic members of the Hungarian national team. Just one
year later the same team came close to winning the 1954 World Cup,
their star player Ferenc Puskás becoming a household name.

It was during this time, as part of the Communist regime's attempt
to "bring sport to the people", that Hungary's largest sporting facility
was built, namely the People's Stadium (Népstadion) a couple of streets
south-east of City Park. The stadium was erected between 1948 and 1953
by Károly Dávid & Associates and could hold a crowd of 76,000. It was also
given a grand approach lined with robust statues in the so-called Socialist
Realism style, which are still in place (see nos. 17 & 39).

This was the golden age of Hungarian football and it was not uncom-
mon for capacity audiences to turn up regularly to watch Honvéd (an
army team based in the working-class district of Kispest) and Ferencváros
(the city's other great working-class club from neighbouring District IX).
Unfortunately, following the 1956 Uprising many of the country's best
players drifted abroad to pursue their careers, including Ferenc Puskás
who went to play for Real Madrid. Despite his departure the Hungarian
team continued to perform well at successive World Cups in 1966,
1978 and 1982, a resounding if controversial 6-0 defeat to the USSR in

Soviet-era sportsmen at the
Ferenc Puskás Stadium

1986 being the last time Hungary graced the world football stage.

Sadly, since this time the domestic game has suffered from supporter apathy, match rigging and under-funding, gradually draining teams of their talent – and the great stadium of its audiences. Today, only major music concerts manage to fill the cavernous arena's thousands of empty seats. However, in 1998 the stadium was renovated for the 1998 European Athletics Championships and in 2002 it was renamed in honour of Hungary's most famous number 10, Ferenc Puskás. Home matches are still played here during two seasons running August-November and March-June.

The Ferenc Puskás Stadium site also includes a sports complex as well as the Hungarian Sport Museum (Sportmúzeum), at Istvánmezei út 3–5, filled with medals, photographs and other mementoes of celebrated Hungarian sports people. Hungary has a proud and very varied sporting tradition and it should not be forgotten that no other country has won as many gold medals per head of population. A prime example is Alfréd Hajós, Hungary's 18-year old swimming gold medallist at the first modern Olympics in Athens in 1896, who in 1935 designed the eponymous National Sports Pool (Hajós Alfréd Nemzeti Sportuszoda) on Margaret Island.

80 Little-known Sights in Old Kőbánya

District X (Kőbánya), the Church of St. László on Szent László tér off Kőrösi Csoma út
M2 to Blaha Lujza tér then Tram 28 to Szent László tér

Between the 17th and the 19th centuries Budapest's little-visited District X was actively worked to extract building stone for the city's new buildings, indeed the district's name of Kőbánya means 'stone quarry'. Today, the 80 kilometres of subterranean galleries that still riddle the area are used for cultivating mushrooms and brewing beer (The Dreher Beer Museum is at Jászberényi út 7–11).

Although well off the tourist route a trip out to Kőbánya is recommended for it contains several little-known sights. Firstly, there is the magnificent and recently restored Church of St. László on Szent László tér. It occupies a site where until 1875 there was a clay pit hence its former name of Bányató, or 'Mine Lake'. Having been filled in the area was renamed Market Square and a church planned to dominate it. Several architects put forward their designs, including Frigyes Feszl, designer of the Vigadó concert hall, who proposed a triple-naved neo-Romanesque basilica, Ödön Lechner, creator of the

Kőbánya's Church
of St. László dominates Szent László tér

A detail of Kőbánya's former synagogue on Cserkész utca

Hungarian Secession (Art Nouveau) style, who suggested a neo-Byzantine domed church, and Elek Barcza, who favoured a multi-steepled cathedral. With such differing designs disagreements were inevitable, or as a newspaper article at the time reported: "It is no wonder that the tempers raised during the building did not calm down, and articles of various emotions followed each other in the press". Not wishing to restrict the design to any one established style it was decided to merge all three concepts and in doing so to create a truly unique Hungarian church building, one that would reflect the mood of a city about to celebrate a thousand years of history. Thus, Feszl got his naves with basilica-like ceiling and Romanesque ground floor windows, Barcza was allowed a magnificent 80-metre high steeple, Gothic-style upper windows and flying buttresses, and in accordance with Lechner's design the whole was decorated and roofed with Zsolnay ceramic bricks and tiles.

Walking away from the church down Halom utca brings the visitor to the Csajkovszkij Park with its tiny Second World War sentry bunker. To the left is the Óhegypark where a whitewashed tower functioned originally as a lookout to prevent thieves stealing grapes from the extensive vineyards that once existed here. To the right is the little-known Firefighting Museum (Tűzoltó Múzeum) at Martinovics tér 12 (the square itself is the geographical centre of Budapest). Located in a working fire station its exhibits include ancient firefighting equipment retrieved from the Roman ruins of Aquincum, a late 19th century horse-drawn engine, as well as the original dry extinguisher invented in 1928 by Kornél Szilvay. Of especial interest is Hungary's first motorised firefighting vehicle brought all the way from England in 1870 by Ödön Széchenyi, instigator of Buda's funicular railway, whose father Count István Széchenyi masterminded the city's famous Chain Bridge (Budapest's other museum devoted to the emergency services, namely the Kresz Géza Ambulance Service Museum (Kresz Géza Mentőmúzeum), is at Markó utca 22 (District V) and includes a portable 'Iron Lung' from the time when *poliomyelitis* was endemic).

Finally, at the junction of nearby Román utca with Cserkész utca, there is Kőbánya's former synagogue now used as a Christian church. Richard Schöntheil designed this striking building with its distinctive low, wide dome and decorative cupolas in 1909–12. Inside the synagogue much of the original Jewish decoration remains so it appears rather strange to see a baptismal font occupying the *bimah* where the *Torah* lectern once stood.

81 Plot 301

District X (Kőbánya), the Kozma utca New Municipal Cemetery
(Kozma utcai Új köztemető) at Kozma utca 8–10
M2 to Blaha Lujza tér, then Tram 28 or 37

Of Budapest's three main municipal cemeteries (*temető*) that of
Kerepesi is certainly the most impressive, with its mausolea to 19th
century Hungarian heroes and crumbling Communist-era monuments
(see no. 58). By contrast, the Farkasréti Cemetery in the Buda Hills
(*Budai-hegység*) is certainly the prettiest, its graves including those
of renowned composers set picturesquely amongst groves of Horse
Chestnut trees (see no. 19). That just leaves the sprawling Kozma
utca New Municipal Cemetery in distant District X, farthest away
from the city centre, not especially attractive and with little in the way
of atmosphere or famous names. However, the cemetery does con-

Wooden markers in the Kozma utca Municipal Cemetery commemorate those
who died in the 1956 Uprising

tain one very important grave that has come to symbolise an important chapter in Hungary's centuries-old struggle against its oppressors, namely that of Prime Minister Imre Nagy (1896–1958), executed for his part in the 1956 Uprising against the Soviets (see no. 37).

The grave of former Prime Minister Imre Nagy

The story of Hungary's rapid transition from Fascism to Communism is an oft-told one, producing its fair share of heroes and villains in the process (see nos. 3, 17 & 69). Imre Nagy was a former Minister of Agriculture and a Reform Communist, one who dreamt of an independent Hungary free from the enforced ultracentralised economic planning of traditional Stalinist Communism; such thoughts had seen him removed from office by the Communist Party in 1955 on account of "deviationism". On Tuesday October 23rd 1956, in support of strikes for reforms occurring in Poland, students and workers gathered to demand similar changes for Hungary. Fighting broke out and Nagy was reinstated as Prime Minister, whereupon he announced Hungary's secession from the Warsaw Pact. Although at first in agreement the Soviet authorities soon feared the worst and brutally suppressed the Uprising, installing their new General Secretary János Kádár (1956–88) soon afterwards. Although Nagy found temporary sanctuary in the Yugoslav Embassy, the KGB soon arrested and imprisoned him. By late December over

200,000 Hungarians (nearly 2% of the population) had fled to escape the reprisals and Cardinal József Mindszenty, Hungary's Catholic primate and renowned critic of both Fascism and Communism, sought refuge in the American Embassy on Szabadság tér, where he famously remained in "internal exile" for fifteen years! Despite a promise of clemency Nagy was tried and executed in secret two years later in June 1958.

Today, the anniversary of the start of the 1956 Uprising (October 23rd) is a public holiday when flags with a hole in the middle can be seen fluttering across the capital. The usually near-empty coach parks of the Kozma utca Cemetery are fleetingly busy as visitors arrive to lay wreathes at Plot 301, where Imre Nagy was buried after his execution: he was only 'officially' reburied there on June 16th 1989 after a State Funeral on Heroes' Square, an event that marked the rebirth of Hungarian democracy. The grave (number 23), together with those of 260 other victims of the Uprising, each marked by a simple carved wooden grave post, lies in the farthest left hand corner of the cemetery, adjacent to György Jovánovics's Central Martyrs' Monument. Far removed from the rest of the cemetery it remains an atmospheric resting place for those who gave their lives "…for an independent, free and democratic Hungary."

82 The Transylvanian Housing Estate

District XIX (Kispest), the Wekerle-telep housing estate at Károly Kós tér on Hungária út
M3 to Határ út then walk down Pannónia utca to Kós Károly tér

A quick glance at any street map of Budapest that includes the outer suburbs will immediately show something rather unusual down in the south-east, far away from the usual tourist hotspots. Here, straddling the border between Districts XIX and XX, can be seen a vast grid-plan of streets, as big as Castle Hill and medieval Pest put together. Forming distinct neighbourhoods and bordered by main thoroughfares these are deliberately planned housing estates (*telep*), laid out in the first half of the 20th century to accomodate the tens of thousands of manual workers and other administrative employees who had arrived to work in the city and the factories of nearby Csepel Island (see no. 84).

A closer look at a map will show that most of these estates comprise streets built monotonously at right angles to each other – but with one exception. In the district of Kispest (District XIX) can be seen a remarkable housing estate whose geometrically planned streets appear more like a tapestry design or spider's web. Known as the Wekerle Housing Estate (Wekerle-telep) it was instigated and named after twice Prime Minister Sándor Wekerle (1892–95 and 1917–18).

The idea for the estate was to build a self-contained garden city in the former village of Kispest, big enough to house 20,000 people, while

Transylvanian architecture at the Wekerle-telep housing estate in Kispest

A rustic detail on a Wekerle-telep house

still retaining something of the rural atmosphere of the village it replaced. That today it remains a self-contained and self-sufficient entity, despite Kispest having been incorporated into Budapest proper along with several other suburbs in 1949, is testament to the fifteen or so architects whose job it was to design the estate. Chief amongst these was Károly Kós (1883–1977), an architect who together with Béla Lajta created a distinctly Hungarian building style that fused the design ideals of Hungarian Art Nouveau (Secession) with the practical demands of Modernism (see no. 67). Unlike Lajta, however, Kós looked to Hungary's medieval folk past for inspiration, as well as to the village architecture of his native Transylvania (he was born in the Bánát region, now in Romania). His folk revival style is thus characterised by distinctive steep gables, tiled turrets and the use of weatherboarding and other rustic details.

Although Kós's most famous work is the Bird House (*madárház*) (1911) in the City Park Zoo (see no. 73), his most important is certainly the Wekerle Housing Estate. Constructed mainly between 1909 and 1929 the estate was designed to provide its inhabitants with all the services they might require, including individual gardens and shops. Kós himself was responsible for designing the centre of the estate where today his statue now stands.

After the First World War and the Treaty of Trianon, under whose terms Hungary lost Transylvania, Kós returned to his homeland and its capital of Kolozsvár, now Cluj, where he devoted his energies to promoting the Transylvanian school of architecture, designing a number of religious and secular buildings, and tirelessly recording his country's cultural heritage.

Those wishing to continue their Transylvanian experience in Budapest might like to visit an authentic folk dance house. At Fonó Budai Zeneház at Sztregova utca 3 (District XI), for example, visitors can enjoy live music, whilst participating in the dancing themselves. Traditional dances were popular a century ago in Transylvania but since the 1970s the tradition has been rekindled and kept alive by enthusiastic Hungarian city-dwellers, both young and old.

83 A Load of Old Junk

District XIX (Kispest), the Ecseri Flea Market (Ecseri
Használtcikkpiac), at Nagykőrösi út 156
Tram 2 to Boráros tér, then Bus 54

Geographically speaking, Hungary lies at the very heart of Europe, in a vast plain known as the Carpathian Basin – and at its own heart is its capital city. With the mighty Danube (*Duna*) flowing right through the city, Budapest, the "Pearl of the Danube" is a microcosm of Hungary's geography: on the west (or right) bank is the old rocky fastness of Buda, its hills representing the last shout of the mountains of Transdanubia (Dunántúl); on the east (or left) bank is the flat commercial expanse of Pest, stretching away to the Great Hungarian Plain (Nagyalföld). Across the centuries this enviable location has attracted merchants and traders from Central Europe and far beyond, the city acting as both end-user and as a stepping-stone for markets farther afield. Indeed it was Charles Robert of Anjou, who as King Charles (Károly) I (1308–42) following the collapse of the Árpádian dynasty declared Buda "a place of call", meaning that no matter from whence they hailed, all merchants had to stop to sell their wares.

However, with entry into the European Union and Budapest's rapid ascension to major commercial and financial hub for Central

Antiques for sale at the Ecseri Flea Market in Kispest

and Eastern Europe, much of the colour of the old trading practices is inevitably vanishing. Witness, for example, the much talked about fate of the Four Tigers' Chinese Market (Józsefvárosi piac) at Kőbányai út 21–23 (District VIII). Throughout the 1990s, on a stretch of waste ground alongside the number 28 tramline, hundreds of Chinese, Vietnamese, Uzbeki and Balkan traders peddled their cheap imported wares here, albeit often without a licence. Come rain or shine these hardy traders would conduct their business from six by eight metre booths seven days a week. The market remained off-limits to government inspectors and was run as a sort of fiefdom by the private security force of a former Interior Minister.

In 2004 the authorities decided to no longer turn a blind eye and an Austrian real estate developer took several hundred of the traders and relocated them to the new eight-storey Asia Center on Szentmihály út (District XV). With its granite and glass walls, gurgling fountains and inevitably higher rents, it resembles a Hong Kong shopping mall. Needless to say, electronic goods, cosmetics and travel agencies have quickly replaced the cheap shoes, kitsch jewellery and Samurai swords still (at the time of writing) being sold in the old market. Incidentally, the Asia Center, which aims to attract high-end producers from Hong Kong, Taiwan and Singapore to consolidate Hungary's role as a regional distribution centre for Far Eastern goods, is Europe's first complex built according to the principles of the ancient Chinese space-arranging tradition of Feng Shui. The architects hope that this will guarantee prosperity and rewarding business relationships.

There are a few places remaining in Budapest, where the visitor can still get a feel for the hustle and bustle of the old way of trading, namely the city's covered markets (see no. 52) and open air flea markets (bolhapiac). Of the latter, the biggest and most famous is the Ecseri Flea Market in the district of Kispest, indeed it is one of the largest in Central Europe. Saturday morning is recommended when there is a boisterous mix of dealers. Whilst the die-hard professionals in their cluttered dens service big buyers from Paris and Milan, weekenders spread out their wares on blankets on the ground, including old gramophones, Soviet cameras, Transylvanian vases, pictures of Lenin and East German toys. Also worth experiencing is the weekend Városliget Flea Market (Városligeti Bolhapiac) at Petőfi Csarnok on Zichy Mihály út in City Park (District XIV) – look out for the Transylvanian peasant women selling their folk embroideries.

84 Red Csepel

District XXI (Csepel-sziget), old factories on Csepel Island
(Csepel-sziget)
Suburban train HÉV from Boráros tér to Szent Imre tér

Csepel Island is surely one of Budapest's least visited tourist attractions and yet it contains much of interest for the explorer. The island is not only the largest in Hungary but also along the entire Danube, being 54 kilometres long, 3–10 kilometres wide and covering an area of 257 square kilometres. Of this only 26.1 kilometres, at the northern tip of the island, actually lies within Budapest's city limits, where it makes up District XXI, known as Csepel.

Archaeological finds demonstrate that Csepel Island was inhabited as early as the 2nd millennium BC (Bronze Age) and was visited later by the Romans during their conquest of Pannonia, the most eastern province of their European Empire; they built a defensive fort here as part of their so-called *limes* border defence (see no. 34).

Csepel next appears in the Latin writings of the medieval scribe known only as Anonymous, whose *Gesta Hungarorum* details how Prince Árpád, who had led the Magyar tribes into the Carpathian Basin in c.900AD, erected a palace on the so-called Great Island, re-naming it

The main entrance to the once mighty Csepel Works

Csepel in honour of his stable master (see no. 77). These early nomadic Magyars were great horsemen who would undertake forays deep into Western Europe (see no. 1).

During the 16th century Serbs fleeing the approaching Ottoman armies also settled on Csepel, although only in the southern part of the island, outside today's modern city limits (see no. 51), an area that is still predominantly rural and noted for its natural history.

The modern settlement of Csepel was officially undertaken in 1712 as an agricultural endeavour but despite its rapid development the Great Flood of 1838 devastated it. Following the Compromise Agreement with Habsburg Austria in 1867, Csepel Island was protected from further flooding by an ambitious programme of river regulation, dyke digging and raising of embankments. The district again began to develop only this time as a centre of increasingly heavy industry. Most significantly the great Jewish industrial magnate Baron Manfréd Weiss, known as the "Hungarian Krupp", established his munitions factory here in 1893. By 1914 the factory was the nation's biggest ammunition manufacturer with 30,000 employees – at a time when the population of Csepel itself was only 15,000! Rapid industrialisation of the district followed and with it came a telegraph agency, radio station transmitters, Suburban Railway (HÉV), and a sports club that produced several Olympic water sports champions. In 1930 the Anglo-Dutch Shell Company built the world's most advanced oil refinery on the island – Hungary having lost many of her oil deposits under the Treaty of Trianon after the Great War – and in 1934 a freeport was established where seagoing vessels could dock, an idea that had been mooted by the forward thinking Count István Széchenyi back in 1843 (see no. 42).

Not surprisingly the factories of Csepel Island saw much activity during the Second World War with the mighty Weiss works commandeered to produce artillery rounds for the *Wehrmacht* until the city fell to the Soviets; tellingly the Weiss family vault now lies abandoned in the Kerepesi Jewish Cemetery (see no. 59). During the last weeks of the war those installations considered useful to the allies (e.g. the Lakihegy radio transmitter) were deliberately destroyed by retreating German troops, whilst allied bombing had already flattened much of the rest (including a factory producing *Messerschmitt* components for the Luftwaffe).

With the arrival of Communism in 1948 the Csepel district was re-developed yet again, this time as a compulsorily industrialised and chimney-filled manufacturing heartland, dominated by heavy machinery and truck factories such as the Red October Tractor Works. For a taste of Red Csepel, as it was nicknamed by the Communist authorities, take the Suburban Railway from Boráros tér to Szent Imre tér and then walk down Tanácsház utca to a factory entrance where a neon sign announces "Csepel Művek" (Csepel Works). Beyond it lies a vast factory complex made up of cavernous empty workshops, abandoned railway lines and soaring disused chimneys. With the collapse of heavy industry after the fall of Communism the old factory was abandoned and parts of it reoccupied by numerous small firms. The vast size of the site, however, still gives a good impression of Csepel's former industrial might.

Back at the railway station can be seen the many tower blocks built to house the thousands of factory workers, the surrounding streets once the scene of much proletarian activism. At the end of the railway line is the station of Csepel itself, where in a corner of Béke tér behind the water tower stands András Beck's Socialist Realist statue depicting the idealised Communist worker, his foot resting atop a pile of bricks whilst reading from a book (see no. 75).

*   *   *   *

Standing on Csepel Island is the perfect place to finish this odyssey during which some of the more unusual and unsung corners of Budapest have been explored. Looking out from this former Communist industrial heartland that was also home to some of Budapest's earliest inhabitants, across the sprawling Danube to the grand boulevards of old Pest and Buda's Castle Hill beyond, gives the satisfied explorer the opportunity to reflect on the myriad cultures and characters that have helped shape this ever-changing city at the heart of Central Europe.

Opening times

(Correct at time of going to press but may be
subject to change)

A38
District XI, Buda side of the Danube 1
50 metres south of Petőfi Bridge, opening times vary
according to the events

Admiral Restaurant
District V, Belgrád rakpart 30, daily noon-11pm

Alabárdos Restaurant
District II, Országház utca 2,
Mon-Fri 7am-11pm, Sat noon-3pm, 7am-11pm

Alexandra Bookstore
District VI, Andrássy út 39, daily 10am-10pm

Amusement Park (Vidámpark)
District XIV, City Park (Városliget), Állatkerti körút 14-16,
visit www.vidampark.hu

Angelika Kávéház
District I, Batthyány tér 7, Apr-Oct
daily 9am-midnight, Nov-Mar daily 9am-11pm

Applied Arts Museum
(Iparművészeti Múzeum)
District IX, Üllői út 33-37, Tue-Sun 10am-6pm

Aquincum Hotel Baths
District III, Árpád fejedelem útja 94,
daily 7am-9pm

Aquincum Museum and Ruins
(Aquincumi Múzeum és Romterület)
District III, Szentendrei út 139,
Apr-Oct Tue-Sun 9am-6pm; museum Apr-Oct Tue-Sun
10am-6pm, Nov-Mar Tue-Sun 10am-4pm

Auguszt Cukrászda
District V, Kossuth Lajos utca 14-16, Mon-Fri 9am-7pm,
Sat 11am-6pm

Bambi Presszó
District II, Frankel Leó út 2-4,
Mon-Sat 7am-10pm

Banknote and Coin Collection
District V, Szabadság tér 8, Hungarian National Bank,
Mon-Wed, Fri 9am-4pm, Thu 9am-6pm

Bartók Memorial House
(Bartók Béla Emlékház)
District II, Csalán út 29, Tue-Sat 10am-5pm

Baths Museum (Fürdőmúzeum)
District III, Flórián tér underpass (Flórián téri aluljáró) 3-5,
15th-30th Apr & Oct Tue-Sun 10am-5pm, May-Sep,
1st-14th Apr & Nov 10am-6pm

Bible Museum (Biblia Múzeum)
District IX, Ráday utca 28, Mon, Tue, Thu & Fri 9am-
5pm, Wed 1-5pm, Sat 9am-1pm (Jul & Aug Mon only)

Biblical World Gallery
District VII, Wesselényi utca 13, Mon-Thu 10am-6pm,
Fri 10am-2pm

Buda Castle Funicular Railway
(Budavári sikló)
District I, lower station at Clark Ádám tér
and upper station at Szent György tér on Castle Hill
(Várhegy), daily 7.30am-10pm except the first,
third and fifth Monday of each month

Buda Castle Labyrinth
(Budavári Labirintus)
District I, Úri utca 9, daily 9.30am-7.30pm

Budapest History Museum
(Budapesti Történeti Múzeum)
District I, Wing E of the Royal Palace (Budavári Palota)
Szent György tér 2,
Nov-Feb 10am-4pm, Mar-Oct 10am-6pm

Budapest Parliament (Országház)
District V, Kossuth Lajos tér 1-3,
Apr-Oct Mon-Fri 8am-6pm, Sat & Sun 8am-4pm,
Nov-Mar daily 8am-4pm

Budapest Zoo and Botanical Gardens
(Fővárosi Állat- és Növénykert) District XIV,
City Park (Városliget), Állatkerti körút 6-12, Jan & Feb
daily 9am-4pm, Mar Mon-Thu 9am-5pm, Fri-Sun 9am-
5.30pm, Apr Mon-Thu 9am-5.30pm, Fri-Sun 9am-6pm,
May-Aug Mon-Thu 9am-6.30pm, Fri-Sun 9am-7pm,
Sep Mon-Thu 9am-5.30pm, Fri-Sun 9am-6pm, Oct
Mon-Thu 9am-5pm, Fri-Sun 9am-5.30pm, Nov & Dec
daily 9am-4pm

Café Callas
District VI, Andrássy út 20, Tue-Fri 8.30am-midnight,
Sat & Sun 10am-midnight

Cave Church (Sziklatemplom/Sziklakápolna)
District XI, just off Verejték utca,
Mon-Sat 9.30am-5pm, 6-7.30pm

Centrál Kávéház
District V, Károlyi utca 9, daily 8am-11pm

Central Market Hall
(Központi Vásárcsarnok)
District IX, Vámház körút 1-3, Mon 6am-5pm,
Tue-Fri 6am-6pm, Sat 6am-3pm

Central Synagogue (Zsinagóga)
District VII, Dohány utca 2-8,
Nov-Feb Sun-Thu 10am-4pm, Fri 10am-3.30pm, Mar-Oct
Sun-Thu 10am-6pm, Fri 10am-4.30pm

Chairlift (Libegő)
District XII, lower station at the corner of Zugligeti út
and Csiga út and end station on János-hegy,
mid May-mid Sep daily 9am-7pm, mid Sep-mid May
daily 10am-4pm

Children's Railway
(Gyermekvasút)
District XII, first station on Széchenyi Hill
(Széchenyi-hegy) and end station at Hűvösvölgy,
mid Mar-mid May Mon-Fri 10am-6pm, Sat & Sun
9am-6.45pm, mid May-mid Jun daily 9am-6.45pm,
mid Jun-Oct Mon-Fri 10am-6pm,
Sat & Sun 9am-6.45pm,
Nov-mid Mar daily 10am-6pm;
Sep-Apr closed Mondays (for full timetable visit
www.gyermekvasut.com)

Church of St. Anne
(Szent Anna-templom)
District I, Batthyány tér 7,
6.45-9am & 4-7pm, Sun 7am-1pm;

Cyrano Restaurant
District V, Kristóf tér 7-8,
daily 8am-midnight

Cogwheel Railway
(Fogaskerekű vasút)
District II, lower station at Budapest Hotel,
Szilágyi Erzsébet fasor 47 and end station
on Széchenyi Hill (Széchenyi-hegy), daily 5am-11pm

Danubius Health Spa Resort
Margitsziget
District XIII, Margitsziget, daily 6.30am-9.30pm;
women only Mon, Wed & Fri noon-3pm

Danubius Hotel Astoria
(Astoria Szálló)
District V, Kossuth Lajos utca 19-21, open to
non-residents at any reasonable time;
Mirror Café & Restaurant, daily 7am-11pm

Dreher Beer Museum
(Dreher Sörmúzeum)
District X, Jászberényi út 7-11, daily 9am-4pm

Ecseri Flea Market
(Ecseri Használtcikkpiac)
District XIX, Nagykőrösi út 156,
Mon-Fri 8am-4pm, Sat 6am-3pm, Sun 8am-1pm

Ethnographic Museum
(Néprajzi Múzeum)
District V, Kossuth Lajos tér 12,
Tue-Sun 10am-6pm

Farkasréti Public Cemetery
(Farkasréti temető)
District XII, Németvölgyi út 99,
Daily 7am-sunset

Ferenc Hopp Museum of
Eastern Asiatic Arts
(Hopp Ferenc Kelet-Ázsiai
Művészeti Múzeum)
District VI, in the György Ráth Villa at Városligeti fasor
12, Fri-Sun 10am-2pm; the Ferenc Hopp Villa is at
Andrássy út 103 and is open Fri-Sun 2am-6pm

Fine Arts Museum
(Szépművészeti Múzeum)
District XIV, Dózsa György út 41, Tue-Sun 10am-6pm

Firefighting Museum
(Tűzoltó Múzeum)
District X, Martinovics tér 12,
Mon-Thu 7.30am-4pm, Fri 7.30am-1.30pm

Flag Museum
(Zászlómúzeum)
District VIII, József körút 68, Tue-Fri 11am-6pm,
Sat & Sun 11am-3pm

Former Royal Post Office Savings Bank
(Magyar Királyi Takarék Pénztár)
District V, Hold utca 4 (entrance from
Szabadság tér), foyer only Mon-Fri; tours
of the building are available once a year
in the third week of September

Foundry Museum
(Öntödei Múzeum)
District II, Bem József utca 20, Thu-Sat 10am-2pm

Four Tigers' Chinese Market
(Józsefvárosi piac)
District VIII, Kőbányai út 21-23,
daily 6am-6pm

Franz Liszt Museum
(Liszt Ferenc Múzeum)
District VI, Vörösmarty utca 35,
Mon-Fri 10am-6pm, Sat 9am-5pm

Gas Museum
(Gázmúzeum)
District VIII, Köztársaság tér 20,
Tue Sun 9am-2pm by appointment only
tel. 0036 (1) 477-1347

Gellért Thermal Baths
(Gellért Gyógyfürdő)
District XI, Danubius Gellért Hotel, Kelenhegyi út 4,
daily 6am-8pm; Mon-Fri thermal baths segregated,
swimming pool mixed; Sat & Sun thermal baths and
swimming pool mixed

Gerbeaud Café
District V, Vörösmarty tér 7, daily 9am-9pm

Golden Eagle Pharmacy Museum
(Arany Sas Patikamúzeum)
District I, Tárnok utca 18,
mid Mar-Oct Tue-Sun 10am-6pm,
Nov-mid Mar Tue-Sun 10am-4pm

Gizi Bajor Theatre Museum
(Bajor Gizi Színészmúzeum)
District XII, Stromfeld Aurél út 16,
Thu-Sun 2pm-6pm

Greek Orthodox Church
(Görögkeleti templom)
District V, Petőfi tér, Sun before 10am service

Gundel's Restaurant
District XIV, Állatkerti körút 2,
Mon-Sat noon-4pm, 6.30-11pm, Sun 11.30am-3pm,
6.30-11pm

Hall of Art-Kunsthalle
(Műcsarnok)
District XIV, Dózsa György út 37,
daily 10am-6pm, Thu noon-8pm

Hat-három (6:3) Borozó
District IX, Lónyay utca 62, Mon-Thu 11am-11pm,
Fri & Sat 11am-midnight

Hercules Villa
District III, Meggyfa utca 19-21,
mid Apr-Oct by appointment only
tel. 0036 (1) 250-1650

Hilton Hotel (Hilton Szálló)
District I, Hess András tér 1-3,
open to non-residents at any reasonable time

Historic Aircraft & Spacecraft Exhibition
(Repüléstörténeti és Űrhajózási Kiállítás)
District XIV, Petőfi Csarnok, Zichy Mihály út 14,
May to mid-Oct Fri 10am-5pm,
Sat & Sun 10am-6pm

Hold utca Market Hall
District V, Hold utca 13, Mon 6.30am-5pm,
Tue-Fri 6.30am-6pm, Sat 6.30am-2pm

Holocaust Memorial Centre
(Holokauszt Emlékközpont)
District IX, Páva utca 39, Tue-Sun 10am-6pm

Horgásztanya vendéglő
District I, Fő utca 27, daily noon-midnight

Hospital in the Rock Museum
(Sziklakórház Múzeum)
District I, Lovas út 4/C, Mon-Sat 10am-8pm,
only with guided tours on the hour

House of Hungarian Art Nouveau
(Magyar Szecesszió Háza)
District V, Honvéd utca 3, Mon-Sat 10am-5pm

House of Terror Museum
(Terror Háza Múzeum)
District VI, Andrássy út 60, Tue-Sun 10am-6pm

Hungarian House of Photographers
in the Mai Manó House
(Magyar Fotográfusok Háza
a Mai Manó Házban)
District VI, Nagymező utca 20, Tue-Sun 10am-6pm

Hungarian Museum of Electrical Engineering
(Magyar Elektrotechnikai Múzeum)
District VII, Kazinczy utca 21,
Tue-Fri 10am-5pm, Sat 10am-4pm

Hungarian Museum of Trade & Tourism (Magyar Kereskedelmi és Vendéglátóipari Múzeum)
District III, Szent Korona tér 1, Tue-Sun 10am-6pm

Hungarian National Gallery (Magyar Nemzeti Galéria)
District I, Wing C of the Royal Palace (Budavári Palota), Szent György tér 2, Tue-Sun 10am-6pm

Hungarian National Museum (Magyar Nemzeti Múzeum)
District VIII, Múzeum körút 14-16, Tue-Sun 10am-6pm

Hungarian Natural History Museum (Magyar Természettudományi Múzeum)
District VIII, Ludovika tér 2, Wed-Mon 10am-6pm

Hungarian Railway History Park (Magyar Vasúttörténeti Park)
District XIV, Tatai út 95, 15th-30th Mar, 5th Nov-2nd Dec Tue-Sun 10am-3pm, 31st Mar-4th Nov Tue-Sun 10am-6pm

Hungarian Sport Museum (Magyar Sportmúzeum)
District XIV, near the Ferenc Puskás Stadium (Puskás Ferenc Stadion) (formerly the People's Stadium (Népstadion)), Istvánmezei út 3-5, daily 10am-5pm

Hungarian State Geological Institute (Magyar Földtani Intézet)
District XIV, Stefánia út 14, visits by appointment only tel. 0036-30-960-0587

Imre Varga Sculpture Museum (Varga Imre Gyűjtemény)
District III, Laktanya utca 7, Tue-Sun 10am-6pm

Inner City Parish Church (Belvárosi plébánia templom)
District V, Március 15 tér, daily 5-7pm

Jégbüfé
District V, Ferenciek tere 10, Mon-Tue, Thu-Sat 7am-9.30pm, Wed 7am-8.30pm, Sun 8am-9.30pm

Jewish Museum (Zsidó Múzeum)
District VII, Dohány utca 2, Mar-Oct Sun-Thu 10am-6pm, Fri 10am-4pm, Nov-Feb Sun-Thu 10am-4pm, Fri 10am-2pm

Kádár étkezde
District VII, Klauzál tér 9, Tue-Sat 11.30am-3.30pm

Károlyi Étterem és Kávéház Restaurant
District V, Károlyi utca 16, daily 11am-10pm

Kárpátia Restaurant
District V, Ferenciek tere 7-8, Mon-Sat 11am-11pm, Sun 5-11pm

Kazinczy utca Synagogue
District VII, Kazinczy utca 29-31, Mon-Thu 10am-3.30pm, Fri & Sun 10am-12.30pm

Kerepesi Cemetery (Kerepesi temető)
District VIII, Fiumei út 16, daily 7am-7pm; Funeral Museum Mon-Fri 9am-5pm, Sat 10am-2pm

Kerepesi Jewish Cemetery (Kerepesi zsidó temető)
District VIII, Salgótarjáni utca, Mon-Fri 8am-3pm; ring bell at gatehouse

Király Thermal Baths (Király Gyógyfürdő)
District II, Fő utca 82-84, daily 9am-9pm, mixed

Kiscelli Museum (Kiscelli Múzeum)
District III, Kiscelli utca 108, Apr-Oct Tue-Sun 10am-6pm, Nov-Mar Tue-Sun 10am-4pm

Kossuth Museum Ship—Old Timer Ship Restaurant (Vénhajó Étterem)
District V, Vigadó tér landing stage, daily 11am-11pm

Kozma utca New Municipal Cemetery (Kozma utcai Új köztemető)
District X, Kozma utca 8-10, daily 7am-7pm

Kozma utca Jewish Cemetery (Kozma utcai zsidó temető)
District X, Kozma utca 6, Summer Sun-Fri 8am-4pm, Winter Sun-Fri 8am-3pm; opening hours can be irregular

Kresz Géza Ambulance Museum (Kresz Géza Mentőmúzeum)
District V, Markó utca 22, Mon-Fri 8am-6pm, Sat 8am-2pm

Légrádi Antique Restaurant
District V, Bárczy István utca 3-5, Mon-Fri noon-3pm, 7pm-midnight, Sat noon-midnight

Lehel tér Market
District XIII, Lehel tér,
daily Mon-Fri 6am-6pm, Sat 6am-2pm

Lukács Cukrászda
District VI, Andrássy út 70,
Mon-Fri 8.30am-7pm, Sat 9am-7pm

Lukács Thermal Baths (Lukács Gyógyfürdő)
District II, Frankel Leó utca 25-29,
daily 6am-9pm, mixed

Margitkert Restaurant
District II, Margit utca 15,
daily noon-midnight

Matteo Restaurant
District II, Pasaréti tér, daily 11.30am-midnight

**Matthias Church/Buda Church of Our Lady
(Mátyás-templom/Budavári
Nagyboldogasszony templom)**
District I, Szentháromság tér 2,
Mon-Fri 9am-5pm, Sat 9am-1pm, Sun 1pm-5pm

Medieval Jewish Prayer House
District I, Táncsics Mihály utca 26,
May-Oct Tue-Sun 10am-6pm

Memento Park (Szoborpark)
District XXII, on the corner of Balatoni út
and Szabadkai utca, daily 10am-5pm

**Miksa Róth Memorial House
(Róth Miksa Emlékház)**
District VII, Nefelejcs utca 26, Tue-Sun 2pm-6pm

Millennium Park (Millenáris Park)
District II, Fény utca 20-22, daily 6am-2am;
Tue-Fri 9am-5pm, Sat & Sun 10am-6pm

Millennium Restaurant
District VI, Andrássy út 76, daily noon-midnight

**Museum of Hungarian Agriculture
(Mezőgazdasági Múzeum)**
District XIV, Vajdahunyad Castle, City Park (Városliget),
Apr-Oct Tue-Sun 10am-5pm,
Nov-Mar Tue-Fri 10am-4pm,
Sat & Sun 10am-5pm

**Museum of Military History
(Hadtörténeti Intézet és Múzeum)**
District I, Tóth Árpád sétány 40,
Apr-Sep Tue-Sun 10am-6pm,
Oct-Mar Tue-Sun 10am-4pm

**Museum of the Milling Industry
(Malomipari Múzeum)**
District IX, Soroksári út 24,
Mon-Thu 9am-2pm

**Music History Museum
(Zenetörténeti Múzeum)**
District I, Erdődy Palace, Táncsics Mihály utca 7,
Tue-Sun 10am-4pm

Művész Kávéház
District VI, Andrássy út 29,
Mon-Sat 9am-10pm, Sun 10am-10pm

Múzeum Kávéház District VIII, Múzeum körút 12,
Mon-Sat 6pm-midnight

Náncsi Néni Vendéglője
District II, Ördögárok út 80, daily noon-11pm

National Széchenyi Library
District I, Wing F of the Royal Palace,
(Budavári Palota), Szent György tér 2,
Tue-Sat 10am-8pm during the academic year

New Theatre (Új Színház)
District VI, junction of Dalszínház utca and Paulay
Ede utca 35, 10am-7pm & until the first interval
of the evening show; closed June-Aug

New York Café
District VI, Erzsébet körút 9-11, daily 9am-midnight

**Nostalgia Train
(Nosztalgia vonat)**
District VI, leaves the Western Railway Station every
Saturday May-Sept at 9.40am heading north to Szob

**Óbuda Local History Museum
(Óbudai helytörténeti gyűjtemény)**
District III, Fő tér 1, Tue-Sun 10am-6pm

Orient Express Restaurant
District I, Krisztina körút,
located in a converted railway carriage outside
Déli Railway Station, daily noon-midnight

Pál-völgy Cave (Pál-völgyi-barlang)
District II, Szépvölgyi út 162,
Jun-Aug Tue-Sat 10am-5pm, Sept-May Tue-Sun
10am-4pm; guided tours every hour

**Petőfi Museum of Literature
(Petőfi Irodalmi Múzeum)**
District V, Károlyi utca 16,
Mon-Thu 9am-4pm, Fri 9am-3pm

Pilvax Restaurant
District V, Pilvax köz 1-3, daily 7am-11pm

Pintér Antik
District V, Falk Miksa utca 10,
Mon-Fri 10am-6pm, Sat 10am-2pm

Planetarium (Planetárium)
District X, Népliget, daily 9.30am-4pm;
laser shows at 7.30pm

**Police History Museum
(Bűnügyi és Rendőrség-történeti Múzeum)**
District VIII, Mosonyi utca 7, Tue-Sun 9am-5pm

Postal Museum (Postamúzeum)
District VI, Benczúr utca 27, Tue-Sun 10am-6pm

Rác Thermal Baths (Rác Gyógyfürdő)
District I, Hadnagy utca 8-10,
part of the soon-to-be opened Rácz Hotel
and Thermal Spa

**Radio and Television Museum
(Rádió- és Televíziótörténeti Múzeum)**
District VIII, Pollack Mihály tér 8-10, Tue-Sat 10am-6pm

Rákóczi tér Market Hall
District VIII, Rákóczi tér,
Mon 6am-4pm, Tue-Fri 6am-6pm, Sat 6am-1pm

Remiz Kávéház és Étterem Restaurant
District II, Budakeszi út 5, daily noon-11pm

Restaurant M
District VII, Kertész utca 48, Mon-Fri 6pm-midnight,
Sat & Sun noon-4pm, 6pm-midnight

Restaurant Robinson
District XIV, City Park, Állatkerti körút 3,
daily noon-5pm, 6pm-midnight

Rivalda Restaurant
District I, Színház utca 5-9, daily 11.30am-11.30pm

Roma Parliament
District VIII, Tavaszmező utca 6,
opening times and admission vary,
www.romaparlament.hu

Romani Design
District V, Szent István tér 3, Mon-Fri noon-8pm

Rudas Thermal Baths (Rudas Gyógyfürdő)
District I, Döbrentei tér 9,
swimming pool daily 6am-8pm, Thu-Sun 6am-8pm,
steam bath daily 6am-8pm; Tue women only, Mon,
Wed, Thu & Fri men only, Sat & Sun mixed

Rumbach Synagogue
District VII, Rumbach Sebestyen utca 11,
Mar-mid Nov Sun-Thu 10am-5.30pm, Fri 10am-4.30pm,
mid Nov-Feb Sun-Thu 10am-3.30pm, Fri 10am-1.30pm

Ruszwurm Cukrászda
District I, Szentháromság utca 7,, daily 10am-7pm

**St. Stephen's Basilica
(Szent István Bazilika)**
District V, Szent István tér,
Mon-Fri 9am-5.15pm, Sat 9am-1pm, Sun 1-5pm;
Sacred Right (Szent Jobb) Apr-Sep Mon-Fri
9.30am-4.30pm, Sun 1-4.30pm, Oct-Mar Mon-Fri
10am-4pm, Sun 1-4.30pm; Cupola Apr-May daily
10am-4pm, Jun-Aug 9.30am-6.30pm, Sep-Oct
10am-7.30pm

Sas Hill (Sas-hegy)
Nature Reserve, District XI, Tájék utca 26,
Mar-Oct Thu, Sat & Sun 10am-6pm;
tours with guide only tel. 0036-30-408-4370

**Semmelweis Museum of Medical History
(Semmelweis Orvostörténeti Múzeum)**
District I, Apród utca 1-3,
Mar-Oct Tue-Sun 10am-6pm,
Nov-Feb Tue-Fri 10am-4pm

**Serbian Orthodox Church of St. George
(Pesti Szerb orthodox templom)**
District V, Szerb utca 2-4,
Sun before 10am service

Spoon Café & Lounge
District V, Vigadó tér landing stage, daily noon-midnight

Stamp Museum (Bélyegmúzeum)
District VII, Hársfa utca 47, Tue-Sun 10am-6pm

Szalai Cukrászda
District V, Balassi Bálint utca 7,
Wed-Mon 8am-7pm

**Széchenyi Thermal Baths
(Széchenyi Gyógyfürdő)**
District XIV, City Park (Városliget), Állatkerti körút 11,
Outdoor swimming pool daily 6am-10pm,
steam bath daily 6am-7pm;
all-weather swimming area is mixed,
steam baths are segregated

**Szemlő-hegy Cave
(Szemlő-hegyi-barlang)**
District II, Pusztaszeri út 35, Wed-Mon 10am-4pm;
guided tours every hour

Szimpla Kert
District VII, Kazinczy utca 14, daily noon-3am

**Telephone Museum
(Telefónia Múzeum)**
District I, Úri utca 49,
Tue-Sun 10am-4pm;
entrance via Országház utca 49 at weekends

Textile Museum (Textilmúzeum)
District III, Lajos utca 136-138, Tue-Sun 10am-6pm

**Tomb of Gül Baba
(Gül Baba türbéje)**
District II, Turbán utca 11/Mecset utca 14,
Mar-Oct daily 10am-6pm, Nov-Feb 10am-4pm

**Trafó House of Contemporary Arts
(Trafó Kortárs Művészetek Háza)**
District IX, corner of Liliom utca 41 and Tűzoltó utca,
Theatre box office daily 4-8pm; Trafó Gallery daily
4-7pm; Trafó Bár Tangó restaurant & lounge daily

**Transport Museum
(Közlekedési Múzeum)**
District XIV, City Park (Városliget),
Városligeti körút 11, May-Sep Tue-Fri 10am-5pm,
Sat & Sun 10am-6pm, Oct-Apr Tue-Fri 10am-4pm,
Sat & Sun 10am-5pm

Tropicarium-Oceanarium
District XXII, in the Campona Shopping Centre
at Nagytétényi út 37-45, daily 10am-8pm

**Újpest Butterfly Museum
(Újpesti Lepkemuzeum)**
District IV, Dessewffy utca 26, Tue-Fri noon-6pm,
Sat & Sun 10am-6pm

**Underground Railway Museum
(Földalatti Vasúti Múzeum)**
District V, Deák Ferenc tér metro station underpass,
Tue-Sun 10am-5pm

**Uránia Astronomical Observatory
(Uránia Csillagvizsgáló)**
District I, Sánc utca 3/B,
Mon, Wed & Thu in clear weather,
for times visit www.urania-budapest.hu

**Uránia National Film Theatre
(Uránia Nemzeti Filmszínház)**
District VIII, Rákóczi út 21,
box office and café daily 10.30am-10.30pm

**Városliget Flea Market
(Városligeti Bolhapiac)**
District XIV, City Park (Városliget), Petőfi Csarnok
Zichy Mihály út, Sat & Sun 7am-2pm

Verne Étterem-Restaurant
District V, Váci utca 60, daily noon-midnight

Virág Judit Gallery
District V, Falk Miksa utca 30,
Mon-Fri 10am-6pm, Sat 10am-1pm

**Zoltán Kodály Memorial Museum
and Archives
(Kodály Zoltán Emlékmúzeum
és Archívum)**
District VI, Kodály körönd 1,
Wed-Fri 10-noon, 2-4.30pm

Zsolnay Café (Zsolnay Kávézó)
District VI, Radisson Blu Béke Hotel,
Teréz körút 43, daily 8am-11pm

**Zsolnay Porcelain Shop
(Zsolnay Porcelánbolt)**
District V, Kígyó utca 4,
Mon-Fri 10am-6pm, Sat 10am-1pm

Bibliography

GUIDEBOOKS

András Török's Budapest – A Critical Guide
(András Török), Park Publishing, 2011

Visible Cities Budapest
(Annabel Barber & Emma Roper-Evans),
Somerset Limited, 2006

Time Out Budapest
(Various), Penguin Books, 2011

Everyman Guides – Budapest
(Various), Everyman Guides, 2004

Eyewitness Travel Guide Budapest
(ed. by Helen Townsend), Dorling Kindersley, 2013

Budapest City Guide
(Adrian Phillips), Bradt Guides, 2012

Rough Guide Budapest
(Charles Hebbert & Dan Richardson), Rough Guides, 2012

ILLUSTRATED BOOKS

Budapest 360° The Capital
From Another Angle
(Tamás D. Vargas and Péter Roth), 360 Art Kft., 2004

ARCHITECTURE AND MONUMENTS

Budapest: A Guide to 20th Century Architecture
(Edwin Heathcote), Batsford, 1998

Castle Walk – Tourist Guide to Buda Castle
(Balázs Dercsényi), Tourism Office of Budapest, 2003

CHURCH, CEMETERY AND MUSEUM GUIDEBOOKS

Budapest Underground Railway Museum
(Miklós Merczi), István Éri, 1996

Folk Culture of the Hungarians
(Attila Selmeczi Kovács and Éva Szacsvay),
Museum of Ethnography, 2003

A Look Into the Workshop – Kodály Zoltán Museum and Archives
(Ferenc Bónis), Péter Erdei/Kodály Institute, 1990

MISCELLANEOUS

A History of Hungary
(László Kontler), Palgrave Macmillan, 2002

Budapest 1900: A Historical Portrait
of a City and its Culture
(John Lukács), Weidenfeld & Nicolson, 1993

The Habsburg Monarchy, 1809-1918
(A. J. P. Taylor), Penguin Books, 1964

The Cooking of Vienna's Empire
(Joseph Wecksberg and Fred Lyon),
Time Life Books, 1979

Between the Woods and the Water
(Patrick Leigh Fermor), John Murray, 1986

A Time of Gifts
(Patrick Leigh Fermor), John Murray, 1977

WEBSITES

www.budapestinfo.hu
(the official Budapest Tourism Office site)

www.budapest.hu
(portal for city listings and other information)

www.budapestinfo.org
(Budapest visitor information)

www.fsz.bme.hu/hungary/budapest
(Budapest visitor information and maps)

www.bkv.hu
(details of Budapest's public transport system)

www.hungary.com
(Hungary tourism site)

www.museum.hu
(details of Hungary and Budapest's many museums)

www.hungary.org
(Hungarian news, culture and country information)

Acknowledgements

First and foremost I would like to thank my Hungarian publisher, JEL-KÉP Kiadó, for realising the first edition of this book, namely Zoltán Farkas, Judit Sós and Ágnes Tóth, also to Anikó B. Nagy for proofreading my original manuscript. I would also like to acknowledge the invaluable part played by Zoltán Csepiga in bringing the project to fruition. Thanks also go to my Viennese publisher, Christian Brandstätter Verlag, for publishing the German language edition, especially Elisabeth Stein (commissioning editor), Else Rieger (editor), Ekke Wolf (design), Brigitte Hilzensauer (German translation), and Helmut Maurer (maps).

For kind permission to take photographs, as well as arranging for access and the provision of information, the following people are very gratefully acknowledged: István Amberg (Kárpáthia Restaurant), Attila Árkosi (Pintér Antik), the caretakers of the Budafok Cemetery, the young staff on the Childrens' Railway, the staff and customers at the Déli Pályaudvar Antikvárium, Dr. István Diós (Baroque Library of the Central Seminary of Pest), the staff at the Dohány utca Central Synagogue, the Ethnographic Museum, Lajos Gál (Budafok), the kind gentleman and the security guard at the Farkasréti Cemetery, the staff at the Golden Eagle Pharmacy Museum, the staff at the Hilton Budapest, Dr. Sándor Jeszensky and the staff at the Hungarian Museum of Electrical Engineering, Éva Kajó (Hungarian National Museum), Kárpáti Kamill (Central Market Hall), Nóra Keskovicz (Postal Museum), the gatekeepers at the Kerepesi Jewish Cemetery (Kerepesi zsidó temető) on Salgótarjáni utca, the staff at the Kiscelli Museum, Éva Kováts (Budapest History Museum), Kornélia Kun (Kurucles), Magdolna Lakatos and the Roma inhabitants of Józsefváros, the Museum of Hungarian Agriculture, László Paszternák (Budapest Tourism Office), Ferenc Polónyi (Tomb of Gül Baba), Noémi Saly (Hungarian Museum of Commerce and Catering), Krisztina Szabó and the staff at the Ferenc Hopp Museum of Eastern Asiatic Arts, the staff at the Textile Museum, Benedek Varga and the staff at the Semmelweis Museum of Medical History, Erika Varga (www.romanidesign.hu), and Mrs. Sarolta Kodály and the staff at the Zoltán Kodály Memorial Museum.

For the supply of film, high-quality processing and technical advice thanks to Foto Wachtl (Vienna).

The following friends, family, colleagues and acquaintances are much appreciated for their support, advice, assistance and inspiration:

In Budapest, Brunó Bitter for his many fascinating facts, Maria Kele and Kata Tirnovan (Cozy Homes, Budapest), Győző and Szabolcs Szivák (for sharing their generous Kőbánya hospitality with me) and Elisabeth Mayer.

In Vienna, Viktoria Hollmann-Kiss for her invaluable translation work, accomodation advice and help in proof-reading Hungarian words and punctuation; also, Dubravka Grujic, Philipp Gufler, Sven Hollmann, Robert Kraska and Christa Bock, Dr. Simon Heathcote-Parker, Martina Horvath and Stefan 'Sy' Gebharter, Dr. Angelika Lenz, James Linkogle and Kristin Teuchtmann, Roland Lohnert, Silvia McDonald (Virtual Vienna), Sophie Menapace, Christian Mikosch, Rostam Neuwirth and

Sanam Salem Haghighi, Manisha Shah and Michael Buttenhauser, Estera Stojanovic, Brigitte Timmermann (Vienna Walks & Talks), Olga Zborowskaja, Josef Schiefer and Lynn-Marie Buenemann-Schiefer and Inge Scholz-Strasser (Sigmund Freud Museum).

Elsewhere, Natascha Backes, Eric Jedrzejek and new arrival Karina Joy (USA), Stephanie Brunner (Austria), Tibor Frank (Canada), Bob and Prue Hinton (Wales), Dániel Jánossy (Transylvania), Zsuzsanna and Tivadar Kiss (Switzerland), Susan von Kloos (USA), Hans Kohlenberg (Munich), Margaret and Keith Orridge (England) and Jan and Melanie Rupp (USA).

Also my great cousin James Dickinson for support, newspaper cuttings and bringing my work to a wider audience – his boundless enthusiasm has been both inspirational and infectious.

Also Roswitha Reisinger for her invaluable assistance in translating German articles, coming up with the title and generally putting up with me and my mania for all things unusual; and not forgetting the Reisinger family in Freistadt, Upper Austria for their affection and unending hospitality.

In England, my loving parents Mary and Trevor, brother Adrian, auntie Catherine and great cousins James, Sally and Janet; also old friends who have sustained me from afar including Philip Adsetts, Peter and Dorothy Askew, Paul Billington and Kerry Newman, Rose and Mike Blackadder, Lisa Blanchflower, Philippa Chapman, Catie Evans and Mark Pitcairn, Jenny Glazebrook, Jean and David Gledhill, Tim and Jane Hale, Judith Hall, Cecilia Harris, Caroline and David Hepworth, Joanne Jagiellowicz, Karen Jagiellowicz and Neil Burkinshaw, Marie-Christine Keith and Bob Barber, Simon, Nadine, Fran and Madeleine Laffoley, Amy Pluckrose and Paul Taylor, Anna Povid, Victor Povid, Marek Pryjomko, Roman Pryjomko, Deniz and Pat Savas, Tom Singer, Jill Sleaford, Nick Smith and Ellie Tordoff, Alan and Pauline Varney, and Tricia and David Ware – my thanks go to you all.

Finally, very special thanks to my father Trevor, not only for proof-reading and correcting my text, but for inspiring me to track down unusual locations in the first place – thanks Dad for making it all such fun!

A window depicting Lajos Kossuth in the Gresham Palace (see nos. 42 & 78)

3rd Revised Edition published by The Urban Explorer, 2014
A division of Duncan J. D. Smith
contact@duncanjdsmith.com
www.onlyinguides.com
www.duncanjdsmith.com

First published by JEL-KÉP Kiadó, 2006

Graphic design: Atelier 21 & Stefan Fuhrer
Typesetting and picture editing: JEL-KÉP Kiadó
Revision typesetting and picture editing: JEL-KÉP Kiadó & Franz Hanns
Maps: APA, Vienna
Printed and bound by GraphyCems, Spain

ISBN 978-3-9503662-7-3

Inlaid floor
bearing the initials
of water manufacturer
Andreas Saxlehner (see no. 66)